Collaboration through Writing and Reading

Institute for the Advancement of Urban Education
NJDHE 1989-91

Collaboration through Writing and Reading

Exploring Possibilities

Edited by
Anne Haas Dyson
University of California, Berkeley

National Council of Teachers of English
1111 Kenyon Road, Urbana, Illinois 61801

In memory of Mary Hurdlow,
a loving teacher,
who turned classroom possibilities
into language-rich realities
for children

NCTE Stock Number 07370-3020

This project was cosponsored by the Center for the Study of Writing and the Center for the Study of Reading and was performed pursuant to grant no. OERI-G-00869 from the Office of Educational Research and Improvement/ Department of Education (OERI/ED) for the Center for the Study of Writing. However, the opinions expressed herein do not necessarily reflect the position or policy of the OERI/ED, and no official endorsement by the OERI/ED should be inferred.

Library of Congress Cataloging-in-Publication Data
Collaboration through writing and reading : exploring possibilities /
    edited by Anne Haas Dyson.
        p. cm.
    Proceedings of a conference, held in Berkeley, Calif., Feb. 14-16,
1986, cosponsored by the Center for the Study of Writing and the
Center for the Study of Reading.
    Includes bibliographies.
    ISBN 0-8141-0737-0
    1. Language arts—United States—Congresses. 2. English language—
Study and teaching—United States—Congresses. I. Dyson, Anne
Haas. II. National Council of Teachers of English. III. University of
California, Berkeley. Center for the Study of Writing.
IV. University of Illinois at Urbana-Champaign. Center for the
Study of Reading.
LB1576.C577   1989
420'.7'073—dc20   89-36233
                                                                      CIP

Contents

Acknowledgments

As is the way with the printed word, the neatly arranged pages that follow belie the talking, writing, reading—and the retalking, rewriting, and rereading—that preceded it. Many contributed their ideas, their energy, and their time to this collaborative work. Sarah Freedman of the Center for the Study of Writing (CSW) and Jana Mason of the Center for the Study of Reading (CSR) organized the conference that first gathered together the people whose voices are heard in this book; they were ably assisted by Jane Powell (CSR) and Sandra Murphy (CSW). The conference participants, many of whom became authors of chapters and prefaces, talked, read, and wrote about talking, writing, and reading with interest and enthusiasm.

In the months following the conference, the chapter authors and I exchanged letters, notes, memos, and drafts as the book envisioned at the conference began to take form. As editor, I was fortunate to work with authors who themselves shared in the vision of the book—and who were good-humored when editor and author seemed to be looking in different directions.

I was equally fortunate to have editorial assistants, who read and talked through the chapters with me, hunted down missing references, and carefully checked each comma and period. Jim Slagel and Mark McCarvel worked with me almost from the beginning. Jeff Maxson helped in the final months, providing good humor and careful proofing and reproofing of the longest bibliography either of us had ever seen. Finally, Carol Heller, whose gifts as writer and editor are humbling, edited my own chapter and helped with the final cleaning up.

Throughout the months of drafting and redrafting, the CSW staff worked through an almost daily deluge of papers to be typed and retyped, always with a smile. I thank Lynnette Harry, Trish Cascardi, and Ernie Grafe.

Conference Participants

Mary Sue Ammon, Department of Educational Psychology, School of Education, University of California, Berkeley

Paul Ammon, Department of Educational Psychology, School of Education, University of California, Berkeley

James Britton, London, England

Bertram (Chip) Bruce, Bolt, Beranek and Newman, Cambridge, Massachusetts

Robert Calfee, School of Education, Stanford University

Rebekah Caplan, University of California, Berkeley

Wallace Chafe, Department of Linguistics, University of California, Santa Barbara

Fran Claggett, Alameda High School, Alameda, California

Geraldine Clifford, Educational Foundations, School of Education, University of California, Berkeley

Jenny Cook-Gumperz, Division of Language and Literacy, School of Education, University of California, Berkeley

Anne Haas Dyson, Division of Language and Literacy, School of Education, University of California, Berkeley

Linnea Ehri, Department of Education, College of Letters and Science, University of California, Davis

Marcia Farr, Department of English, University of Illinois at Chicago

Lily Wong Fillmore, Division of Language and Literacy, School of Education, University of California, Berkeley

Laury Fischer, Washington High School, Fremont, California

Linda Flower, Department of English, Carnegie-Mellon Institute

Sarah Freedman, Division of Language and Literacy, School of Education, University of California, Berkeley

James Gray, Bay Area Writing Project, University of California, Berkeley

Alfred Grommon, Portola Valley, California

Norton Grubb, School of Education, University of California, Berkeley

John Gumperz, Department of Anthropology, University of California, Berkeley

Mary K. Healy, Puente Project, University of California, Berkeley

Mary Hurdlow, Sunset School, Livermore, California

Ken Lane, School of Education, University of California, Berkeley

Judith Langer, School of Education, Stanford University

Jana Mason, Center for the Study of Reading, University of Illinois at Urbana-Champaign

Don McQuade, Department of English, University of California, Berkeley

James Moffett, Mariposa, California

Sandra Murphy, Department of Secondary/Post Secondary Education, School of Education, San Francisco State University

Jean Osborn, Center for the Study of Reading, University of Illinois at Urbana-Champaign

Art Peterson, Lowell High School, San Francisco, California

Robert Ruddell, Division of Language and Literacy, School of Education, University of California, Berkeley

Leo Ruth, Division of Language and Literacy, School of Education, University of California, Berkeley

Herbert Simons, Division of Language and Literacy, School of Education, University of California, Berkeley

Rob Tierney, Center for the Study of Reading, University of Illinois at Urbana-Champaign

1 Introduction

On Collaboration

Anne Haas Dyson

The boys at the back table are arguing loudly. Six-year-old Jake
has written a story about a jet that bombs a desert and thus
creates a volcano. His readers—his classmates—are divided over
whether or not such a thing could happen. Manuel settles the
argument in a way that allows all to save face: "Well, anyway,
it's a pretend story. In real life, it may [not] be true."

Jake's written text was thus given social and intellectual life by the
collaboration of the writing, reading, and talking processes and, through
those processes, by the collaboration of people themselves. Jake and
his friends joined together through language not only to communicate
with each other, but to explore the world around them.[1]

Similarly, this book has taken life from, and indeed defines as its
topic, the concept of collaboration. By collaboration, I refer both to
the collaboration of the *language arts*, particularly of writing and
reading, in school, and to the collaboration of *people* through language
use. For literacy is a tool that allows people—writers and readers—to
join together, even across expanses of time and space.

Throughout the history of American schooling, educators have
periodically called for the integration of the language arts—for writing,
reading, talking, and listening to become collaborative processes in
classroom activities, thereby furthering the development of each process
and, more importantly, furthering children's learning about themselves
and their world. And yet that ideal seems to remain just that, an ideal
broadly praised, yet not broadly attained. Educators may claim curricular time, space, and materials for each language process or, as is often
the case for writing and talking, decry the lack of adequate housing.

In recent years research, theory, and pedagogical innovations have
contributed to a renewal of our commitment as language educators to
the ideal. But the segmentation of instruction in the classroom has a

I thank Carol Heller, Julie Jensen, and Sarah Freedman for their helpful comments
on earlier drafts of this chapter.

counterpart in the segmentation of the literature informing our efforts to unite the language arts. In particular, studies of the interrelationships among writing, reading, and learning have been carried out by researchers operating from a wide range of theoretical perspectives, methodological paradigms, and practical aims.

To this collage of separate pieces in practice and research, we might add the traditional divisions among the efforts of elementary, secondary, and college teachers and between those who primarily work as researchers and those who primarily work as teachers. Thus the seemingly natural flowing of talking, writing, and reading—so evident in Jake's classroom—appears to lack a coherent framework within which it might be understood and fostered.

Separation of people, like separation of the language arts, is engendered by differences in roles and status.[2] To promote the flowing of language among people, one must promote in them a sense of collegiality—a feeling of community, of being involved with each other and with common ends. An example of such a sense of collegiality— of people and of writing and reading—can in fact be found in the early history of our country. The literate common citizenry, including working-class people, were the readers of popular periodicals or newspapers, but they were also the writers, contributing reports of opinions or events, how-to accounts, and letters. As Shirley Heath notes, when writing became more formalized—and "would-be writers . . . warned [that] they must learn to think"—the role of writer became separated from that of reader.[3]

Such ideas about becoming a member of a literate community— and thus beginning to "read like a writer" and "write like a reader"— are prevalent in many theoretical and pedagogical discussions of writing-reading relationships.[4] Certainly in the opening anecdote, Jake's peers were reading his text as writers, questioning his decisions. Moreover, they were bringing to bear upon his text information about volcanoes and the composition of the earth and, in addition, a sense of what was possible in stories, information and sense that they had gained in part through reading (or, more accurately, being read to).

This book, *Collaboration through Writing and Reading: Exploring Possibilities*, results from a joint effort to promote integration of the language arts within the classroom. Through their own talking, writing, and reading, the book's contributors have aimed to draw together information on writing and reading and their interrelationships. They have focused on information that, in their view, is rich in its implications for literacy teaching and learning and thus might inform the daily curricular and instructional decisions educators must make.

In the sections to follow, I describe the working conference that brought the contributors together, the differing perspectives of those contributors, their products—the chapters that appear in this book— and the common themes that linked them and that link those products. Throughout this discussion, I draw upon illustrations from my own experiences in order to clarify these perspectives and themes. Finally, I explain how the contributors to this book hope to collaborate with you, our readers, as you turn to your own experiences to make sense of these ideas.

Collaborating through Writing, Reading, and Talking: The Planning Conference

To assist in the profession's efforts to bring together writing and reading in the classroom, the Center for the Study of Writing and the Center for the Study of Reading brought together a group of people concerned with literacy teaching and learning. This interdisciplinary group met together in Berkeley on February 14, 15, and 16, 1986, for a working conference on writing-reading interrelationships.

The participants represented a variety of interests and roles in schooling. "Writing" people and "reading" people came together, as did people from primarily "social" and from "cognitive" perspectives, as well as university and classroom teachers. Collaboration was thus not easy. In their thinking about writing and reading, individuals brought to mind different sorts of images—writers and readers of different ages and backgrounds engaged in different activities.

For example, for some participants, the whole notion of talking about "writing" and "reading" seemed inappropriate; their interest was in how literacy was organized in particular communities—the purposes for which people used (wrote, read, talked about) varied kinds of texts. For others, "writing" and "reading" brought to mind individuals sitting alone, engaged in what might be similar but by no means inseparable mental activities. Some participants were excited by recent theoretical and instructional ideas about writing-reading interrelationships—the concepts that both writing and reading are active ways of constructing meaning and that both processes can contribute to learning across the curriculum. Others viewed recent attention to the integration of writing and reading as yet another occurrence of an old theme in our professional history.

Differing images can make communication difficult, particularly when those images are not themselves articulated, but rather remain in the background, silently informing that which is articulated. People who feel that "literacy is a social activity" tend to travel in different circles than do those who feel that "literacy is a cognitive activity"; people who envision small children, like Jake and his peers, chatting their way through tasks tend to commerce separately from those who envision people in study cubicles sipping coffee in the wee hours as they puzzle themselves through a task.

To begin to communicate successfully among ourselves, it was necessary, then, to talk in specifics. Talking about writing and reading and their interrelationships was difficult unless speakers articulated their own images—who is the writer or reader? what exactly is being done? where? why? (In fact, this pushing for specificity is how, in this paper's opening anecdote, Manuel settled the argument about volcanoes—he pointed out that the particular volcano in question was *pretend*.)

Talking specifically, rather than in abstractions, seemed important for at least three reasons. First, it is easier to share referents than it is to share meaning.[5] For example, young children do not necessarily share the same meaning of words as do the adults around them. Yet in a specific situation—a specific context—adults and young children do communicate.[6] Conversationally building scenes for discussed literacy activities—sharing our "referents" and avoiding overly simplistic statements about "writing" or "reading"—seemed to help create a common frame for discussion.

Second, specificity in conversation seemed important because of the very nature of language processes. Like oral language, written language is a tool with distinctive properties and potentialities, a tool for constructing meaning. But the way we use both oral and written language varies with the purposes that motivate us and the situations within which we act. So the interrelationships between these processes—their similarities, differences, ways of supporting each other and furthering learning across the curriculum—must vary. Specificity therefore seemed important, so that potential insights into writing-reading interrelationships were neither overgeneralized nor summarily dismissed.[7]

Finally, specificity in conversation seemed important to develop precisely those needed common insights. To use Katherine Nelson's term, we develop "shared meaning systems"—systems that allow us to communicate with each other—through exchanging meanings.[8] As argued above, the lack of collaboration among writing and reading may well be related to the lack of collaboration among people—and such collaboration is encouraged by the common understandings brought about as people talk, write, and read together.

The conference participants, then, built contexts for each other "upon a sea of talk."[9] The three chairpersons (Sarah Warshauer Freedman, Jana Mason, and I) had a goal—to synthesize the literature on the interrelationships between writing and reading—and an outline of what seemed sensible areas for such a synthesis to cover. But no more than that. The jobs of defining or redefining these areas, fleshing them out, and actually interweaving any theoretical threads were carried out by the conference participants as a group.

After a sketchy introduction to possible areas for discussion, conference participants divided into working groups and began to formulate the content of this book. Back and forth the participants went, from small group huddles to whole group hashings-out. Writing and reading were important parts of this process. Groups organized and summarized their thoughts before the whole group meetings by writing and reading. In the large group, all group reports were read and the relationships of the chapters to each other were discussed.

The conference resulted in detailed outlines of the proposed chapters. Each group came up with its own design for producing its chapter. In some groups, the chapter was written primarily by the group leader; in others, the chapter was written collaboratively by many group members.

As was evident in working on these chapters, it is not easy to talk of "relationships"; it is much easier to speak of "writing" or "reading." Vygotsky wrote of the similar dilemma posed by attempting to understand the relationship between thinking and speaking. Separating each from the other—and then searching for a relationship—is not possible, he explained. One needs to examine a unit that preserves the relationship between the two; and so he turned to word meaning, the word being a symbol of both thought and of social interchange.[10]

The word will not do as a unit for studying the relationship between writing and reading. It is too narrow a focal point to accommodate the myriad of images of writers and readers that populate this book. Perhaps the unit that allows writing and reading to maintain their true relationship is the sort of unit the contributors were trying to become—not a symbol, but a group of symbol users who share some common concerns, values, and rules and who need writing and reading to act on those common concerns. Heath's term *textual communities* seems a possibility: a group of people who talk about knowledge they have gained through reading and writing. "The process of learning from written materials includes reflecting on the meaning of such knowledge for changed values and behaviors."[11]

As illustrated within the chapters to follow, these communities of people—including the community that forms within the classroom itself—are influenced by a complex interplay of broad historical and cultural forces, the properties and potentialities of writing and reading as social acts and cognitive processes, and, most specifically, within the classroom itself, by the ways in which those processes are used by teachers and students in particular literacy activities. Ultimately, writing and reading are used by people to participate in the life around them. For educators, the key to the collaboration of writing and reading may be, not so much in focusing on these processes themselves, as in understanding how, through these processes, students and teachers can collaboratively accomplish larger social ends.

Examining Collaboration: The Chapters

What Is the History of the Interrelationships
between Writing and Reading in the Schools?

Our current professional concerns about the integration of the language arts, particularly writing and reading, are not new. Throughout the twentieth century, calls for integration have periodically occurred. The conference planning group for this chapter confronted the issues raised by the "discovery" of the potential integration of the language arts by past generations of language educators. Group chairperson Geraldine Clifford reflected during the conference on the group's changing sense of purpose:

> My expectation . . . was that we were going to be looking histor-
> ically at how reading and writing have been related in the
> classroom. And what we've instead done here is to contrast
> reading and writing historically. . . . Maybe this is because these
> have been largely separate entities, and they have their separate
> histories. And there is [historically] very little combined pedagogy.

Thus, as group member Jenny Cook-Gumperz commented, the group used its social history to ask causally, "Why are these two being kept separate?"

And the answer to that question, argues Clifford in chapter 2, is that the forces that have led to these recurrent calls for integration are the very forces that make integration difficult. Included in these forces are the democratization of schooling, the professionalization of education, technological change, the pragmatic character of American culture, and liberationist ideologies, all of which may contribute to the recurrent calls for a holistic approach to literacy instruction, but all of which have been "essentially fragmenting in their effects."

To take but one example, organizations are critical to our professional growth, for they further the network of people and information that allows for the development and sharing of ideas. Certainly organizations like the National Council of Teachers of English and the International Reading Association have been strong advocates of an integrated approach to literacy instruction.

Yet organizations may also divide the curriculum and educators. Classroom teachers, administrators, university professors, and educational researchers all have their own organizations, journals, textbook materials, and teacher and student evaluation requirements. The same is true of elementary teachers, secondary teachers, English teachers, reading teachers, writing teachers, remedial reading teachers, basic writing teachers, and on the list goes. As we naturally seek association with those whose concerns are most like our own and as we search for information about specific and very real problems, how do we maintain the holistic image of language use—and whole language users talking, writing, and reading to accomplish legitimate ends? As professionals we face a problem similar to that which we face as individuals: How do we as individuals or groups figure into the social whole (of language and literacy education)? As argued earlier, the collaboration of language processes may be furthered or hindered by the collaboration of people.

How Do Writing and Reading Figure into the Life of the Community?

Just as social forces have influenced how, through time, schools have structured writing and reading instruction, so too have social forces influenced how writing and reading are organized outside the classroom. Writing and reading will collaborate—or not collaborate—as literacy demands and opportunities arise in the home, on the job, and in the community at large. And again, the collaboration of people living, working, and playing together may contribute to the forms that writing-reading collaboration will assume.

For example, in many organizations and small communities, the writing and reading of small news publications are reciprocal processes that support relationships among people. To illustrate, in the small rural village of Spring Green, Wisconsin, townspeople read and contribute to the weekly newspaper, which chronicles well the life of the village—births and deaths, marriages and family reunions, village board meetings and school budget debates, dueling letters of citizens on opposite sides of issues, columns of birthday greetings, and cards of thanks. During June (dairy month) 1986, dairy farmers—whose jobs certainly do not demand essays—wrote poetically of the rural life, with its "cows in their tranquil ways . . ., the bubbling noises in the milk line, . . . a newborn calf eyeing the world with trust and a little naughtiness," and of course with its possibilities of "drought, early frost, hail, tornado, or flood."[12]

And so in different ways writing and reading can be woven into and interweave the lives of people in homes and communities. Our children come to us from the community and, we hope, will find a satisfying role in their lives outside of school. To best take advantage of the literacy experience students bring with them and best prepare them for their lives ahead, we would do well to understand the interrelatedness of writing and reading outside of school.

In our diverse society, however, understanding writing and reading in the community is an enormously complex task. As Marcia Farr, a planning group member for chapter 3, explained to the conference participants, this understanding entails a thinking about writing-reading interrelationships "from a language and cultural perspective; in other words, language and culture as a base" from which people use literacy. And so, in chapter 3, Robert Gundlach, Marcia Farr, and Jenny Cook-Gumperz explore literacy uses outside of school, in diverse homes, communities, and workplaces. As these authors note, "Writing and reading are each, finally, umbrella terms for specific culturally bound activities that vary in character, consequence, and significance."

The authors of chapter 3 illustrate that, as educators, we must decide not only what writing and reading skills students must learn, but what roles as writers and readers students should experience. Further, by calling our attention to the interrelatedness of writing and reading in contexts outside the school, these authors illustrate the importance not only of joining writing and reading—and writers and readers—in the school, but also of joining educators with other community members. All of us—parents, teachers, employees, and the broad spectrum of community members—must talk, read, and write together, to share the information and insight necessary to smooth the critical transitions from home to school, from school to workplace.[13]

What Cognitive Processes Are Involved as Individuals Negotiate between Writing and Reading?

To this point, we have seen that the interrelationships between writing and reading are influenced by an interplay of historical, cultural, and ongoing situational and social forces. Thus we can assume that the sorts of cognitive or mental processes individuals engage in as they write and read are influenced by the purposes motivating them and the situations in which they are acting.

Consider, for example, the purposes guiding the reading that occurs during the writing process. Jake, as a first grader, struggled to spell and then to read his own journal entries. As he explained, he tended to "memorize" what he had written and thereby to at least minimize his decoding difficulties. In the second grade, his struggle with the written language system eased, and at the same time he displayed a new purpose for reading during writing. He no longer worried if he had correctly read what he had written, but rather if what he had written would read "correctly"—or at least seem sensible—to others. While rereading he now said, "That doesn't make any sense," rather than, "What does that say?"

The authors of chapter 4 would refer to Jake's described processes as ways to "solve the problem" of constructing meaning as a writer and a reader. They are concerned with how individuals might conceive of and carry out literacy tasks at different ages and in different situations. Chip Bruce, a member of this chapter's planning group, explained his group's concern that we "have a place where we could talk about looking at the individual learner," a place where we could examine both writing and reading "as constructive processes."

In chapter 4, then, Ann Rosebery and colleagues at Bolt, Beranek, and Newman, and Linda Flower and colleagues at Carnegie-Mellon focus on individuals' purposeful use of written language. They stress, first of all, the compatibility of writing and reading. Basing their illustrations on studies of literacy processes, they present vignettes of students writing and reading in response to varied academic literacy tasks. Through these vignettes, the authors demonstrate that, in such tasks, both writing and reading involve consideration of purpose, construction of meaning, and the monitoring, evaluation, and revision of those emerging constructions. Moreover, they demonstrate how writing may further the articulation of ideas read—and reading the critical assessment of ideas written.

The authors stress too, as do authors of earlier chapters, the collaboration of people that is implicit in both processes. Writers and readers work together most effectively when they share compatible standards and goals. Imagine, for example, five-year-old Christopher preparing a birthday card for his friend Alex. He folds a piece of paper and then, before writing his friend's name, carefully searches for a red crayon—because "I think red's his favorite color." Christopher thus displays his implicit awareness that pleasing his eventual reader is essential if his purpose—to make a card for this friend—is to be satisfactorily fulfilled. Conversely, Alex will be able to fully appreciate the text—the red-crayoned ALEX—and thereby Christopher's thoughtfulness only because he understands the writer's purpose and shares the writer's appreciation of color. This observed sensitivity to purpose is not unusual but critical to language learning.[14]

While the authors of chapter 3 stress children's initiation into purposeful literacy in homes, chapter 4 authors emphasize the increasingly deliberate consideration of purpose and situation possible as students develop over the school years. Yet there is danger that through the process of schooling—where skills such as summarizing or critically interpreting a text may be pulled out of a sensible, meaningful context—students will lose this understanding that writers and readers "are linked in a communicative interaction." How, then, do we help students develop the sorts of literacy skills perceived as necessary for academic success—skills such as summarizing earth science texts and composing a critical analysis of a literary text—*without* inadvertently helping them lose this purposeful sense that so many have at the beginning of the schooling process?

How Might Writing and Reading Work Together in the Classroom?

While all chapter authors consider how students might interrelate writing and reading—and become collaborative writers and readers—chapter 5 authors focus specifically on this concern. Further, they consider the potential benefits that accrue from different sorts of writing-reading collaborations by elementary and secondary students—collaborations that can occur across the curriculum.

In writing this chapter, authors Rob Tierney, Rebekah Caplan, Linnea Ehri, Mary K. Healy, and Mary Hurdlow drew upon their own experiences as educators to illustrate and extend the literature on writing-reading interrelationships. Their intention was to share their own experiences through writing and reading among themselves. As Rob Tierney explained at the conference, they wanted to "make sure that . . . the way we involve people in our text is consistent" with the theme of that text—that writing and reading can serve each other as both processes are used by individuals to serve some broader goal.

Their inclusion of their own experiences in their chapter was also a way of acknowledging the insight into writing-reading interrelationships that has come from the accumulated experiences of teachers. As classroom teacher and conference participant Art Peterson commented,

"These are *not* ivory tower ideas that researchers have dreamed up. These are things that real teachers are doing."

In the discussion of examples presented in chapter 5, we see, as in the previous chapter, that exactly how writing and reading work together is influenced by the purposes guiding individuals and by the nature of writing and reading themselves. Further, those purposes vary not only across situations, but, within any one situation, across individuals with differing degrees of developmental skill. The chapter 5 authors illustrate in detail the sorts of developmental benefits that can result from this working together; that is, how writing can benefit the development of reading, and reading, the development of writing.

After taking readers into elementary classrooms and into secondary English, biology, and science classes, chapter 5 authors close with a statement that leads directly to the book's final chapter, chapter 6. They point out that, although they have focused on the nature of literacy activities, those activities exist amidst "various facets of classroom life [that] support some of the outcomes we have described. Indeed, most of the examples involve writing and reading supported by a rich rather than sterile classroom environment."

What Characterizes Classrooms Where the Language Arts Are Integrated?

The authors of both chapters 4 and 5 emphasize the centrality of purpose to the interrelationships between writing and reading and between writers and readers. When students adopt the roles of both writer and reader of a particular kind of discourse, they may gain insight into the mutually dependent purposes of writers and readers.

This sense of purpose is not something that can simply be assigned by the teacher: "Your mission is to _____." Such dictating of purpose is likely to result in—to borrow a line from a television program—a "mission impossible." How, then, does one engender language activities that are "authentic" from the students' points of view—language events they themselves regard as addressing purposes of their own, beyond simply that of fulfilling another assignment?[15]

In chapter 6, James Britton addresses this difficult question. At the writing-reading conference, Britton summarized his planning group's intention to present many examples of good practice that would illustrate "reading and writing enabl[ing] him/her to make a unique contribution to a satisfying whole"—to the fulfillment of some purpose. The group intended to induce from these examples characteristics of classrooms evidencing successful collaboration of writing and reading in diverse areas of the curriculum and across levels of schooling.

The most dominant characteristic illustrated in chapter 6 (as in the book as a whole) is the importance of building collaboration among people—of creating a sense of community—thus enabling genuine collaboration of writing and reading to occur. Indeed, writing and reading both contribute to and benefit from such communities, because through these processes teachers and students can come to know each other and each other's worlds.[16]

However, Britton not only discusses the importance of the collaboration among students and teachers; he discusses how forces outside the classroom may both limit and foster the ability of teachers to develop activities that unite writing and reading—and writers and readers. In this way, he returns us in the book's final chapter to the themes Clifford developed in chapter 2.

Specifically, Britton argues that teachers must be allowed opportunity within the school day to consult with—to collaborate with—each other, as they discuss the need for and explore the possibilities of writing and reading collaboration in all areas of the curriculum. Yet teachers' ability to organize for change and implement it is furthered or hampered by their ability to collaborate with administrators within the school system itself, with parents and other community members outside the school, and with teacher education programs at universities and colleges.

Those who have not experienced the possibilities and the problems that classroom teachers encounter may not understand teachers' purposes for seeking changes in the potentially limiting aspects of educational bureaucracy discussed in chapter 2—curriculum objectives, textbook materials, evaluation requirements, and so on. Conversely, teachers may not have had the opportunities to gain an understanding of the purposes of these others. Mutual understanding is an essential framework within which all such concerns may be more adequately addressed. Only the *exchange* of meanings can lead to the *sharing* of meaning necessary for clear communication about and planning for strong language programs in our schools. Thus again, in chapter 6, as throughout the book, it is collaboration among people that is the key to the collaboration of the language arts.

Promoting Collaboration: Writers and Readers

When this project began, I envisioned the planning conference resulting in a book with a rather neatly ordered discussion of the interrelationships between writing and reading. Yet when participants began actually talking, writing, and reading, I soon realized that, just as there is no neat summary of the interrelationships between oral and written language, my own neat summary was not to be.

Before researchers began to study how people in a range of situations actually use print, it was relatively easy to discuss the relationships between oral and written language. Yet as the uses of literacy were explored in the community, the very nature of oral and of written language was questioned.[17] "Written" language is not always written—people at times talk like a book. "Oral" language is not always oral—people sometimes write conversationally. Further, talking and reading and writing are often interwoven, as in many of the examples presented in this book.[18] The interrelationships between writing and talking, like the interrelationships between writing and reading, depend on the individuals engaged in those processes. The clear message is that how individuals use language—the purposes guiding their efforts—determines precisely how language processes serve each other and learning in general.

That message is reflected in this book. Thus issues related to context or development are not confined to particular chapters, for writing-reading interrelationships depend upon the who, what, where, when, and why of the writers and readers. Such specificity matters if we are to flesh out the range of ways that writing and reading may be intertwined, the potential benefits that may ensue, and the sorts of school and classroom environments that support such intertwining.

Ultimately, we, as authors of this book, aim to contribute to this intertwining of the language arts in the schools. Yet we do not give simple prescriptions for such integration. As Mary K. Healy pointed out at the conference:

> You can't *give* people strategies. You have to set up a framework from within which they can make some discoveries, it seems to me. And they make a discovery, and then they have to have an opportunity to *reflect* upon the discovery and discuss it, and *then* it can be fit into a larger context.

We hope that this book offers a framework which might engender discussion and exploration. That framework sets writing and reading within the context of people—most immediately, within the social relationships between and among teachers and students. What purposes do we want students to be able to fulfill through written language? What roles do we want them to be able to serve as writers and as readers? The answers to those questions will no doubt lead us—and students—to a range of kinds of discourse. More broadly, the framework should focus our attention on the sorts of "textual communities" within which we want students to participate comfortably with some degree of involvement, including those communities formed by particular academic disciplines with particular languages—those of the scientists, the literary artists, the business communities. Students' writing and reading will mutually benefit the development of each process and learning itself when they serve as reciprocal processes within specific activities energized by social interchange.

Yet, while we see the integration of the language arts as influenced by the interactions among teachers and students, we know that classroom life itself is influenced by the experiences students and teachers bring with them from their homes and communities and by the ever present expectations of a widening circle of institutions, from the school to society as a whole. Thus the title of our book— *Collaboration through Writing and Reading: Exploring Possibilities*—ends with the phrase "exploring *possibilities*." The word *possibilities* is our acknowledgment that the collaboration of writing and reading in the classroom is not a simple accomplishment. It will entail the collaboration of people playing diverse roles in the schooling of our children. For teachers need more than the sorts of information we offer in this book; they need time, organizational space, and institutional support for infusing language—writing, reading, and talking—throughout the curriculum. In brief, to realize these possibilities we as educators are dependent upon each other and upon the public, whose children we seek to serve; our collaborative talking, writing, and reading outside the classroom supports the collaboration of those processes within the classroom. We thus invite you, our readers, to explore with us the interrelationships among the language arts.

Notes

1. Jake was one of eight children in a study that examined, in part, how children's written texts are shaped by and also shape their ongoing relationships with each other. See Dyson, A. Haas (in press). *The multiple worlds of child writers: A study of friends learning to write*. New York: Teachers College Press, Columbia University.

2. Szwed, J.F. (1981). The ethnography of literacy. In M.F. Whiteman (Ed.), *Writing: The nature, development, and teaching of written communication: Vol. 1. Variation in writing: Functional and linguistic-cultural differences* (pp. 13–24). Hillsdale, NJ: Erlbaum.

3. Heath, S.B. (1981). Toward an ethnohistory of writing in American education. In M.F. Whiteman (Ed.); see note 2, p. 31.

4. Smith, F. (1984). Reading like a writer. In J.M. Jensen (Ed.), *Composing and comprehending* (pp. 47–56). Urbana, IL: ERIC Clearinghouse on Reading and Communication Skills and National Conference on Research in English.

   Holt, S.L., and Vacca, J.L. (1984). Reading with a sense of writer: Writing with a sense of reader. In J.M. Jensen (Ed.), pp. 177–184.

5. I thank Courtney Cazden for reminding me of Vygotsky's reference to this notion of sharing referents rather than meaning. See Vygotsky, L.S. (1962). *Thought and language.* Cambridge, MA: M.I.T. Press. (Original work published 1934.)

6. Nelson, K. (1985). *Making sense: The acquisition of shared meaning.* Orlando, FL: Academic Press.

7. Hymes, D. (1974). *Foundations of sociolinguistics: An ethnographic approach.* Philadelphia: University of Pennsylvania Press.

   This concept of language variation has been applied mainly to oral language, but certainly it applies to written language as well. For example, how children read, including their use of varied strategies for discovering meaning, is dependent upon their purpose for reading (pleasure, information, performance), the kind of reading material (their own writing, a favorite trade book, a "linguistic" reader), their interest in and knowledge about the content and style of that material, and the audience for the reading (self, a friend, a teacher). Similarly, in writing, purpose and situation influence the words that are used, the ways words are arranged in sentences and larger structures (for example, stories)—even the ways they are spelled. (We worry more about our spellings in some situations and for some audiences than we do for others.)

8. Nelson (1985); see note 6, p. 10.

9. Britton, J. (1970). *Language and learning.* Harmondsworth, England: Penguin Press.

10. I thank Sarah W. Freedman for reminding me of yet another link to Vygotsky's work. See Vygotsky (1962), note 5.

11. Heath, S.B. (1986). Critical factors in literacy development. In S. de-Castell, A. Luke, and K. Egan (Eds.), *Literacy, society, and schooling: A reader* (p. 228). Cambridge: Cambridge University Press.

12. Gentes, H. (1986, June 18). The importance of dairy farming. *Home News,* p. 7.

13. Moffett, J. (1985). Hidden impediments to improving English teaching. *Phi Delta Kappan, 67,* 50–56.

14. Donaldson, M. (1978). *Children's minds.* New York: Norton.

15. The concept of "authenticity" in language use is discussed in:

    Edelsky, C., and Smith, K. (1984). Is that writing—Or are those marks just a figment of your curriculum? *Language Arts, 61,* 24–32.

    Goodman, K.S. (1986). *What's whole in whole language?* Exeter, NH: Heinemann.

16. For an engaging discussion of the role of dialogue in learning, see Shuy, R.W. (1987). Research currents: Dialogue as the heart of learning. *Language Arts, 64,* 890–897.

17. Shuman, A. (1986). *Storytelling rights: The uses of oral and written language by urban adolescents.* Cambridge: Cambridge University Press.
    Tannen, D. (1985). Relative focus on involvement in oral and written discourse. In D.R. Olson, N. Torrance, and A. Hildyard (Eds.), *Literacy, language, and learning* (pp. 124–147). New York: Cambridge University Press.

18. Heath, S.B. (1982b). Protean shapes in literacy events: Ever-shifting oral and literate traditions. In D. Tannen (Ed.), *Spoken and written language: Exploring orality and literacy* (pp. 91–118). Norwood, NJ: Ablex.

2 A Sisyphean Task: Historical Perspectives

Planning Group Members

Gerald Joncich Clifford, Chair
Fran Claggett
Marcia Farr
James Gray
Alfred Grommon
Jenny Cook-Gumperz
Mary K. Healy
Kenneth Lane
Robert Ruddell
Leo Ruth

Introduction

James Moffett

I have long felt, and said, that the predominance of reading over writing is a major fault of the curriculum, though the problem is rarely discussed. This chapter documents that this favoritism has been criticized periodically over the generations, but to no avail. Righting the imbalance has been all the more difficult, no doubt, because the language arts have never been integrated except in theory. Reading itself has suffered, ironically, since it is far better taught when reading, writing, and oral language activities are all brought to bear on each other. This lack of integration, too, has been deplored cyclically for the last century or longer, but never corrected despite sporadic prophecies of reform.

By dealing with these two chronic complaints in five different educational contexts, Geraldine Clifford helps us think about why correcting them should be such "A Sisyphean Task." I have a few thoughts about why, but I offer them mostly as an invitation to other educators to use this chapter as stimulus for their own analysis.

Though invented, we are told, about 3000 B.C., writing was discovered only about 1975—in American schools. An even more recent archaeological find was "critical thinking." Of course both have been professed goals all along, but must be unearthed from time to time precisely because of bias built in against them. In favoring reading over writing, schools have not only made both harder to master, but have necessarily also made students more the consumers of others' thinking than original thinkers themselves. To read is to think, of course, but to author is to conceptualize and verbalize more for oneself. And the various kinds of writing (many of them seldom taught in school) correspond to various ways of thinking. A full and well-grounded course of writing is automatically a course in thinking, critical and other. But the traditional teaching of composition bears a bias within itself exactly parallel to the predominance of reading over writing. This imbalance disturbs the fundamental complementarity

21

between inductive reasoning—from particular to general—and deductive reasoning—from general to particular.

The common approach to composition is far more deductive than inductive and, because of this, serious distortion militates against the development of critical thinking, while actually setting it up as the ultimate goal. That is, we teachers have most often framed assignments so that students must start with a generality and dig downward for examples and evidence. The prompts are *topics*—some name, phrase, or statement that preconceptualizes content and indeed often serves as a composition title, such as "Euthanasia," "Fate in Macbeth," or "Modern Revolutions Start Left and Move Right" ("Discuss. You have forty-five minutes."). As prompts, topics come from current popular debates, quotations from the greats, teachers' lectures, concepts central to a school course, and other sources in the public domain.

The deductive approach usually aims, through topic prompts, to habituate students to writing about some given content—either course material to be mastered and tested or certain issues we think students should be thinking about. When not simply didactic, the purpose may be moralistic at bottom, in keeping with the fact that English courses arose in the nineteenth century at about the time that religion courses were being phased out of public schools. Similarly, literary criticism took up where Biblical exegesis left off, which explains why a sermon on "the text for today" so closely resembles the *explication de texte*, why classics are sometimes referred to as the "canon," and why literature professors act like hierophants. At any rate, deductive assignments allow adults more control over the content of student writing and thinking, just as a reading bias fosters reception over production. It is a more authoritarian approach.

Using a given generalization as a probe to explore some content is of itself a valid and valuable way to proceed in building one's own knowledge. Deduction is in fact one half of the reasoning faculty. Since the composing process is, after all, a way to externalize the thinking process, we would expect deduction to be necessary for working out the implications and applications of some generalization already inferred. The thinker runs a hypothesis back down into more concrete reality to see what it can turn up. Thus from one generalization the thinker may deduce others and build chains of reasoning, structures of knowledge. A problem arises only when the complementary way of reasoning is slighted.

By contrast, when writing inductively, students begin with particulars and have to forge from them their own generalizations. While ensuring that this way of reasoning is not unduly short-circuited by others' previous abstractions, these assignments ask students to work up their own material from memory and fresh investigation of the world around them. Inductive writing puts students in the position of working from plenty instead of from paucity. Constant nagging for details and examples becomes unnecessary because these are the author's point of departure. Teachers should not prefer inductive writing either, but for novice writers it may be the kind to emphasize *first*, since it will prepare for deductive writing by bridging into higher abstraction.

Ironically, riding herd too soon on deductive, topic writing undermines the very kinds of expository and persuasive writing that colleges put such a premium on. In fact, universities have shown so little respect for any writing besides that required for term papers and essay exams that they have balefully influenced school writing to settle into a narrow range of the whole repertory. All through school, writing mostly just serves as study aids for given content or becomes a testing instrument to monitor the reading program.

Together, the predominance of reading over writing and of deductive over inductive writing place the inculcative possibilities of literacy over the investigative possibilities. (There goes "critical thinking.") The public—all of us—fears loss of control over youth, their minds and their behavior, and hence loss of control over the course of the society. Reading is dangerous enough, but reading matter is easy to control in school. By choosing the content, adults can use books to transmit the old values and modes of thought. Though potentially more dangerous, writing too can be used to transmit to students if they write about the reading or about other given content. (Study aids again.) But if students choose what they read—and especially what they write—ah well, who knows where that will end. The young may transform rather than transmit the world we know.

Teachers have the additional problem of controlling the classroom itself. How would one *manage* all this choice? And if students read and write things I know nothing about, how am I any longer an expert, and what role is left for me? The fact is that people learn to write and think well only in the measure that they are licensed to make decisions. We cannot have it both ways—to spoonfeed students for twelve years and then expect them in college to think for themselves. Authors must control matter and means. The perceiving of alternatives, the playing with possibilities, which makes a critical thinker, comes likewise from constantly experiencing choice. Powerless people quit thinking because nothing can come of it. If we teachers cannot empower, we cannot improve.

Prating on about the "process approach" and "critical thinking" will merely turn over again the cycle you will read of in this chapter unless both the public and the profession acknowledge that the curriculum stays unbalanced because we remain ambivalent about literacy. The secret reason that schools have had students read about writing and write about reading is that this neutralizes both. Our society keeps literacy skewed toward reading and deductive writing because, unconsciously, it is trying to maintain literacy as a one-way channel from adults to youth, because, freely given, reading and writing threaten adult security and identity. Part of us does not really want children to see and think for themselves. But one generation sometime has to fish or cut bait, has to *mean* it when it posts its noble goals, has to face the fear of actually achieving what it says it wants for its young. Are we that generation, or will we just provide more instances in the pattern of history you are now going to read about?

A Sisyphean Task: Historical Perspectives on Writing and Reading Instruction

Geraldine Jonçich Clifford[1]

"The mind has a thousand eyes," and like Argus, education must look at life through every one of them!

Mr. Hosic was the gallant Theseus who liberated distressed curriculum from this cramping limitation and made possible expansion and literation of the materials of instruction.

Given their classical educations, the first several generations of "modern" English language educators were more inclined than we are to view pedagogical reform in the terms of epic struggles. The two examples above were drawn from a 1936 publication of the National Council of Teachers of English, *A Correlated Curriculum*, which advocated the integration of writing, reading, speaking, and listening activities in the schools.[2] In truth, the battles to improve teaching and learning in the language arts were often mere skirmishes, the results neither victory nor defeat but stalemates. Sisyphus, not Hercules, is the hero of most school wars. To see this more clearly we now turn from Greek mythology to history, which is itself a tamer version of myth-making. History will give us better insight into the confounded and often cyclical nature of reform in education. The title chosen for this chapter reflects that fact, using the imagery of the Corinthian ruler condemned to push a heavy object up a steep hill. His was a task with which teachers can readily identify.

Introduction

You are living during a time that in our profession will be known as the beginning of the most thoroughgoing revolutionary development in the teaching of English in the 20th century. What will you do? Whether you yourself participate in that revolution, catch the caboose as the train rolls by, or simply sit and watch—that is up to you.[3]

This confident challenge was issued in 1964 by Professor Harold Allen of the University of Minnesota. It reminds one of another, equally confident prediction made during that same decade about the impending role of instructional technology: "Elementary, high school, or college teachers . . . who rely exclusively upon the teacher-centered lecture, demonstration, or explaining technique . . . now find themselves virtually expendable with the advent of television teaching."[4] Both men, of course, saw the events that they wanted to see and invested more vitality, or historicity, in them than proved warranted. These were, however, errors of judgment that we, too, will probably make about change in our own times.

The closer integration of writing and reading instruction is at present a popular topic. In describing the trends that characterize reading research developments during the 1970s, Jeanne Chall and Steven Stahl point to an increased interest for the past two decades in writing and in the relationship between writing and reading.[5] Janet Emig, an active participant in that movement, states her conviction that that movement is appropriate and seemingly inevitable. She argues:

> For learning and teaching writing and the other language arts cannot sensibly be regarded discretely and in isolation from one another. Reading impinges on writing, which in turn is transformed by listening and talking. Sponsorship of wholly autonomous research inquiries and curricular ventures into any one of the four language processes is now theoretically and empirically suspect.[6]

Will assessments like Emig's be sustained by future developments? Or will some later historian of language education liken them to the fate of those early 1950s futurists who confidently predicted that every home would soon have its own helicopter pad?

The Uses of the History of Education

The study of our past offers some protection against a tendency to view the immediate events of one's present as indicative of a trend. A trend is, ironically, only a mental construct used by historians and similar seekers after tidiness.[7] That fact explains why the past always appears more orderly than one's present. "History never looks like history when you are living through it," John Gardner once reminded us; rather, "It always looks confusing and messy, and it always feels uncomfortable."[8]

In addition, many a trend proves to be *partly reversible*—at least over the short run—if the forces supporting it are repudiated or diverted into other channels. So, in a sketch of the history of composition in American education, Alvina Treut Burrows aptly refers to the "crosscurrents and strong headwinds" that obstruct progress, of regressions, of action followed by reaction.[9] There is ample evidence from history to support this view.

It is therefore tempting to view history as a series of cycles endlessly repeated. Another common metaphor likens history to a pendulum. This is misleading, since a pendulum returns to the place from which it began its swing. This is not true of social events. For example, today's quest for "back to basics" in education cannot, and does not intend to, return us to that single and even undeterminable place where we somehow went wrong. Too much else has changed in the interim, and the standards of the past would no longer be acceptable even to the critics of present arrangements. Today's "basic literacy," for example, incorporates expectations that far exceed those that satisfied our forebears.[10] A United States Commissioner of Education at the turn of this century, William T. Harris, is rumored to have described the course of educational progress as "a zigzag, from one extreme to another." But hindsight shows us that the reversals were not as extreme as they then appeared. Still, the fact that Harris spoke thus is instructive about the course of educational developments. If we can be reasonably certain about anything, it is that our successors will draw similar conclusions about their own times.

The Plan of This Chapter

The thesis of this chapter is that cycles of concern for an integrated, holistic approach to English language instruction have periodically emerged in reaction to historical forces that are essentially fragmenting in their effects. We will explore events in twentieth-century American educational theory, research, and practice that illustrate and explain two fundamental and long-persisting facts about English language education in the schools. First, writing has been subordinated to reading and the other language skills. Second, language skills have been separated from one another; in particular, reading has been isolated from writing. The approach we take will be *thematic*, not chronological. There are better places to look for a systematic, sequential, time-oriented review of the major landmarks in the history of English language education, notably Arthur N. Applebee's 1974 work, *Tradition and Reform in the Teaching of English*,[11] and H. Alan Robinson's briefer 1977 collection, *Reading and Writing Instruction in the United States*.[12]

Ours is an essay using perspectives drawn from American educational and social history. It identifies five forces—the democratization of schooling, the professionalization of educators, technological change, the functionalist or pragmatic character of American culture, and liberationist ideologies—and probes their analytically separable but interacting influences on English language education. We will see that these influences promoted both separation and integration of the teaching of writing and reading. First, however, comes (1) a summary of the evidence for the assertions that writing has been dominated by reading in schools and that writing and reading have been separated for most of their histories; (2) next, illustrations of the prevailing opinion that integration in language education is the proper approach, giving rise to cycles of reform aimed at such integration; and (3) then an overview of the emergence in the nineteenth century of English as an identifiable subject of the school and college curriculum.

Writing and Reading in the Curriculum

The Low Estate of Writing in the Schools

The very first report that considered issues of secondary schooling in a national context—the 1894 report of the Committee of Ten—both declared that writing and reading are equal in importance and recommended that literature receive double the time that composition should have. No such landmark document exists for elementary education, but in a present-day work on interrelating writing and reading in the elementary school, the authors contend that "reading has dominated the scene in language arts instruction, research, and funding." Furthermore, "In most elementary classrooms, reading instruction dominates the day, starts the instructional agenda, controls grouping, and dictates schedules."[13] Years of studies of how classroom time is spent support this contention. In grades one, three, and five in the mid-1980s, only 15 percent of the school day was spent on writing; of that, two-thirds was spent on word-for-word copying in workbooks.[14] Investigations of secondary schools by the National Council of Teachers of English (NCTE) have repeatedly shown that more time was spent on literature than on all other aspects of the English curriculum *combined*; in the early 1980s, national reports indicated that less than 10 percent of a student's time in English was spent writing connected prose.[15] A study of 168 exemplary American high schools during the early 1960s—schools with high state or national reputations—reported that reading (that is, literature) received roughly three and a half times more attention than writing (that is, composition) in English classrooms. Moreover, English teachers were spending more time "teaching" composition through marking student papers at home than they were engaging in actual classroom writing instruction; further, most of their marking was of the proofreading kind.[16] Add to this distribution the far greater amount of reading than writing in the other content subjects of the curriculum, and the subordination of writing to reading becomes even more evident.

Another kind of domination of writing by reading is the longtime proclivity of upper-grade teachers to assign writing in response to literature; that is, to make writing a test of whether students have read and (perhaps) comprehended the reading. An early complaint about this relationship was articulated in 1913:

> For a considerable period the desire to unify the course in English, and especially the literature and composition, led to forced relations that were not to the advantage of either. Pupils were required to write too frequently on literary subjects that were beyond their grasp, with the result that the compositions were insincere and futile, and the pupil's love of literature hindered rather than helped.[17]

To try to remedy this situation, in 1909 the National Conference on College Entrance Requirements in English, comprised of high school and college teachers, adopted a report recommending that composition, instead, be substantially built upon "such experiences as come within the pupil's daily life and observation."[18] That this recommendation was only partly accepted is clear from the Anglo-American Dartmouth Conference held fifty-five years later: some of the members of the Dartmouth seminar group on literature still clung to the view that response to literature was the best means to improving writing.[19] In fact, the 1960s appear to represent a period when literature, from *Charlotte's Web* through *The Ox-Bow Incident*, was rather generally held to provide "eminently suitable and endless topics for writing."[20]

When Purdue University developed materials for the teaching of seventh grade English, a curriculum funded by the United States Office of Education under the 1960s Project English, it was described as "opus-centered" in its approach to language integration. The authors wrote:

> Literature is our target language. We steep pupils in reading; then we involve them in writing and speaking about what they have read. We also involve them in writing and speaking about their personal experiences that the literary work echoes.[21]

Purdue's effort led to an amalgam of the traditional literary emphasis plus references to students' own needs and experiences. In fact, both emphases recur and compete *throughout* the history of English language education in the past two centuries.

Literary essays have been generally accepted, even by advocates of enlarging writing's place in schooling, as long as they do not exclude other writing.[22] Writing experts do not consider the book report as an attempt to connect school writing and reading, composition and literature. This writing is usually, instead, an artifact intended to check on reading. In James Moffett's blunt words, this commonplace assignment puts writing and reading in "a stupefyingly negative relationship to each other that makes students want to avoid both." Unwittingly, teachers have accepted practices that make writing a punishment for reading.[23]

By the 1980s the National Assessment of Educational Progress examinations gave focused publicity to writing deficiencies. Despite this, the place of writing has not apparently grown much. The most recent large survey—The National Study of Writing in the Secondary School, sponsored by the National Institute of Education—discovered that school and homework writing activities were limited in both time and scope. Although about 40 percent of class time was spent in paper-and-pencil work, only 3 percent of students' class and homework time was spent on composing text of paragraph or greater length.[24] Furthermore, students in the lower tracks of the high schools generally had still fewer opportunities to write. Since the conventional wisdom of the English profession is that one learns to write by writing, the restricted amounts of opportunity for instruction and practice have been lamented for decades.

Another indicator of the relative status of writing and reading in the history of American schooling is the attention that authors have paid to each. The annual publications of the National Society for the Study of Education are a reasonably reliable barometer of their relative activity and importance. To date, the Society has published eighty-five two-volume yearbooks. Nine have been devoted to reading, six others to all other aspects of English language education: in 1906, 1923, 1944, 1970, 1977, and 1986. Only two, a 1923 and a 1986 volume, considered composition exclusively. Also, as Shirley Brice Heath has observed, published histories of education give far more attention to the teaching of reading than to the teaching of writing.[25] In fact, most historical index entries for *writing* refer to penmanship rather than to composition. Furthermore, although histories do not make this fact explicit, such important school problems as truancy, "retardation" (failure to be promoted), and early school leaving ("dropping out") were related to reading rather than to writing achievement. This is not surprising, given the consistently greater attention that reading and literature have received in both mass and elite education. In their quest to reconstruct the past, a major source for historians is school-books. Unlike the hornbooks, primers, and "eclectic" readers (anthologies) of the colonial and national periods and the ubiquitous spellers of the nineteenth century, composition books were not present except for rhetoric texts used in the colleges.

It has been said of American education that "if it's not tested, it's not taught!" As a consequence, some exponents of writing have periodically tried to develop tests of expository and imaginative writing abilities in order to *legitimize* this area. The movement for objective (quick-scoring), standardized tests of school subjects began around 1910. One after another field was quickly targeted, but reading tests were consistently the most widely used. This occurred for two reasons. First, great importance was placed on reading in the elementary schools, which enrolled the vast majority of all American school children before World War II. Second, vocabulary knowledge, which could be readily tested, appeared to be a reliable proxy measure for assessing reading competence in general.

A somewhat different situation existed in secondary schools. Although theirs was a "word field"—like reading, spelling, shorthand, and foreign language instruction—many teachers of literature have been consistently unsympathetic to standardized tests. They were offended by the aesthetics and logic of the procedure. Moreover, by being concentrated in the high schools, where the pressures for accountability were far less than in mass (elementary) education, literature teachers were somewhat protected. Therefore, externally imposed tests were fewer and less consequential in the professional lives of secondary English teachers. This did not save them from criticism, however. For example, in the 1930s the supervisor of the New York City Schools' program in remedial education singled out English teachers for their "wont to arrogate to themselves the holy mission of spreading the gospel of beauty and truth," for their "belletristic bias," for their deplorable concern "with 'Creativism' in all its forms at the expense of basic instruction in reading."[26] What has been said of the difficulties of testing literature and getting teacher support for such testing was even more true of composition, as we shall see later in this chapter.

Perhaps the best measure of the different status of writing and reading instruction is the weight of their respective research traditions. No field surpasses reading as a subject of investigation. By 1960, "Some 4,000 careful, scientific studies of the sociology, psychology, and teaching of reading" already existed.[27] Through the 1960s, when educational research was relatively well funded, 350 reading studies were filed annually.[28] In contrast, between 1955 and 1980, a total of only 156 studies was completed in the United States on writing in the elementary grades, and most of these were unpublished dissertations. Further, most writing studies were surveys of practices and other descriptive investigations of teacher preparation, censorship cases, and so on, rather than experimental or qualitative studies.[29] Except for one study on the weak relationship between studying grammar and improved writing, the research was generally inconclusive; teachers got little of value to go on.[30] At the height of funding for educational research, writing got less than one-tenth of one percent of all educational research dollars. Calculating all public school spending on textbooks, personnel, and materials related to writing and reading, Donald Graves concluded that "for every $3000 spent on children's ability to receive information, $1.00 was spent on their power to send it in writing."[31] Reporting in the 1982 *Encyclopedia of Educational Research* on writing, composition, and rhetoric, Janet Emig concluded that these three areas did not even constitute a field of research before 1970, since they were not "the subjects and objects of wide and systematic inquiry." Further, almost no studies had been undertaken on the important questions surrounding writing across the curriculum.[32]

A manifestation of the recent effort to raise the educational and research status of writing is to stress the process and not the product of writing, to enhance its equivalency to reading, to study composing and not the composition. As Burton Hatlin has put it, "'Process' suggests change, fluidity, indeterminacy: all positive values in a society that has prided itself on its presumed freedom from fixed hierarchies, which admires 'self-made' people, and which throughout its history hymned the open road."[33] Reading has that status among many educators; why not writing?

The Separation of Reading from Writing

In a 1986 review of theory and research conducted by the Center for the Study of Reading, the authors comment on the persisting separation of writing and reading instruction in the schools:

> They are commonly taught as individual subjects and in quite different ways. The way they are tested is usually quite different. Reading performance is often scored with multiple choice test items as either right or wrong; writing performance is often scored using qualitative comparisons.[34]

Many teachers continued to favor this separation, however. In 1957 the California State Department of Education surveyed secondary school teachers. It found that the majority favored separating the time devoted to the teaching of literature from that given to composition and oral language.[35] Even under the pressure of various school reform movements and given developments in language-related disciplines, separatism persisted. For example, the curriculum used in Portland, Oregon, schools offered six discrete language-study units during the four-year high school program. The language units were not correlated with one another or with speech, and only slightly with composition or literature. In 1964 Portland's was described as the "principal functional language-content school program in the United States."[36] What it lacked in language integration it supposedly made up for in high student consciousness of language. But instructional atomism probably reached its peak, to date, during the craze of the 1970s for behavioral objectives. Critics pointed to one city whose school board "had set 1200 of these objectives in the language arts alone; none of the 1200 suggested that the students might read a book or write a page describing their understanding of a trip to a museum or solve a word problem in mathematics."[37]

Observations about the fragmentation of the curriculum antedate these illustrations, however. In elementary school basal readers, teachers' manuals, and workbooks throughout this century it was persistently noted that writing of text was seldom called for; the writing that was required typically consisted of underlining, circling, and supplying one-word responses. In the early years of this century, reforms in the teaching of reading turned the emphasis from oral to silent reading and from word-calling to thought-getting; even these reforms did not ordinarily involve writing. In 1913, in an era when, to most teachers and to the public, writing meant penmanship rather than composing text, there was some discussion of writing in relation to speech and motor development but little in relation to reading.[38] What is the explanation? In substantial measure writing was overlooked or rejected in elementary schools because of ignorance of children's early writing. It was the general belief that writing must be delayed until reading and handwriting skills were secure, perhaps to the third grade or later. Postponement often meant neglect, however.

Given the research that showed statistical interrelationships of language skills, a prominent reading expert wondered, "Would the relationships found to exist among the various language arts areas and abilities be changed if instructional procedures were actually designed to reinforce and facilitate the learnings in other areas?"[39] Twice, in the

1930s and the 1950s, NCTE tried to promote greater instructional linkages between the language areas. The volumes of the NCTE Commission on the English Curriculum—in 1952, 1954, and 1956— placed particular emphasis on writing in an integrated language arts approach. But since complaints continued about the isolation existing among the language areas in the curriculum, there is presumptive evidence that these two language arts movements had limited influence on teaching practices at all levels.

Moreover, countervailing forces were at work. For example, believing that there was an overemphasis on language and composition in the federally funded projects launched during the post-Sputnik years, the College Entrance Examination Board (CEEB) appointed its own Commission on English. It proposed a tripartite division of high school English into language, literature, and composition; reading and other skills were ignored.[40] Both this commission and the federal government sponsored summer institutes for English teachers based on this tripartite pattern, sometimes with a workshop that aimed to provide some integration across the areas. The workshops were reported to be the weakest element in the whole program.[41]

As economic and social change made attendance at the American high school a universal experience of adolescence, comprehensive and vocational senior high schools began to add reading courses, reading teachers, and reading programs. The term *developmental reading* was coined to describe this new obligation of the high school, instead of *remedial reading*, which many teachers, students, and parents believed it to be. Like those celebrated critics of "dumbing down" the curriculum and textbooks, Bertrand Evans and James Lynch, many English teachers drew a distinction between "reading materials" and "literature."[42] If high schools had such a program, and many did not, teachers of developmental reading might be grouped apart from the English department faculty.[43] If developmental reading teachers were not separated, there still might be questions as to whether the budget for their programs should be a part of the English budget. Rarely did writing instruction profit from this appearance of reading instruction in the high schools.

Whether they taught literature or composition or both, English teachers tended *not* to belong to the International Reading Association (IRA). They tended not to know of the existence of one of the largest circulation journals in all of education, *The Reading Teacher*. For their part, IRA members might be oblivious of the journal *Language Arts*. Here were yet other signs of the isolation of writing and reading. In this case it was reinforced by the chasm that effectively separates elementary from secondary school teachers. We will have more to say about this later in this chapter.

Cycles of Interest in Relating the Language Arts

Regardless of the practices followed in the schools, one can find evidence that opinion leaders in English education throughout the twentieth century have favored the integrated teaching and practice of the language skills. For the entry on composition in the 1913 *A Cyclopedia of Education*, the nation's first such reference book, the author opined that in the high school "the divorce between English composition and other subjects is an evidence that our systems are still imperfect."[44] In the 1930s the term for enhancing the desired writing-reading relationships was *integration*. In 1950 A. Sterl Artley, subsequently a president of the International Reading Association, recalled the efforts made in the 1930s by NCTE's Commission on the English Curriculum to promote interrelationships among the language processes taught in elementary and secondary schools. He called them the "initial steps in a transition from the compartmentalized subject matter areas of reading, oral and written composition, spelling, and handwriting to an integrated or fused language arts or communications program."[45] Artley acknowledged, however, that it was easier to adopt the language arts label than to institute the required changes in teaching practices and that traditions of separatism still flourished. This was true despite the occasional appearance of basal reading series, professional books, and school district courses of study that espoused such approaches.[46] In many cases integrated programs existed in name only, "since it is the practice to teach two weeks of writing, followed by two weeks of 'oral composition,' followed by two weeks of something else," Artley conceded.

A quarter century later, in the late 1970s, in commenting on the calls for "back to basics," NCTE's political action group—SLATE: Support for Learning and Teaching of English—reiterated the case for integrated language instruction, thinking that it saw promising new signs of such a development:

> The movement has been decidedly away from the teaching of skills in isolation and the traditional emphasis upon grammar exercises, sentence parsing, and other drillwork. Instead, NCTE advocates the importance of language arts skills being used to reinforce each other. In this process of reinforcement, students explore a wide range of reading interests, get involved in a variety of related learning activities, and thereby develop a firmer grasp of all of the necessary language competencies.[47]

In this latest reform cycle, NCTE was being driven by events largely external to the schools: by the economic, social, cultural, and political forces that give context to education in any society. But professional developments also figure in that context. One such development was the state of research on writing-reading relationships. When the first *Handbook of Research on Teaching* was published in 1963, a small corpus of investigations and theory existed to support the opinions of many prominent English educators about the value of integrated language arts.[48] Although reading specialists were less concerned with the issue, they too were informed that writing activities such as note-taking, outlining, and summarizing improved reading comprehension scores and that good readers were likely to do more creative writing.[49] Twenty years later, in *Becoming Readers in a Complex Society*, a publication of the National Society for the Study of Education, another pair of reading specialists was ready to take a more systematic look. They concluded that only the first steps had been taken to develop a research base: "Connections between writing and reading are only now beginning to enjoy avid research attention, so that little of substance is as yet known about ways in which writing can enhance reading comprehension."[50] Here, again, is that tendency, noted in the beginning of this chapter, for each generation to *think* it perceives a change but which a later generation claims for *its* own time.

In the soft social and behavioral sciences that constitute educational research, standards for judging the adequacy of research vary widely. In 1984 the authors of *Becoming a Nation of Readers*, the Commission on Reading of the National Academy of Education, reviewed theory and research in psycholinguistics, cognitive psychology, and child development. They concluded that this literature supported writing's contribution to more effective reading, as well as to its importance in its own right.[51] What was most encouraging to supporters of writing instruction was the new research on the processes and components of writing. This was a departure from the focus of the 1920s, for example, when studies investigated length of sentences, ratio of complete to incomplete sentences, numbers of words written in relation to extent of different words, and similar matters.[52] Like other English language educators over the decades, June Birnbaum thought that "despite a surge of interest in the relationship of reading and writing, in-depth study has only begun." Yet, in her opinion, teachers and researchers should go ahead and take important strides in "rejoining the naturally related processes of reading and writing."[53]

By the 1980s, theory-building was also making new connections between the processes of writing and reading. Once again it was noted that readers write (in making marginal notes or preparing outlines or précis, for example) and that writers must read (their own notes and drafts and, often, some other resources). More original, however, were descriptions of reading itself as a composing activity: comprehension is an act of constructing meaning, and one that can be made more effective by the understanding of such elements of the writing process as planning, drafting, and revising.[54] The earliest writings of young children were becoming dignified as researchers studied "invented spellings" and "story grammar." Such study offered more possibilities of "unifying the acquisition of writing and reading skills" in the early grades.[55] Integration in the high schools depended on other insights. If educators were again optimistic, perhaps this time the integrated English language curriculum sought almost from the first appearance of English as a school and college subject might finally be achieved.

The Emergence of English as a Curriculum Subject

The history of Anglo-American education is littered with references to English. One was to the "good English education" espoused by reformers of various stripe, from Puritan and Presbyterian dissenters in the Mother Country to the utilitarian Benjamin Franklin, all of whom established English-language academies as alternatives to the Latin grammar schools. Another reference was to the "common English education" that dominated the "common branches"—reading, 'riting, and 'rithmetic—of the prototypical eight-year nineteenth-century American public school. Yet another was to the "English course" of the later nineteenth- and early twentieth-century high school and college. At first a suspect alternative to the "classical course" (Latin and Greek required) and the "scientific course" (substituting German and French), the English course eventually triumphed. Still, the staying power of the classics is indicated by the 1902 survey of the United States Commissioner of Education, which showed more high school students studying Latin than English.[56]

By the early twentieth century, English clearly dominated the elementary school curriculum, largely in the form of instruction in reading. English subsequently became the most required subject in the secondary school. Through the cycles of relaxation and tightening of academic discipline that have marked this century, English requirements for (and in) the college and university have consistently fared better than requirements in science, mathematics, and foreign languages. Yet for all its prominence, for being a shared experience of millions of

Americans, the meaning of *school English* still confuses the public and, perhaps, some professionals.[57] It is clearly one of the "solids" of the modern high school, but is it a skills subject or a content subject? If the former, how is the responsibility for its development to be divided between the English department and all those other faculty who teach it? If it is both skill and content, which aspect is to predominate? Is it grammar and spelling? What about handwriting? Literature? Creative writing? In part, the confusion stems from the fact that English has not ordinarily been experienced as a unified school subject, and schooled Americans have received uneven portions of its diverse elements. This in itself reflects the several streams that fed into the new subject of English—a subject that emerged in the United States as a discrete, if not unified, entity only in the late nineteenth century.

A Gathering of Many Traditions

The history of English as a school subject is entangled in the Protestant Reformation, the rise of the nation-state, colonialism, the invention of printing, and the emergence of modern science. (This was also true, of course, of the study of other vernacular languages: of French in France, German in Germany, Italian in Italy—each having to nudge out Latin and Greek as the objects of a "real" school or university education.)[58] Suffice it to say here of the United States, that by the early nineteenth century, when the common (public) school was spreading out of New England on its way to vanquishing most other approaches to making children literate, three facts were most pertinent. First, the basic elements of an English education—the abilities to read and write English—were accepted as a necessary standard for all white Americans, both boys and girls. Second, a body of American writing, much of it patriotic utterances associated with the American Revolution, had been packaged into books for children, beginning a corpus of American literature and history that children were increasingly required to study. Third, declaring America's cultural independence, Noah Webster was creating school spellers and dictionaries of American English; these would standardize orthography, limit variations in pronunciation, set standards of correct usage, and provide additional English content for the curriculum.[59]

There was still, of course, a great deal of tinkering and packaging to do, especially to define and redefine what it meant to read and to write English. For generations many teachers and parents were content with *reading* defined operationally as the ability to say the words aloud. They were especially impressed when practice resulted in memorized recitations of prose and poetry; wide, silent reading had little popular appeal in schools. The meaning of the ability to write was even more unclear and slow to develop, in large measure because less time was given to writing. In everyone's mind, writing meant the ability to sign one's name. This was the first, and for centuries the only, writing task that people had striven to master; for many children, one's name remains the first word one writes and reads, although not necessarily the first word one sees. Writing also meant penmanship. For the colonial and early national periods, most of the entries for *writing* in Lawrence Cremin's masterful histories refer to penmanship and signing; there is no entry for *composition* in his first volume and few references in the second.[60]

Writing was coming to mean more, however. Nineteenth-century rural and urban schools gave children ample practice in writing short contracts, invoices, and receipts; how much youngsters learned to compose these, rather than to copy and master by rote teacher-provided models, is difficult to judge with certainty. Then, as later, student writing apparently existed to display penmanship or knowledge, not ideas. Those older children who remained in school longer wrote letters and essays, often doing little beyond copying models. Yet functional literacy—in the forms of personal and business correspondence, diaries, and autobiographies—has left its traces in the millions of pieces of manuscripts to be found in libraries and personal collections. But we simply do not know how typical was schoolmaster George Moore of Grantham, New Hampshire, who wrote in his diary on December 25, 1828 (a regular school day), "[I] informed scholars for the first time that *compositions* would be required of them weekly."[61] Nor do we know what Moore meant by *compositions*.

Twentieth-century concepts of composition writing appear surprisingly early. For example, in his 1749 proposals for an English School in Philadelphia, Benjamin Franklin specified that all the students (adolescent boys) "should be taught to write a *fair Hand*, and swift, as that is useful to All," be taught the English language by grammar, and more:

> To form their Stile they should be put to writing Letters to each other, making Abstracts of what they read; or writing the same Things in their own Words: telling or writing Stories lately read, in their own Expressions. All to be revised and corrected by the Tutor, who should give his Reasons, and explain the Force and Import of Words, &c.
> To form their Pronunciation, they may be put on making Declamations, repeating Speeches, delivering Orations, &c. The

Tutor assisting at the Rehearsals, teaching, advising, correcting
their Accent, &c.[62]

English academies like Franklin's embodied a new hybrid: a modern
core of English, certain other practical studies, and grammar and
rhetoric, borrowed from the colleges. The methods being used elsewhere to teach Latin grammar were, however, transferred to the
teaching of English. Pupils learned pages of rules that described Latin
rather than English grammar and parsed sentences by Latin methods.[63]

The perennially fragmented character of later English education
owes something to the fact that schools like Franklin's added new
elements to the several other distinct educational traditions that were
merged to form school English by 1900. Reading, the most likely
language skill after speech and signing to be learned at home, represents
a tradition of literacy in the native language that was becoming a
universal requirement for participation in modern society. The teaching
of writing, as handwriting, had once been a monopoly of scribes—
whose chief function before the days of printing had been to preserve
learning by copying and illustrating manuscripts. The Church long
enforced prohibitions against scribes teaching reading and schoolmasters teaching writing. This distinction collapsed, however, under the
influence of the Reformation, the spread of printed books, the growth
of commerce. It became common, in England and later in North
America, to find schools and teachers offering both writing and reading
instruction, as well as schools that remained specialized.[64]

Still, as late as 1800, reading and writing had different uses—reading
motivated chiefly by religious and, later, political pressures, writing by
economic change. As a sign of this, handwriting exercises were far
more likely to be found in a textbook along with arithmetic (which
also had commercial value) than to be included in reading books.
Writing and reading had different constituencies; women were, for
example, thought not to need writing even after they were permitted
reading. It is not surprising therefore that, before about 1830, many
teachers of beginning reading were women, but teachers of penmanship
(scriveners), of more advanced English subjects, and of ciphering were
almost always men. Further, given the tradition of being taught by
different teachers, writing and reading were commonly learned at
different ages: learning to read as young children, learning to write
later, if at all.

Examples of this fragmentation are revealed in many accounts that
have survived to the present. Like countless others, John Griscom
(1774–1852), a native of New Jersey, was sent for short periods to
several schools by his father, a literate saddle and harness maker. One

schoolmaster taught him spelling and another how to compose letters to his parents. Still, at age seventeen, he began teaching school himself, without much knowledge of grammar; further, although "twas certain I could write, and cipher too,—but in reality, as to my penmanship, . . . it was very awkward and clumsy, for I had never had a teacher who had inspired me with any ambition to acquire a good hand."[65] Through much of the nineteenth century, American adolescents and adults who had never attended school or who had left before mastering writing answered the advertisements of writing teachers or subscribed to a few weeks of instruction in "writing schools" offered by itinerant teachers. Susan Grant warned a younger brother in 1841: "Do not think it is a matter of little consequence *how* you write, for many a young man has lost a chance for a good clerkship, because he was a poor writer."[66] How much their improvement in handwriting came through composing rather than copying and how much their better handwriting caused them to produce more writing is hard to determine. We do know that, as late as the 1870 census, those claiming reading literacy were 50 percent more numerous than those professing any ability to write.[67]

Influences from the Education of Elites

In 1895, after surveying a number of American colleges and universities, the editor of a prominent national magazine, *The Dial*, concluded that it had established "beyond question the claims of English as a proper subject of university study."[68] The classical secondary schools and the colleges and universities of Europe and North America had long had their own language studies, notably Latin and Greek grammar and rhetoric; these subjects had been the preserve of elites in the Church, learned professions, and gentry. Since the Renaissance those of scholarly disposition among the upper classes had studied and practiced the principles of oral and written expression in the ancient languages. By the nineteenth century, however, American colleges were being visited by the same modernizing forces that had already made English language studies a popular alternative to the study of ancient languages in secondary schools. Rhetoric and oratory (using English texts), a Latinized English grammar, philology, and, more gradually, English literary history were appearing in the curriculum as alternatives to the Greek etymology, Hebrew grammar, and practice in Chaldee found in the curriculum of the colonial colleges.

The pathway to this change was initially cleared by the literary societies that students formed, more than by adventuresome professors.

In these societies, the members read modern literature that they collected in their own society libraries, wrote and criticized one another's essays, and prepared and performed orations for their members and for other societies.[69] The practice received in writing declamations and delivering Class Day and commencement addresses benefited the aspiring ministers and lawyers who predominated among American college students. But America was becoming daily less an oral and more a print culture. As one historian puts it, "Decision making in business and government was more and more to rely on the impersonal printed word, rather than face-to-face contact."[70]

Before 1900 most American colleges began instituting courses in composition for freshmen. Even small, local colleges, like Beloit for men and Rockford for women in Illinois, moved composition from fortnightly or Saturday exercises to a nine-credit requirement.[71] The larger, ambitious institutions embarked on a process of faculty and curriculum specialization that in the twentieth century would place oratory in a speech department and poetry in an English department and would make freshman composition a de facto course in technical writing for the aspiring business person. Practice in writing was associated with the requirements of business, professional, or social life.[72] This very usefulness of writing made it less prestigious, however, than literature was coming to be; literature was to be studied as an end in itself. In 1900, after Harvard converted to a fully elective system, its sole prescribed course was freshman composition.[73] This was not because composition was valued on its own terms, but because it was *not*; that which was valued was made elective, something for the discriminating student.[74]

The universities' changing values influenced the high schools. In a period when individual colleges set examinations to determine who was eligible to enroll, rather than use a diploma from an accredited high school or a standardized external examination like the College Boards, college entrance requirements told the high school faculty what to emphasize. In 1819 Princeton College had asked applicants for "acquaintance" with the Latinate English grammar and, in 1870, for demonstration of the ability to write a "short and simple English composition"; other colleges followed suit. In 1874 Harvard College's specification went still further by linking composition to specific literary texts. Candidates for admission were to "write a short English Composition, correct in spelling, punctuation, grammar, and expression, the subject to be taken from such works of standard authors as shall be announced from time to time."[75] Other colleges developed their own lists, and the resulting chaos eventually led, in 1893, to a voluntary

Conference on Uniform Entrance Requirements in English. Literature
was enhanced as a school subject in the process.

These events moved the high schools and colleges toward a stable
literary canon. There were serious drawbacks, however, in this new
marriage of literature and composition: literature was frequently man-
handled in order to furnish a subject for teaching composition, while
composition became hedged in; the results were stilted literary essays.[76]
In 1893 Harvard established a Committee on Composition and Rhetoric,
which concluded that its students were lamentable writers, a criticism
that would be periodically echoed in subsequent decades.

An earlier effort to reform composition had come in the 1830s and
1840s when educational leaders like Horace Mann objected to rote
learning of grammar and pressed for teaching methods that ensured
understanding of rules, models, and definitions. Teachers were urged
to ensure that pupils could apply grammatical rules in composing
sentences and essays. These reforms did eventually produce more of
what was then called "consecutive writing." In 1913 Franklin T. Baker
could report some progress:

> Within the past twenty-five years the art of composition has
> assumed far greater importance than before. . . . It is now usual
> to find composition given a large share of the time of the program,
> and taught as a vital subject rather than in the occasional and
> perfunctory fashion of former days. It is now recognized as a
> subject of the greatest utility, inasmuch as every one depends for
> his pleasure and success in part upon his ability to express his
> ideas agreeably and effectively. It conduces to clearness and
> definiteness in one's thoughts, to care in ordering and expressing
> them. To have tried conscientiously to say things well helps in
> the appreciation of things well said, and therefore adds to the
> enjoyment of literature. And command of one's native speech
> puts one into closer touch with the social and national life about
> him.
>
> Especially noteworthy are the changes in the methods of
> instruction. . . . The earlier teaching aimed at a sort of lifeless
> accuracy. Verbal and grammatical correctness, propriety in spelling
> and punctuation were sufficient. The present-day teaching of the
> better sort judges the child's efforts not only for these things, but
> for the interest and general effectiveness of the whole composi-
> tion.[77]

Although Baker's assessment overstated both the progress made and
the bright prospects ahead, school writing had indeed progressed if
judged relatively. And, while Baker's language and references are
rooted in the social and pedagogical temper of the early progressive
era, modern teachers and theorists of writing will find concepts there
they can endorse.

Something of a backdrop has now been established for a consideration of those social, cultural, political, and economic developments that appear to explain both the constancy and the pressures for change in English education. That their influence was not limited to this part of the school curriculum will also be obvious to the reader.

The Democratization of Schooling

The political decisions to ensure the schooling of all the children of all the people began in the nineteenth century. By 1900 the states of the United States, each sovereign with respect to education, had taken some or all of the following actions: establishing provisions for voters to found and maintain local public schools, supplementing locally raised funds with state monies, making public schools free, setting minimum standards for schoolhouses, broadening curriculum, approving textbooks, addressing teacher education and selection, and enacting and enforcing compulsory school attendance laws. The Northeast had gone the farthest and the South and rural states generally lagged. But so widespread and successful were these policies that about 90 percent of the nation's school children were in public schools before the turn of the century. Public school students included the majority of those whose parents could have paid for private schooling and would have done so in earlier eras. The children of immigrants were similarly drawn into this system of universal education, some in Catholic or Lutheran school systems, the majority in the public system. America's major racial minorities—blacks, Native Americans, and Mexican Americans—were also receiving public schooling, but often in inferior schools, almost always under deliberate policies of segregation, and with less regularity and longevity of attendance, given prevailing educational discrimination and social prejudice.

The High School: The "People's College"

The public high school appeared in some cities before the Civil War and had spread by 1880 to enroll most secondary school students, dooming the private academy and seminary to virtual extinction; yet it educated a small fraction of all school children before 1920. Most youngsters left school at the end of the eighth grade or earlier, drawn into the labor market by the availability of unskilled jobs or repelled by the mandatory entrance examinations and academic classicalism of the high school curriculum. In 1890 only 6.7 percent of youngsters aged fourteen to seventeen were attending secondary schools. The majority of the graduates were girls, some planning to become teachers; many of the rest, boys and girls, were headed for the still more elite institution of the college or university.

Yet the processes of social, economic, and political change that had created universal elementary schooling were already evident, and they would eventually spread and democratize secondary education as well.[78] Rising standards of living in the American population generally and status-striving in the growing middle class attracted progressively more children into high schools. Heavy immigration, technological change, and the campaigns of social reformers and organized labor were also constricting employment opportunities for youth, especially for those under age fifteen or so. Academic qualifications for high school admission gradually disappeared, except for a handful of selective, examination high schools. Increasingly, one was promoted to high school as one was promoted from grade to grade: on the basis of age.

In 1930 half of the youngsters aged fourteen to sixteen were in high school; by 1940 the proportion was two-thirds. Despite high attrition before graduation, status-conscious and subject-matter-oriented high schools had to deal with the consequences of becoming institutions of universal instruction. To relieve some of the pressure, high schools adopted alternative curricula to the college-oriented academic course—trade and commercial education, home economics, and finally the general track that eventually came to enroll most students. They also instituted ability-grouping. The extracurriculum, the relaxed disciplinary standards, and a more informal climate were accommodations of the system to the social and intellectual diversity of an often restive clientele. Students who were not book-minded had been "frozen out, as early as possible" in the old days, recalled one educator in 1940; now "we reduce the amount of book and language activity in the school to the minimum at which we can keep our self-respect."[79] In 1956, by which time the majority of students persisted to graduation, the NCTE Commission on the English Curriculum was forced to consider literature in reference to the needs of widely diverse students and even to give attention to reading instruction:

> Improvement of reading in the secondary school has in recent years become the common concern of all teachers. Conditions of life in the mid-twentieth century place increasing demands upon every individual to be able to read intelligently. More and more pupils in the lower ranges of ability are now in high school. Research has revealed the complex nature of reading and the necessity for adapting skills learned in the early grades to the

more mature tasks of the high school. This challenge is being met by recognizing the need for both a developmental and a remedial program.[80]

The position of NCTE reflected official opinion favoring a holistic approach to English language education, a strategy rooted in pupil experience. This movement paralleled the popularization of the high school. As part of the American response to the launching of the Soviet Sputnik in 1957, however, NCTE's Conference on Basic Issues in the Teaching of English retreated: it endorsed more formal, book-centered teaching styles and more traditional curriculum units—in line with the public outcry, Congressional alarm, and the rush of academic disciplines to get on the bandwagon to save the American way of life. The majority of NCTE conference members represented Eastern colleges and preparatory schools, or those with classical leanings.[81] Heavier university influence on the theory of English education also came through the Modern Language Association and the Commission on English of the College Entrance Examination Board (CEEB). However, through its 1965 report, *Freedom and Discipline*, CEEB tried to compromise. In its report, CEEB acknowledged both children's experience-based mastery of English grammar (which was attested to by linguists) and the obligations of English teachers and professors to maintain standards of usage. While formed "to propose standards of achievement for college preparatory students and to suggest ways of meeting them," CEEB stated that its efforts "though aimed at one group, are intended to influence all tracks and all levels."[82] Thus by the mid-1960s, American secondary education seemed to be returning to its older, college-oriented posture.

From "Uniform Lists" for the Few to Experience for the Many

It had been reaction against college influence (some said "domination") over the curriculum and pedagogy of the high school that led in 1911 to the formation of a professional body, the National Council of Teachers of English. NCTE's first target was the hold exerted on high schools by the 1894 recommendations of the National Education Association's Committee of Ten, a body chaired by Harvard University president Charles W. Eliot. University spokesmen had been gratified by an increase of students wishing to prepare themselves in college for the new opportunities in the professions, science, technology, and business. But the Committee of Ten reflected collegiate unease, given the less aristocratic backgrounds and weaker academic motivations of their new students, many of them products of public high schools rather than of academies run by the elite colleges' own graduates. The private sector's share had gone down from preparing 32 percent of college students in 1890 to a mere 7 percent in 1930. By setting uniform college entrance requirements and issuing pronouncements, the colleges tried to improve English education in the high schools. To do so, the colleges promoted the analysis of English literary classics through required lists and urged teachers to focus upon correctness in spelling, grammar, and handwriting in student essays and proper usage and delivery in their oral utterances.

The rebuttal to the Committee of Ten came in 1917. Another committee, differently constituted, issued a ringing challenge: "After more than half a century of struggle, the public high school has definitely established itself as a continuation of common-school education, as a finishing school (in the good sense of that term) rather than as a fitting school."[83] This declaration of independence from the colleges was the report of the joint committee of the National Council of Teachers of English and the Commission on the Reorganization of Secondary Education of the National Education Association. Unlike the Conference on English of the Committee of Ten—seven professors and three schoolmen—this body was dominated by representatives of schools and was chaired by James F. Hosic. The committee's 1917 *Reorganization of English in Secondary Schools* concluded that the demands of college preparation created "monotonous and unintelligent uniformity in the secondary schools."[84] Hosic, professor of English at Chicago Teachers College, summarized the new orientation intended for the high school: "The chief problem of articulation is not how to connect the high school and the college but how to connect the high school with the elementary school."[85] High schools were urged to develop the students' faculties of sensitivity, thinking, and interpretation; to enrich their imaginative lives; to stress appreciation and enjoyment in reading; to view learning in instrumental terms as promoting socially responsible, well-rounded lives.

The spirit of the new science of child development and the confidence of the progressive era in rational reform and social adjustment were evident in this report, which was the first comprehensive curriculum statement in the history of English language instruction in the United States. The committee believed that the articulation of writing and reading were mandated by the social nature of language, as well as by psychological principles:

> The chief function of language is communication. Hence . . . the pupil must speak or write to or for somebody, with a consciously conceived purpose to inform, convince, inspire, or entertain. The

> English course should be so arranged as to couple speaking and
> writing for practical purposes with reading of the same character,
> and speaking and writing for pleasure and inspiration with the
> study of the novelists, the playwrights, and the poets.[86]

While the report did not repudiate prevailing recommendations in
literature, it envisioned a broadened curriculum and greater choice.
Although the influence of the Hosic report was uneven, certain practices
did become commonplace: writing assignments freed from literary
themes, extensive and even "free" reading, the use of magazines and
newspapers to engage reluctant readers and to connect school to life,
and providing practice in language skills associated with student
government, drama, assemblies, and school publications.

Some of the distinctions between elementary and secondary education were indeed breaking down, as were those between reading
and literature, creative and functional writing, oral and written language. The concept of *language arts* made common cause with John
Dewey's philosophical attack upon all dualisms: mind versus body,
individual versus society, art versus science, subject matter versus life,
knowledge versus skills—even text versus reader or writer versus
reader.

The 1920s and 1930s introduced other challenges to old pieties, in
the forms of Freudian and gestalt psychology. New NCTE committees
and commissions published two works that endorsed the "sturdy
common sense and vigorous statements" of Hosic's report.[87] Both the
1935 *An Experience Curriculum in English* and the 1939 *Conducting
Experiences in English* emphasized pupils' prior knowledge and interests
as the starting point and promoted experience as the organizational
principle of curriculum and teaching from kindergarten through graduate school.[88] Experience was an antidote to the fragmenting effects
of specialization and the elective system. "The cause of the malady is
the artificial separation of one subject from another, and, even more
potently, the divorce of all school study and drill from dynamic
experience."[89] We must present students with a "carefully integrated
curriculum so taught that the connection of each subject with every
other subject and with the whole of life will be unmistakable," declared
another NCTE committee, in *A Correlated Curriculum*.[90] But it was
premature for the committee to conclude that "the day of educational
segments is definitely done."[91] While elementary schools were more
susceptible to such reforms, for reasons to be discussed later, many
teachers in primary and even more in secondary schools adhered to
traditional schedules, textbooks, and assignments, drilled students on
grammar, and religiously compartmentalized their teaching of English.

Moreover, when teachers succumbed to the ideology of experience as a basis of writing, was it often, as Robert Connors claims, because such essays are easier for the overworked teacher to read?[92]

The Popularization of the College and New Questions about Standards

Higher education was itself slowly changing after 1900. It was becoming increasingly specialized in its curricula and faculty. The faculty, many with doctorates in subfields of the disciplines, were less able to agree on the essentials of a collegiate education and hence tended to relax requirements altogether for undergraduates. Conservatives charged that the universities, and even many so-called liberal arts colleges, were more responsive to explicitly utilitarian than to liberal and cultural values. Yielding to expediency, early in the century the colleges abandoned their own entrance examinations in favor of admitting students on the basis of class standing and graduation from accredited high schools. As high schools proliferated and became increasingly diverse in their products, the more selective colleges also began using nationally standardized scholastic aptitude tests to provide a supplementary screen.

Entrance requirements were also loosening. In 1894 the president of Bowdoin College insisted that "Latin is the Thermopylae where the modern Greeks must take their stand, determined to withstand the Barbarians or perish in the attempt."[93] Latin did perish, however. Between 1915 and 1965 the percentage of high school students studying Latin went from 37 percent to 1 percent. A significant indicator of the capitulation to modernism was the decision of that bastion of academic conservatism, Yale University, to drop Latin as an admissions requirement in 1919. The modern foreign languages also fared poorly. The very large high school enrollments in German collapsed during World War I and never recouped; the Romance languages failed to pick up much of the slack. In 1950 fewer than a quarter of high school students studied any foreign language. As a consequence of these several actions—the elimination of the composition requirement along with college admissions tests, the general decline in language studies, the capitulation to the principle of electives—there is reason to believe that writing and language study declined relative to literature and oral language and that English generally competed less well with other school subjects and activities despite the colleges' retention of English as an entrance requirement.

The "G.I. Bill of Rights" (Servicemen's Readjustment Act of 1944) began the real rush of Americans to colleges and universities, however.

Tertiary education, which had enrolled 3.9 percent of the age group in 1900, attracted 33.9 percent by 1960. Fearful of rising competition for clean and secure jobs, Depression-reared parents increasingly encouraged their children to plan for college and wondered aloud whether the high schools provided an adequate preparation for the youth who were the first in their families to attempt higher education. Socially prestigious institutions, like Harvard and Stanford, raised their entrance requirements to become academically as well as socially elite; so did the stronger public universities. For the first time, nonselective state, private, and junior colleges faced much of the range of student abilities and interests encountered in the comprehensive high school. Remedial reading and writing courses served many college students. The Council for Basic Education, founded in 1956, lambasted progressivism and "life adjustment" education for having debased the curriculum and academic standards of public schools.

In the loud reaction against a half-century of often timid educational "reform," English education was not exempt. Critics singled out the "word method" of teaching reading, high school units in "talking on the telephone" and "writing thank you notes," and college majors in "communications." While business and industry claimed that their production and service employees could not read well, management trainees were faulted for their inability to write well. The academic elite got particular attention from the critics between 1950 and 1965. The Advanced Placement Program was inaugurated by the College Board in 1952 for "secondary school students who are capable of doing college-level work" and for high schools "interested in giving such students the chance to work up to capacity."[94] In his widely cited 1959 report, *The American High School Today*, James B. Conant advocated two reform strategies: (1) enlarging small high schools so that broad and challenging programs of general, vocational, and academic classes would be available to all; and (2) instituting more demanding courses and requirements for the 15 to 20 percent of the age group who are academically talented. He thought both strategies were consistent with America's democratic ideals.[95]

For a long time, to many Americans democracy in education meant the chance for their children to climb the social and economic ladder of success. Good usage in language had long been an important social marker. It functioned to set the educated and cultivated apart and provided a standard against which to measure the acceptability of the upwardly mobile. With the establishment and formalization of English studies around the turn of the century, the educated American was subjected, through the study of the written and oral language, to "a certain version of the native language, a version that tended to coincide with the dialect of the upper middle class, the group that had customarily attended college." After about 1870 in the United States, in the words of James Berlin, "Composition teachers became the caretakers of the English tongue, and more important, the gatekeepers on the road to the good things in life, as defined by the professional class."[96] Rhetoric's traditional emphasis upon persuasion and analysis was transformed into "a narrow concern for convention," a "stultifying hunt" by the composition teacher for students' errors in the mechanics of writing.[97] Efforts to reduce this orientation had limited success, however. And, given the renewed emphasis of the 1950s and early 1960s upon correctness and the elimination of errors in writing or speech, attempts to integrate writing and reading were a distraction at best.

After 1950 the civil rights movement and affirmative action programs added their own complications. In the long tradition of joining the advantaged by emulating them, some speakers of nonstandard English certainly wanted such corrective attention by the gatekeepers. But the more militant (white, brown, and black) have argued more forcefully in recent times that "Black is Beautiful" and that retention of one's native language and culture is more important than melting into the mainstream. Linguists endorsed the rule-governed character of non-standard dialects. The "disadvantaged," they pointed out, came to school "completely fluent (like all human beings of their age)" and teachers' claims about their linguistic incompetence were called ill-informed.[98] In the universities, ethnic studies (and women's studies) departments also challenged once-entrenched values and ideas of what truth and beauty are.

Two other manifestations of the latter-day democratization of American schooling bear on the issues of the relative status and relationship of writing and reading. Bilingual education has not yet proven to be a friendly environment for writing. With rare exceptions,[99] the overwhelming emphasis is on oral language competence, with a secondary focus on the reading of English. Writing, when it goes beyond mere copying, is often confined to teachers asking students to make sentences using words written on the blackboard; this leads to mechanical, formulaic products—*table*: "The table is big"; *flower*: "The flower is big"; *pen*: The pen is not big." Students are seldom asked to write anything generative of more than two or three sentences. Bilingual classes provide even fewer writing opportunities than do those for native English speakers, where the readers, workbooks, and teachers' manuals persist in suggesting limited writing activities: underlining, circling, numbering in sequence, filling one-word blanks.[100]

The Right to Read program, a large federally funded attack on functional illiteracy announced in 1969, represented the shift, however short-lived, from concern with excellence to that of promoting equity.[101] In proposing a national strategy for attacking the reading problem, the authors of the 1975 *Toward a Literate Society* wrote that it would be tragic and counterproductive if so much attention were given to the teaching of reading that writing and other language skills were slighted.[102] This happened, however. Like standards for minimum competencies, those for reading skills were decidedly emphasized. Right to Read also perpetuated isolation, as do categorical programs in general, since program leaders are fearful of losing funding if they lose their identity by attempting to attack more than one problem at a time. Such single-issue campaigns support the fragmentation and specialization that have moved through society, only now and then challenged or checked.

The Professionalization of Educators

Professionalization is a major product of the linked advances of technological change, occupational differentiation, and formal education.[103] It fosters the development and aggrandizement of distinctive "subcultures" of like-minded interest groups. In education, subcultures divide teachers from administrators, and both groups from university professors and educational researchers. Subcultures divide elementary from secondary teachers, English teachers from other teachers, writing teachers and *their* specialists from reading teachers and *their* specialists. They even separate the faculties of English departments in the colleges: the lower status faculty who teach composition are kept at arm's length by the "regular faculty," whom Thomas Newkirk calls the "mandarinate that looked upon us with such disdain."[104] Professional subcultures are defined and maintained by the professional educations of their members, their disciplinary or work orientations, their organizations, and their publications. Textbooks and allied materials, examinations, and the research corpora perpetuate the divisions among teachers of the different fields and levels of schooling.

The Education and Socialization of Teachers

In the last century much has changed in the institutional arrangements for teacher education. The normal schools and state teachers colleges that once educated the majority of elementary school teachers have disappeared or been transformed into multipurpose colleges and universities. Elementary teachers, like their high school counterparts, are now college graduates. But this convergence of experiences should not obscure persisting differences in the recruitment, socialization, and professional education among America's teachers. The self-contained classroom has tended to attract persons to elementary teaching whose interests are not, or do not remain, subject-specific. To the high school English teachers who would say, "I teach English," they would reply, "I teach children." Their training and socialization almost always differ accordingly, even when the elementary school teacher majored in English. Because of the great emphasis placed on reading instruction, the elementary teacher is pulled by professional training and by the school culture to stress reading; writing suffers accordingly. The colleges have not helped to redress the balance, for composition enjoys low status among English department faculty, and this "menial task" is often assigned to junior or temporary staff. Various studies show that many elementary school teachers have had no instruction in writing beyond freshman composition.[105]

This same disdain for composition has afflicted English majors generally, as their professors pursued more elevated interests in literary history or the New Criticism. Composition was associated in their minds with secondary or remedial education, with requirements, with practical skills—not with thinking, specialization, or culture.[106] Hence English majors planning to teach English were steeped in literature and sometimes little else, ill-prepared to give either basic reading or writing instruction. Thus the professional interests of university English faculty have superseded the needs of future teachers and their students, as they have of English students generally.[107] Thomas Newkirk tells of the uproar that ensued in 1975, after two professors submitted a resolution that all regular members of the English department faculty at the University of Texas be required to teach at least one section of freshman composition every three semesters.[108] In 1961, at a time when James B. Conant was recommending that half of high school English time be given to composition, the NCTE Committee on the National Interest reported that 60 percent of English majors were not required to take any advanced composition.[109] Neither the earlier emphasis upon historical knowledge of literature nor the New Criticism has satisfied those educational reformers who espouse teaching responsive reading and expressive writing in the elementary and secondary schools.

Nor, as James Moffett points out, are many professors in other subjects interested in teaching writing; they view student writing primarily as a vehicle to test whether their assigned reading was done.[110] It should therefore not be surprising that the guidelines for teacher certification in English—drafted in 1965 by the Modern Language Association, NCTE, and the National Association of State Directors of Teacher Education—preserved "the traditional divisions of English into language, literature, and composition."[111] Reports during the 1960s on the further education of teachers were equally discouraging; teachers averaged 0.4 semester hours in composition and 0.7 in language during nine years of teaching.[112]

The foregoing are in addition to other criticisms of the preparation of those who became English teachers: the attraction of English programs for college students who drift into the field by reason of having no clear direction or because of a liking to read or for failing elsewhere. "It is unfortunately true that a great many English teachers have failed to demonstrate that they are genuinely expert and deserve the consideration due someone who is professionally competent in his field," wrote a Project English participant.[113]

The Different Worlds of the Elementary and High School

In 1952, in one of history's many overoptimistic projections of trends toward linking the language arts, NCTE's Commission on the Curriculum thought it observed progress at all three levels: in elementary school units that sprang from normal language integration, rather than twenty-minute segments on language, spelling, and composition; in secondary schools that abandoned semester courses segregating reading and literature from oral and written expression; and in college courses in communications.[114] The same commission, in its 1956 *The English Language Arts in the Secondary School*, described courses concentrating upon only one of the language arts as being remedial programs for retarded students or enrichment courses for superior students; the "normal" course, it maintained, was integrated.[115] But as the Hatfield Commission had observed twenty years before, the correlation of reading with other language activities and with the rest of the curriculum is structurally easier for the elementary than for the secondary teacher. The division of the school day into periods of equal length and the organization of the schools into functional responsibility according to disciplines promote fragmentation and make it improbable that "teachers of all subjects should be, to some extent, teachers of English."[116] And composition suffers most when teachers have more than one hundred students daily, as NCTE has repeatedly warned.[117]

A critical difference between elementary and secondary teachers is that the former must be *generalists*. This helps explain the great dependence of elementary schoolteachers on basal reading series and their teachers' manuals; a 1979 survey found that 95 percent rely on them.[118] Esmor Jones of Britain's National Association for the Teaching of English noted the enormous difficulty of interesting primary teachers in his organization: "It is much easier to interest the specialist English teacher in a 'subject' association than it is to interest the teacher who spends only a part of his time teaching English."[119] In reporting on professional English associations in the United States at the 1965 International Conference on the Teaching of English, Ralph Staiger neglected to mention his own International Reading Association, probably because most of its members, though not generalists, were concerned with elementary education.[120]

In 1924 a new journal, *The Elementary English Review* (now *Language Arts*), was founded in the belief that NCTE did not serve the interests of those who taught or studied English in the elementary schools, that interest in the education of young children "was unorganized, lacking a nucleus and a means of expression."[121] Thus English teachers became even more organizationally divided, in part by the level at which they teach. While observers sometimes acknowledged the arbitrariness of these divisions and proposed greater communication between levels, their members clung to them because they truly represented natural communities of interest related to the sociology of their work.

This fact is vitally important in understanding schooling and its resistance to change. George Henry, in 1986, reminded English educators that to understand this teaching field requires "the fundamental probing of instruction, which lies not solely in overt, externally observed 'method' but also in the internalized arrangement of ideas, most of which are predetermined by the nature of the discipline or by the teacher's expectations of the nature of the discipline."[122] There are additional elements in the teacher's conceptual structure, however, many of which distinguish elementary from secondary teachers (or in high schools, teachers of general science or math from physics or algebra teachers). At the same time that they have more balls to juggle, elementary teachers (and high school teachers of "suspect" fields like reading) also have fewer sacred texts, fewer sacred rules, fewer sacred cows. Hence one should expect different responses to external pressures, including those that come from "expert professional opinion." As I have argued elsewhere,

> Curriculum fields that enroll students, for instruction in introductory (elementary) level basic skills and knowledge, and that are taught by teachers with the most general academic credentials will be more susceptible to new theories and practices in pedagogy

than other combinations of student, subject-matter, and teacher characteristics. . . . There is relatively less to be lost in opting for the uncertainty of change; there are relatively fewer privileges to protect. Lacking high scholastic status, such fields and their teachers may seek a second identity, perhaps the reputation of being pioneering, venturesome, creative, forward-looking. . . . Even if teaching universal and elementary subjects does not present more difficulties, these difficulties are at least more "public" and visible. This visibility can heighten a sense of dissatisfaction with the status quo.[123]

It is not surprising, then, that in his 1984 attempt to reconstruct, historically, *How Teachers Taught*, Larry Cuban found that elementary school teachers have consistently been the greater risk-takers.[124]

Teachers and Their Organizations

Professional associations collect people with shared interests. As arenas for the exchange of information and assistance, including career advancement, they also serve to increase and reinforce in-group identity. Among college educators, the Modern Language Association is oriented toward literature and belletristic studies, leaving rhetoric and composition to the College Conference on Composition and Communication (The Four Cs) of NCTE. From 1911 to 1947 most teachers (and "experts") of writing and reading belonged to the same organization—the National Council of Teachers of English—and they read the NCTE journals, *Elementary English* (from 1942 to 1975, now *Language Arts*), *English Journal*, and *Research in the Teaching of English*. In 1955, however, reading acquired *its* own organization, the International Reading Association (IRA), formed from the merger of two new, short-lived professional associations.

Janet Emig describes the break in the ranks of English teachers as beginning with the departure of a disaffected group of remedial reading teachers. There is certainly little reason to imagine that this ambitious specialization could have long remained content in NCTE, where it lacked an adequate forum for sharing and publishing its concerns.[125] One of the participants in founding the National Association of Remedial Teachers, Constance McCullough, later recalled that remedial reading was ambitious, ready to pass from being a parent's despair and a teacher's frustration to being the object of concerted efforts in the society as a whole.[126] Meanwhile, as the remedial teachers were organizing, another group was forming among English educators. An organizational meeting of thirty-four persons centered around Temple University founded the International Council for the Improvement of Reading Instruction (ICIRI) in 1947; it had two hundred members when it began publishing *The Reading Teacher* in 1951. "I Cry" merged with the young National Association of Remedial Teachers on January 1, 1955, forming the International Reading Association (IRA).

The rapidly growing IRA purchased the *Journal of Developmental Reading* (now *Journal of Reading*) from its publishers, the English Department of Purdue University, in order to better attract and serve those concerned with secondary, college, and adult reading. By the tenth anniversary of the organization, the print orders for the two IRA journals were 39,000 and 9,000, respectively, and plans were afoot for a journal to serve scholars and researchers, *The Reading Research Quarterly*. By its thirtieth anniversary, IRA had 50,000 members, reflecting its popularity among elementary school teachers, reading specialists and supervisors, reading researchers, publishers, and clinicians. A 1969 survey discovered, however, that only 6 percent of IRA members were senior high school teachers; they had *their* organization already, in NCTE.

IRA and NCTE have collaborated, of course. They jointly published a service bulletin, *Reading and Linguistics*. In 1980, when Yetta Goodman was president of NCTE and Kenneth Goodman of IRA, the two organizations began sponsoring sessions at one another's national and regional meetings. Such practices, however, will prove easier than the larger objective in view: the uniting of writing and reading in teaching and research.

Remaking English

The disciplines that are available to researchers in contemporary English education include cognitive psychology, linguistics, child language development, artificial intelligence, brain study, semiotics, rhetoric, anthropology, literature, and philosophy. Kenneth Goodman, a major figure in the effort to reintegrate reading with the other language arts, characterized the research activity as multidisciplinary rather than interdisciplinary, since "there is little crossing over from discipline to discipline."[127] The relative insularity of English education scholars from those in other fields resembles the isolation of reading researchers, much the largest group, from those investigating other language areas. The "sociology of expertise" also affects instructional organization. Thus the elementary school orientation of leaders in the field of reading has been used to explain why secondary school reading remains isolated from the content area classes, sometimes from English itself. The experience of reading experts promotes a view of reading "as a separate subject, with reading skills as the curriculum."[128] At the 1956 annual meeting of IRA, for example, George Mallinson recommended an extension of the basal program in high school English and communications classes, something not calculated to appeal to many English teachers, no matter how desperate they might feel about the challenges of teaching English.[129]

"English teaching is not a profession but a predicament," declared the College Board's Commission on English in 1965.[130] Albert Kitzhaber complained that "English in the schools has become less a curriculum than a receptacle; everything gets dumped into it."[131] The California State Department of Education reportedly accepted 217 courses as English.[132] The identity crisis of the "wastebasket" field of English was only intensified when other disciplines actively organized themselves, in the wake of the Soviet Sputnik, to tap the resources of the federal government and various foundations for curriculum development. The professional pride of English educators was at issue, as well as the threat to the place of English in the curriculum as a result of the new mathematics, science, and foreign language curriculum packages, textbooks, and equipment. Under the influence of the psychological theories of Jerome Bruner, educators in English also began to talk of the "spiral curriculum," whereby previously taught skills and knowledge were reintroduced in cognitively more sophisticated forms. Like their counterparts in other fields, English educators discovered the "discovery method," whereby students learned the basic ideas that compose the "structure of the discipline." Linguistics and a new rhetoric were also enlisted in the 1960s' effort to reconsider and revive English as a field of knowledge.[133]

Project English, funded in 1961 by the United States Office of Education, created more than twenty curriculum study and demonstration centers by 1966; Squire called them "without question the most influential developments in curriculum during recent years."[134] Some, like those programs in New Haven and at the Universities of Indiana and Nebraska and the Carnegie Institute of Technology, tried to attend to the interrelations of literature, composition, and language; others were traditional, reflecting the wider educational conservatism of the period.[135] Through expansion of the National Defense Education Act (NDEA), money was available to support teacher reeducation in reading, English, and other school subjects.

Institutes were offered to elementary and secondary teachers of English, beginning in 1962 under sponsorship of the College Board and then through Project English and NDEA. They proved inadequate, however, to sustain curricular and pedagogical experimentation—including efforts to exploit the potentialities of writing and to relate writing to the other language arts. For one thing, not enough teachers were reached by the institutes. Perhaps 20,000 enrolled at the height of the movement; this was only 20 percent of English teachers.[136] Another problem was that, despite the auspicious beginnings of Project English, English "reform" shared something of the general weaknesses of the other curriculum reforms of the 1960s: the institute programs and the curriculum packages were not conceived with adequate or sustained attention to the realities of the public schools, to the "culture" of the teaching profession, and to the needs and wishes of teachers.[137] In a few years, even among teachers who had attended the institutes, older teaching practices resurfaced.

Technological Change

It is said of today's children that they "are as much immersed in written language as in speech."[138] This was not true in the nineteenth century. Breakfast, for example, did not come out of packages with labels. It came out of wheat fields, chickens, cows, and mother's oven; all were innocent of print. Yet already the revolution begun by Gutenberg had influenced society, causing literacy—and eventually schools—to gain historically unprecedented influence over daily life. By the middle of the last century, Daniel Calhoun writes, even rural Americans experienced a "fluctuating equilibrium between two styles of life—between a communal, personalistic style that required literacy only in its leaders, and a commercial, argumentative style in which literacy was needed to maintain a standard of decision between men."[139] Literacy rates first became high precisely in those communities with market economies, and writing and arithmetic for economic ends joined reading for religious purposes in the expansion of schooling.[140] This helps to explain those nineteenth-century school exercises that children had in writing IOUs and invoices.

The technology of print presented problems as well as opportunities for teachers and learners. Before print, the spelling of English words was governed by pronunciation. After printing reached England, however, the spelling was fixed (a convenience to printers), and subsequent changes in pronunciation left many words with irregular spellings that had to be mastered by rote.[141] Newly standardized spelling also created the need for spelling books and lessons, fixing spelling in the school curriculum. For decades spelling received a considerable share of the school day, far more than it now enjoys.

A direct and immediate outcome of this new reliance on the written word was the appearance and proliferation of schoolbooks of all kinds.

Their use replaced much of the oral methods and memorization that had been so prominent in both formal and informal education from the earliest recorded history of education. By the American centennial the growing system of schooling was also being subjected to calls for better management. The additional technologies of "objective" testing and rational management (bureaucracy) were becoming visible. The new profession of psychology offered a succession of theories about how to manage learning and assessment better. Finally, the isolation of generations of youngsters for increasingly long periods of time in institutions called schools and colleges started the elaboration of a youth culture, one that has become relatively autonomous of parents and teachers through the electronic media of communication and entertainment.

The Textbook Revolution

The revolutionary effects of the printing press could not be fully realized until wood pulp replaced rags in the production of paper. Until then, paper costs made books expensive and also discouraged casual writing. By the late nineteenth century, however, it was feasible for either parents or taxpayers to provide children with uniform textbooks and with writing paper in lieu of slates. Pencils and steel-tipped pens replaced the quills that earlier generations of schoolmasters had tediously sharpened and whose use limited the writing assigned.

Reading instruction was also freed to expand. In 1898 Charles W. Eliot had calculated that an entire six-year elementary school curriculum could be read in forty-six hours; because they read so little, it was small wonder that schoolchildren could learn so much by heart. Indeed, the popular children's magazine, *Youth's Companion*, contained more reading than an entire series of school reading books.[142] The twentieth century added to the profusion of written materials, with graded textbooks, supplementary readers, anthologies, scholastic dictionaries and magazines, and workbooks. Next came paperbacks, to destroy the coherence of the English curriculum or to free it from the tyranny of the textbook—depending on one's point of view. James Squire has called this paperback revolution another version of the older pedagogical debate between intensive and extensive reading.[143]

Cheaper schoolbooks made it possible to group children more easily for instruction, another change from earlier patterns. For example, Connecticut had discovered in 1846 that more than 215 different texts were being used in its common schools.[144] The new technology changed that: when the teacher asked children to take out their reading or history books, they could all have the same book, rather than one brought from home that some distant ancestor had acquired or that some overambitious parents had selected to push their child ahead.[145] This removed a common grievance of earlier teachers. The complaint that a book was too simple or too difficult for a given student was answered by authoring multiple versions of the same graded text; all fifth graders could have a fifth reader, at some level of difficulty, sparing some students excessive pride and others shame—or so it was thought.

Schoolbooks continued to be criticized, however. Given the lofty diction of their texts—"Every man became a mortal; a horse, a courser or a steed; a glass, a crystal vase; the moon, Pale Diana"—it was said that teachers were tempted to try to teach their students "to write like John Milton."[146] That criticism passed as the language of many schoolbooks was simplified to deal with mass education and with research showing that relatively few words carried the bulk of ordinary communication in language; "overlearning" the most frequently used words in English became the dominant pedagogical principle, at least in the elementary school years.

More recently, the poor writing model that many secondary school textbooks present to students—through their trivial character, errors, and inconsistencies—caused Tierney to recommend that students become critics and editors of their textbooks, learning comprehension and metacomprehension skills in the process.[147] The system of authorship and marketing of textbooks also tended to produce discrete texts for the several language arts, and this divisiveness is carried over into the construction of lessons. In so doing, textbook production has reinforced the language arts as separate entities, each to be studied in relative isolation through its own text.

As far as writing is concerned, the use of skill-building workbooks is the product of the textbook revolution that comes in for sharpest attack. The reform that brought silent reading to the fore also led to elementary students spending considerable time in seat work, completing workbooks and skill sheets—more time than they received in instruction from the teacher. These "independent" activities ordinarily make few demands on comprehension skills and produce little or no writing.[148] The authors of the 1985 Breaking Ground: Teachers Relate Reading and Writing in the Elementary School emphasize that writing process instruction "is incompatible with the philosophy behind reading worksheets, tests, basals" and with the practice of subordinating workbooks to books.[149] Meanwhile, secondary students in the lower tracks sometimes find workbooks dominating their composition programs. They are part of what George Henry characterizes as the crude, efficiency-seeking scientism that has driven "imagination, feeling, and transcendence" from education.[150] Nor have the colleges been free from this tendency, as the composition handbooks testify.[151]

Testing

The commercially prepared standardized tests and the state testing programs so familiar to writing and reading teachers have traditionally determined curriculum, book selection, and students' school and university placements in the United States much less than in Japan and Western Europe.[152] The recent growth of state-mandated testing programs is, however, beginning to raise teachers' complaints about class time spent on "teaching for the test."

Despite an occasionally expressed belief that advances in diagnostic testing procedures were promising, English teachers have consistently professed skepticism of such tests. Tests of literature and writing were late in being included in the National Assessment of Educational Progress (NAEP), the federally supported attempt to create measures of the nation's "gross national educational product." Indeed, at the same time that standardized tests were being used for more purposes, writing teachers and researchers were experimenting with holistic assessment.

The assessment of writing achievement remains a particularly thorny issue. The latest edition of *Handbook of Research on Teaching* does not even talk about testing as conventionally understood.[153] Composition scales appeared before 1915 but were dismissed as unreliable. As a result, efforts to rate compositions became one of the major projects in the modest amount of research done on teaching composition. Abandoning its earlier essay tests, in the 1960s the College Board expressed confidence in its new English Composition Test: two twenty-minute objective exercises that "have proved to be good indicators of skill in composition," along with twenty minutes of "actual writing."[154] Nonetheless, other researchers concluded that, whether made by teachers or testers, objective tests of writing are little more than measures of spelling, punctuation, capitalization, and usage.[155] These are precisely the mechanics that the National Assessment of Educational Progress has shown to be fairly well mastered by students, in contrast to their poor performance in syntactical and rhetorical areas.

It has been pointed out that writing and reading are not only commonly taught differently, but that they are tested differently: reading by multiple-choice items and writing by qualitative assessments.[156] This is an overstatement. A similar testing format is used in both areas, and their tests raise some of the same criticisms. Although reading tests are more widely used and accepted, they are still faulted for not requiring strategies that are important in ordinary reading and critical thinking in reading. And, despite the prevailing scorn of standardized tests in English, studies show that teacher-made tests, the widely available end-of-unit tests in language textbooks, and classroom questions in literature, composition, and language were like external examinations in concentrating upon knowledge and not upon comprehension.[157]

External examinations are commonly blamed for shaping the ways that teachers teach or for causing an activity such as writing to be largely overlooked because it is not amenable to traditional teaching forms. It is worth considering, however, that tests and teacher practices alike reflect larger social and cultural expectations. In this view, tests are themselves a consequence and not a cause of technocratic impulses in schooling. They are sustained by the large classes that also assure that, if teachers assign frequent writing, many will grade the themes on the basis of their mechanical correctness.

Management Systems: Bureaucracies and Psychologies

Technology is not so much its products as it is a way of working, a method of attacking problems through planning and precision. In one prominent educator's words, technique "converts spontaneous and unreflective behavior into behavior that is deliberate and rationalized."[158] Between 1910 and 1930, in the interests of order and efficiency, school managers borrowed "scientific management" principles of people- and paper-processing from American business and industry. As the functions of the schools came to include providing lunch programs, transportation, recreation, and vocational and adult education, the technologies of management also grew to coordinate them.

Standardization is associated with bureaucratic systems. An early manifestation of standards-setting was the acceptance, where population density permitted, of the graded school. This hastened the adoption of graded series of schoolbooks. Previously, lessons were merely graded by difficulty within a single book and, later, among books in a single series. The subsequent step in rationalization was to achieve some uniformity across series so that the Third Reader (or the First Grammar) in one publisher's series was equivalent in difficulty to that in other series. Uniformity in texts and later in curriculum packages was a form of "teacher-proofing": an effort to secure acceptable (that is, standard) results, despite the suspicion that many teachers in a mass and rapidly growing system were ill-trained, inexperienced, or incompetent.

Supervision and examination were part of the same process. As early as 1864 the Regents of the State of New York substituted written tests in various school subjects for oral tests and principals' recommendations to determine whether a student had completed the elementary school course. Their confidence in this new, "objective" procedure was vindicated when students' passage rates dropped to half their previous level.[159] Imitating the colleges, elementary and secondary schools adopted written examinations to replace much of the older system of recitation and oral examination. This was testimony to the society's passion for objectification and accountability, and reflected rising expectations of written literacy as well.

From the beginnings of the movement to construct a rational base for setting educational standards and achieving uniformity in teaching practices, the still-young science of psychology seemed to hold the most promise. Psychology might determine whether selections for a literary anthology had pedagogical merit—as well as moral or aesthetic value. It might indicate the pace at which average children should move from writing words to writing sentences and paragraphs. It might determine the amount of practice that was optimal in achieving and maintaining some acceptable standard of legibility in penmanship. In the search for such guidance, theory and practice in the teaching of English have been successively influenced by various psychologies: the connectionism of Edward L. Thorndike, the more purposive paradigm of the followers of John Dewey, gestalt theory, the ideas of Jerome Bruner, and the stages of cognitive development of Jean Piaget.[160]

Thinking or problem-solving has figured prominently in twentieth-century American educational theory and rhetoric. It is not surprising, then, that the NCTE Commission on English stated in 1956 that "writing should help the young student to observe and to organize his experience—in other words, to think."[161] When the cognitive psychologists and the psycholinguists came on the scene, they were greeted with some of the confidence that their predecessors had gained—and lost. By the 1980s their fascination with the technologies of artificial intelligence enlisted interest in the use of computers in the teaching of writing. A few generative and interactive computer programs are today being cited as applying the new theories on writing and reading processes and their interactions.[162]

A Product of Schools and Technology: The Autonomous Youth Culture

Before "Sesame Street" and Head Start programs were created, pre-schoolers' knowledge of English letter names was a good predictor of their reading achievement in the primary grades. With television, however, deliberate teaching of letter names is becoming a part of the shared culture, rather than a characteristic of child rearing in certain social classes.[163] This is one example of the many ways that television and the other modern media of communication impinge on schooling. The electronic media of communication have also strengthened a youth culture, one that extended the peer group from a school-bounded age cohort into a national and international phenomenon. The cultural referees for most youth have become characters in television programs and music and sports stars, rather than those found in books or their teachers, preachers, and parents, as once was the case.

In the face-to-face society of nineteenth-century America, which James Coleman describes as "experience rich and information poor," books read at home, in school, or in Sunday school were windows onto the larger world.[164] So were letters received from distant kin and friends. But radio, film, and television annihilated such provincialism even more than did the automobile and the airplane. Schools lost their monopoly on dispensing information to youth. They also lost something of their authority as the custodians of culture. By the 1950s, as noted in the pages of *Language Arts* as well as in the popular press, television was replacing comic books as the perceived threat to desirable social learning.

Similarly, it is predicted that the microelectronics revolution will alter further how people acquire and process information, how they learn and relearn, and how they communicate. No longer is it assumed that youth is the period for acquiring the permanent base of habits and skills of a lifetime; this diminishes the importance attached to schools. What the telephone has done to personal writing, television has apparently done to reading. But these delegitimating effects of the media are wider still: A culture of play and consumption has been spread across the world, a counterculture to the school culture, one that treats all work as a "middle-class hang-up," including class- and homework.

Three decades of decrying the effects of television have proved futile. Therefore, some educators stopped worrying about competing with the media as entertainment and distraction. They began to think, *once again*, of how teaching might respond to a view of learning as interactive, not receptive. Their numbers and their optimism about both student collaboration in learning and the integration of different language activities were reportedly greater in Britain and Canada than in the United States, however. Here, a view of English as a skills subject—"the iron grip" of the basic skills mentality—was harder to shake. In the words of one American respondent to an international survey: "It is the skills aspect of English which keeps it required, and if it were only there for humanizing effect, it could easily go the way of art and music: nice stuff but frills compared to the real business of preparing kids for the cold, cruel world."[165]

Functionalism: Language and American Culture

Complaints about the pinched character of American culture antedate the Revolution. Thus a teacher complained in 1727 of his "Country People" who wished only as much writing and arithmetic in their schools as would "serve the Common occasions of vulgar People."[166] William Brown's 1826 school copybook combined essays on "Independence" and "Intemperance" with Cowper's poetry and "Forms Used in Transacting Business."[167] Robert Connors describes this century's required course in composition as being, more than any other subject, one "shaped by perceived social and cultural needs."[168] Because of this utilitarian tradition, a survey of American research on writing published in the mid-1980s concludes, "Even a moderately optimistic forecast would have to allow that the teaching of writing will probably continue to take place in a relatively uncongenial cultural environment."[169]

It is not surprising, then, that the educators at the 1966 Anglo-American Conference discovered, despite their shared language and history, consistent differences among themselves in the teaching of English. The British (and Canadians) reportedly gave more attention to creative writing and to the student's inner-life "as a means to self-discovery, self-fulfillment, self-enhancement." In contrast, the Americans taught more grammar and defined reform as the development of uniform language and literature sequences from first to twelfth grade. Herbert J. Muller made an attempt to compromise these differing values, arguing that "practical hard-headed men need to be reminded that good creative writing is a product of thought and hard work, not merely of imagination."[170]

"Functional Literacy"

In its 1926 *The Place of English in American Life*, an NCTE committee updated the society's historic cultural preference for the useful over the "merely ornamental" by recommending that more attention be given to language activities that present difficulties in a heterogeneous society. The list included preparing reports for a superior and instructions for subordinates, conversation at social gatherings, writing memos for one's self, making introductions, listening at a public meeting, and telephone talk.[171] A half century later, some educators feared that technological advances would usurp the place of reading and writing. Folklorist John Szwed noted of many businesses that "it is a mark of success not to be directly responsible for one's own communications in written form—secretaries are employed to turn oral statements into acceptable written ones."[172] This would represent an interesting historical reversal, with functionaries called upon to be ever more able readers and writers, while bosses receive information by listening to employees and peers and giving oral direction to subordinates.

Scholars may debate who the principal intended recipients are of employers' demands for better writers, but there is little doubt that the demands of functional literacy have risen greatly in this century. Consistently more people work in clerical and service jobs, where written and oral language skills are at a premium. Apart from employment demands, ordinary participation in society (including consumerism) requires knowledge and skills in writing and reading that exceed the older criterion of functional literacy: successful completion of five years of schooling. Many written materials of daily life surpass grade twelve difficulty. But at the same time, the concept of functional literacy emphasizes reading competency—not writing. And in practice both economic and social functioning place more demands on people to read than to write. The net effect of this is, again, to concentrate instruction upon reading, to neglect writing, and to judge the utility of writing by its contribution to skillful reading or to thinking—better yet to problem-solving, which has high value in this culture.

The Dominance of Expository Writing

In 1913 Frank N. Freeman observed that, historically, penmanship had degenerated from a fine art to one of the educational disciplines.[173] But writing always contained within it a strong element of the utilitarian, and it was certainly espoused as a school subject chiefly for its ability to support memory and to display learning. Early in its history as a discrete subject of instruction, composition was described as consisting of four types: narration (telling a story), description (appealing to the visual imagination), argument (proving some proposition), and exposition (explaining a meaning).[174] The dominant rhetorical tradition in the colleges at the end of the nineteenth century also became the unquestioned paradigm for teaching writing until the 1960s: it made argument and exposition the chief business of writing classes. While emotion was assigned to oratory and imagination to literature, reason and objectivity were assigned to composition.

A tempering of this tradition in the interests of the experience curriculum came by the 1930s, as educators recommended that topics for expository writing be related to student interest. Still, "Interminable senior essays and long articles prepared for contest themes, unrelated to the experience or interest of the writer, have probably done more to check normal expression and to foster plagiarism than any other activity in school," noted the authors of *The English Language Arts* in 1952.[175] As increasing numbers of high school graduates headed for college, expository writing was required for larger proportions of secondary school students, and oftentimes without regard to earlier warnings. So by the 1950s English teachers began to be cautioned about their earlier "overstress on the writing of personal experiences, imaginative compositions, letters, or other forms of composition."[176] For example, curriculum development at the University of Georgia, under Project English, was based on the principle that elementary school children were doing too much writing from personal experience, imaginative composition, and letters at the expense of expository writing; the remedy was "continuous practice in writing that requires skill in thinking, planning, organizing, and composing, especially writing that requires the extended development of a single idea or point of view."[177] Disregarding the repeated advice of college composition teachers that high school composition programs focus on short compositions, not lengthy research papers, many English teachers imitated university professors in assigning research reports. By the late 1950s, 65 percent of course outlines for grades eleven and twelve recommended writing a research paper.[178]

Even as the link between school composition and college work was being strengthened—"This is practical preparation for papers and tests in college, and you may need it on the job"—voices were again being raised against the dominance of exposition. It was pointed out that creative writing stopped too soon in American schools, around grade five, and that the subsequent "conventional assignments in expository writing and drill in mechanics" had, as its outcome, only rebellion against writing.[179] In 1966 NCTE's Commission on the English Curriculum reported that some teachers believe that "expository writing is not the only or even the best way" to achieve the goals of writing. Nonetheless, questioning its practical value proved difficult:

> As a form of writing, exposition seems ideal to achieve the most important ends of composition, particularly in high school and college. It is useful in school as well as in adult life. It can be a way of teaching the adequacy, precision, and order of ideas; it can be a way, indeed, of discerning ideas. Through it a writer can come to know himself.[180]

Once again, by the 1970s, a sufficient sentiment favoring "expressive writing" was gathering. In their disagreement with the dominant tradition, some critics again related writing to reading. Nor was expressive writing "impractical." Its proponents contended that writing to learn, "speculative writing," is different from writing to communicate, but hardly less practical in a changing society.[181] What one sees in this example is that both the reformers and the exponents of the status quo accept the culture's practical values and argue their different agenda from that point of implicit agreement.

Liberationist Movements: Language and Freedom

Since the nineteenth century, critics have faulted schooling in the United States that was satisfied with mechanical reading ("parrot reading") and stilted writing and that produced students who ciphered by rote-learned rules, who could rattle off the imports and exports of Brazil but were stymied when asked, "What are the *exports* of your father's farm?" or "What does he *import*?" Along with their criticisms, the critics proposed an alternative pedagogy.

Progressive Education

In his 1835 *The School-Master's Friend,* Theodore Dwight, Jr., offered advice on selecting material for initial instruction in reading that was to be echoed by subsequent generations of educators:

> Familiar lessons should first be used in reading; and the more familiar the better. Even sentences composed by the scholars themselves, corrected if they need it by the master, may well serve for early lessons. Children should first be made to read what they understand, and something that relates to their own circumstances, and interests their feelings.[182]

Historian Daniel Calhoun calls this principle one that "in later years and in other hands was to lead both to the most insipid and to the most radical of texts."[183]

During the era of pedagogical freedom (some said "license") known as progressive education, Dwight's idea of "experience charts" was widely recommended and frequently used. Children composed collaborative accounts of their activities in the primary reading program and in social studies and science lessons. Experience charts provided practice in writing and reading, linking them in a way that was consistent with the language experience philosophy. Experience charts posted on classroom walls also gave public testimony to the wealth of "activities" and "units of study" that enlivened the school day and to the "child-centeredness" that animated the teacher. These tenets of progressive pedagogy were the conventional wisdom from before 1920 to about 1955—despite the snipings of cranky reactionaries and the failure of many teachers to observe them in practice, certainly in most secondary schools.

The elementary school was the natural environment of progressive education—for the reasons already suggested and, perhaps, because of greater parental permissiveness in the education of young children, at least in the white middle class. Because of the parallel movement to limit children's reading vocabulary to commonly encountered and well-understood words, the experience chart method did produce stories that sounded no more like children's natural language than did their basal series. Imitating the style of first grade texts, teachers helped children compose their own dry-as-dust *reading material*: "We went to the park. We saw the big trees. We had fun." In 1954 the Commission on the English Curriculum offered a richer example of a teacher guiding children's spontaneous expressions into another story about a park visit:

> Lots of leaves are on the ground.
> Yellow leaves! Red leaves!
> We pile the leaves up.
> We kick the leaves down.
> We get hot! We have fun![184]

Freedom from the style and the assumptions of vocabulary-controlled books—and an expanded conception of the relationships of writing and reading—could have come earlier had the progressives understood that young children can and do write before they are considered to have mastered the fundamentals of reading. They did not understand this, however. Witness Henry Suzzallo, a professor and later a university president. In 1913 he described modern teachers as those who ensured that children had the requisite experience and vocabulary to read a text by such prereading activities as story-telling, conversational lessons, action work, and picture writing; writing itself did not figure in his thinking about reading readiness.[185] Four decades later, in 1954, the book *Language Arts for Today's Children* reiterated the accepted view that "impression precedes expression; intake precedes outflow in all aspects of language learning." This meant writing only *after* reading. These authors did observe preschoolers' scribblings—imitations of adults seen writing. They also concluded that "writing becomes a necessary tool for school experience with the beginning of the primary years," and offered examples of sensible correlations of writing and reading in the existing model.[186] Nevertheless, their limited conception of early writing and the relations of composing writing to comprehending reading showed little advance over the past half century. The reigning assumption remained one of sequential development: hearing words -> speaking words -> seeing words -> recognizing words (reading) -> spelling words -> writing words. Of the skills of the language arts cycle, writing is the last of all.

The Dartmouth Conference

Regardless of what has been said so far, the high schools had not been entirely impervious to aspects of progressive education. The language experience approach to the teaching of literature, for example, dictated that texts be selected for their correspondence with youths' experiences (content over form). In their oral or written literary analyses, students were often asked to comment on a work's personal significance rather than on its structure or place in literary history. Yet when fifty British and American educators met at Dartmouth College in the summer of 1966 under the sponsorship of the Carnegie Corporation, considerable dissatisfaction with high school English was unleashed in the name of liberating English by encouraging responsive reading and expressive writing. The various work groups decried the estrangement of school English from the culture *as the student knows it*, although they did not pay much attention to the issues of cultural diversity that were soon to become commonplace. Participants heard pleas for a kind of teaching that facilitated, or at least did not inhibit, the dialogic relationship of reader and text: "What is vital is the interplay between his personal world and the world of the writer."[187]

The interaction of reader and writer through the text was not the only joining to be promoted. The conferees attacked the dissection of the English curriculum into composition periods, language periods, literature periods, and perhaps poetry periods. John Dixon thought that the conference's "decision to advocate a unitary rather than a fragmented approach to English" was especially significant. It reaffirmed aspects of human experience as the unifying principle of English education, articulated by NCTE in the 1930s, and called on flexible teaching strategies instead of rigid lesson plans. Conference participants discussed talk and drama as resources for a revitalized writing. Revealing examples of young children's writing were shared, leading some of the participants to think more than they had before about the writing process and youthful writing as "embryonic literature." Finally, the conference recommended that teachers at all levels "should have more opportunities to enjoy and refresh themselves in their subject, using language in operation for all its central purposes—in imaginative drama, writing and speech, as well as the response to literature."[188]

The idea that teachers, too, become writers was implemented in the next decade in the Bay Area Writing Project. There is little evidence of a direct influence of the Dartmouth Conference upon practice, however. In the Foreword to the 1975 edition of *Growth through English*, James Squire and James Britton tried to explain why so many expectations spawned at Dartmouth remained unfulfilled. One factor was certainly the end of federal funding, as policymakers' attention was transferred to civil-rights-inspired school improvement and then to the Vietnam War. The place to find the impact of *the Dartmouth ideal*, they concluded, was in the enterprise of individuals, the existence of small networks of teacher groups, the writings of teachers not directly touched by the conference.[189] Much the same could be said about the effect of earlier ideals, previous commissions and their reports, other seminal thinkers—all refracted through the stubborn realities of humans and their institutions.

Writing and Reading, Reconsidered

Revisionist historians of education, especially those with anarchist or Marxist leanings, have included literacy campaigns and school expansion in their radical critiques of contemporary developed societies.[190] They argue that modern nation-states substitute schooled-language for natural language as a means of extending political control over their citizens. Form becomes superior to substance. Experience loses status to books, and adults without academic credentials are consigned to society's margins. Meanwhile, children's "proper literacy" and common-sensical understanding are eroded by the schools' emphasis on reading ability and vicarious mastery, this according to linguist Wayne O'Neil.[191] Like the earliest exponents of biblical literacy, the partisans of all other literacies—including scientific literacy and computer literacy—have in mind wider access to what the Resnicks call the "received wisdom" and "the love of the familiar." Greg Myers raises similar issues of ideology in his commentary on Sterling Leonard's 1917 *English Composition as a Social Problem* and on contemporary reform movements in the teaching of writing.[192]

In such exposés of literacy's "true meaning," it is common to find writing and reading distinguished in their effects. While reading is called consensual and conservative, writing is described as egocentric and change oriented; reading connotes dependence and vulnerability, writing its opposites; the one transmits, the other transforms. The schools and curricular tracks that educate the children of the power-elite feature more writing for the reasons that the United States Navy offers instruction in reading to enlisted personnel and instruction in writing to officers.[193] The type of reading assigned, especially in the lower tracks in schools and in adult functional literacy programs, features such printed materials as "instructions, labels, signs, forms, and form letters—types of communication generally intended to elicit passive behaviors or to encourage conformist responses that reproduce or further institutionalize existing social relations," in the words of British sociologist Kenneth Levine. Public schools, and even universities, would lose support if they stressed anything but the most academic writing since, by its nature, "writing conveys and records innovation, dissent, and criticism; above all, it can give access to political mechanisms and the political process generally, where many of the possibilities of personal and social transformation lie."[194]

Is this true of writing? Is writing as revolutionary as these theorists claim? Not necessarily. If writing entails putting together "details from personal sensory experience, from vicarious experience (reading, listening, viewing), and from inferences,"[195] it has ample opportunity to transmit little or nothing more than that which was received; and the more technically skilled in mechanics the writer is, the more effective in transmitting the received wisdom. (This observation may remind the reader of copywriters in advertising agencies or paid publicists; James Moffett dismisses writers of this sort as paraphrasers rather than authentic authors.) If the majority of a conservative public wishes to control what is read, it desires the same of the content of writing. Assigned writing, as well as assigned reading, ensures that many students will be unengaged by the creative possibilities that inhere in comprehending and composing. When public reaction to the student protest movements of the 1960s and early 1970s is considered, there is some reason to agree with Moffett:

> Both laity and educators fear the liberation of thought and behavior that students would achieve if talking, reading, and writing were taught most effectively—that is, if these powerful tools were freely given to youngsters for their personal investigation.[196]

Yet there are those—parents, politicians, teachers, and researchers—who do welcome in *both* writing and reading the possibilities of creativity, critical thinking, and empowerment.

For some, like Moffett, their conviction means teaching writing and reading socially, as speaking and listening are learned, and engaging the home and the community in the process. These men and women remind us of the progressives of an earlier generation. For others it may mean exploiting the new technologies to provide unparalleled opportunities for independent and individualized instruction. The ideas of the Dartmouth seminar—a renewed interest in learners, their development, and the processes of using language to learn—were clearly taking on new life in the 1980s. If they often sound familiar, they also contain certain new elements. Moreover, these ideals are being reworked in a world *not quite like* that which has ever been known before. And of such threads is tomorrow's history being woven.

Notes

1. I am indebted to Judith Orlemann, who assisted in the research; to Leo Ruth, Kenneth Lane, Robert Ruddell, James Gray, Mary K. Healy, and Marcia Farr, who provided indispensable suggestions and lent works from their own libraries; to the participants at the Reading–Writing Planning Conference, especially Jenny Cook-Gumperz, Alfred Grommon, and Fran Claggett, for their ideas and gracious tolerance of the incursions into the history of *their* field by an outsider; to Julie M. Jensen for her thorough review; and to Sylvia Staller, who helped with the manuscript.

2. National Council of Teachers of English (NCTE) Committee on Correlation (1936). *A correlated curriculum.* New York: Appleton-Century.

   Similar predictions were made for such earlier technologies as the typewriter and radio, each a change agent in society but not in schools. See Clifford, G.J. (1987). The impact of technology in American education. In S. Bruchey and J. Cotton (Eds.), *Technology, the economy, and society: The American experience* (pp. 251–277). New York: Columbia University Press.

3. Project English (1964). Project English curriculum studies: A progress report. In *Iowa English Yearbook: Vol. 9* (p. 9). Iowa City, IA: Iowa Council of Teachers of English.

4. Stiles, L. (1969). Revolution in instruction. In E.D. Hemsing (Compiler), *A decade of thought on teacher education. The Charles W. Hunt Lectures, 1960–1969* (p. 44). Washington, DC: American Association of Colleges for Teacher Education.

5. Chall, J.S., and Stahl, S.A. (1982). Reading. In H.E. Mitzel (Ed.), *Encyclopedia of educational research* (5th ed.) (pp. 1535–1536). New York: Free Press.

6. Emig, J. (1982). Writing, composition, and rhetoric. In H.E. Mitzel (Ed.); see note 5, p. 2031.

7. Clifford, G.J. (1981). Past is prologue. In K. Cirincioni-Coles (Ed.), *The future of education: Policy issues and challenges* (pp. 25–34). Beverly Hills, CA: Sage.

8. Gardner, J. (1968). *No easy victories* (p. 169). New York: Harper & Row.

9. Burrows, A.T. (1977). Composition: Prospect and retrospect. In H.A. Robinson (Ed.), *Reading and writing instruction in the United States: Historical trends* (p. 35). Newark, DE: International Reading Association.

10. Resnick, D.P., and Resnick, L. (1977). The nature of literacy: An historical explanation. *Harvard Educational Review, 47,* 370–385.

11. Applebee, A.N. (1974). *Tradition and reform in the teaching of English: A history.* Urbana, IL: National Council of Teachers of English.

12. Robinson, H.A. (Ed.) (1977). *Reading and writing instruction in the United States: Historical trends.* Newark, DE: International Reading Association.

13. Hansen, J., Newkirk, T., and Graves, D. (1985). *Breaking ground: Teachers relate reading and writing in the elementary school* (p. 169). Portsmouth, NH: Heinemann.

14. Anderson, R.C., Hiebert, E.H., Scott, J., and Wilkinson, I.A.G. (1984). *Becoming a nation of readers.* Washington, DC: National Institute of Education, National Academy of Education, Commission on Reading.

15. Hansen, Newkirk, and Graves (1985); see note 13.

16. Squire, J.R., and Applebee, R.K. (1968). *High school English instruction today: The national study of high school English programs.* New York: Appleton-Century-Crofts.

17. Baker, F.T. (1913). Composition. In P. Monroe (Ed.), *A cyclopedia of education: Vol. 2* (p. 167). New York: Macmillan.

18. Baker (1913), pp. 167–168.

19. Muller, H.J. (1967). *The uses of English.* New York: Holt, Rinehart, & Winston.

20. Frazier, A. (Ed.), and NCTE Commission on the English Curriculum (1966). *Ends and issues: 1965–66* (p. 12). Urbana, IL: National Council of Teachers of English.

21. Shugrue, M.F. (1966). New materials for the teaching of English: The English program of the USOE. *Publications of the Modern Language Association of America, 81,* 1–36, p. 32.

22. Corbett, E.P.J. (1981). The status of writing in our society. In M.F. Whiteman (Ed.), *Writing: The nature, development, and teaching of written communication: Vol. 1. Variation in writing: Functional and linguistic-cultural differences* (pp. 47–52). Hillsdale, NJ: Erlbaum.

     Newkirk, T. (1986). Background and introduction. In T. Newkirk (Ed.), *Only connect: Uniting reading and writing* (pp. 1–10). Upper Montclair, NJ: Boynton/Cook.

     Hatlin, B. (1986). Old wine and new bottles: A dialectical encounter between the old rhetoric and the new. In T. Newkirk (Ed.), pp. 59–86.

23. Moffett, J. (1985). Hidden impediments to improving English teaching. *Phi Delta Kappan, 67,* 50–56, p. 54.

24. Applebee, A.N. (1984a). Writing and reasoning. *Review of Educational Research, 54,* 577–596.

25. Heath, S.B. (1981). Toward an ethnohistory of writing in American education. In M.F. Whiteman (Ed.); see note 22, pp. 25–46.

26. Quoted in Clifford, G.J. (1978). Words for schools: The applications in education of the vocabulary researches of Edward L. Thorndike. In P. Suppes (Ed.), *Impact of research on education: Some case studies* (p. 171). Washington, DC: National Academy of Education.

27. Harris, T.L. (1969). Reading. In R.L. Ebel (Ed.), *Encyclopedia of educational research* (4th ed.) (pp. 1069–1104). New York: Macmillan.

     Russell, D., and Fea, H.R. (1963). Research on teaching reading. In N.L. Gage (Ed.), *Handbook of research on teaching* (p. 865). Chicago: Rand McNally.

28. Robinson, H.M. (1971). Reading instruction: Research. In L.C. Deighton (Ed.), *Encyclopedia of education: Vol. 7* (pp. 406–412). New York: Macmillan.

29. Blount, N.S. (1973). Research on teaching literature, language, and composition. In R.M.W. Travers (Ed.), *Second handbook of research on teaching* (pp. 1072–1097). Chicago: Rand McNally.

30. Muller (1967); see note 19.

31. Graves, D.H. (1980). A new look at writing research. *Language Arts, 57,* 913–918, p. 914.

32. Emig (1982); see note 6, p. 2021.

33. Hatlin (1986); see note 22, p. 67.

34. Tierney, R.J., and Leys, M. (1986). What is the value of connecting reading and writing? In B. Peterson (Ed.), *Convergences: Essays on reading, writing, and literacy* (p. 14). Urbana, IL: National Council of Teachers of English.

35. Meckel, H.C. (1963). Research on teaching composition and literature. In N.L. Gage (Ed.); see note 27, pp. 966–1000.

36. Project English (1964); see note 3, p. 11.

37. Purves, A.C. (1984). The challenge of education to produce literate students. In A.C. Purves and O.S. Niles (Eds.), *Becoming readers in a complex society. 83rd Yearbook of the National Society for the Study of Education* (p. 9). Chicago: University of Chicago Press.

38. Freeman, F.N. (1913). Writing: Historic evolution. In P. Monroe (Ed.); see note 17, *Vol. 5,* pp. 819–827.

39. Artley, A.S. (1950). Research concerning interrelationships among the language arts. *Elementary English, 27,* 527–537, pp. 533–534.
40. Jenkins, W.A. (1977). Changing patterns in teacher education. In J.R. Squire (Ed.), *The teaching of English. 76th Yearbook of the National Society for the Study of Education* (pp. 260–281). Chicago: University of Chicago Press.
41. Squire, J.R. (1969). English literature. In H.E. Mitzel (Ed.), *Encyclopedia of educational research* (4th ed.) (pp. 461–473). New York: Free Press.
42. Evans, B., and Lynch, J.J. (1960). *Dialogues on the teaching of literature.* New York: Bookman.
43. Devine, T.G. (1971). Reading in high schools. In L.C. Deighton (Ed.); see note 28, pp. 402–406.
44. Baker (1913); see note 17, p. 167.
45. Artley (1950); see note 39, p. 527.
46. Smith, N.B. (1965). *American reading instruction.* Newark, DE: International Reading Association.
47. NCTE Steering Committee on Social and Political Concerns (1976). What are the basics of English? *Slate Newsletter, 1,* 1–4.
48. Meckel (1963); see note 35.
49. Robinson (1977); see note 12.
    Russell and Fea (1963); see note 27.
50. Robinson, H.A., and Schatzberg, K. (1984). The development of effective teaching. In A.C. Purves and O.S. Niles (Eds.); see note 37, p. 250.
51. Anderson, Hiebert, Scott, and Wilkinson (1984); see note 14.
52. Burrows (1977); see note 9.
53. Birnbaum, J.C. (1982). The reading and composing behavior of selected fourth- and seventh-grade students. *Research in the Teaching of English, 16,* 241–261, pp. 257–258.
54. Rosenblatt, L. (1978). *The reader, the text, the poem.* Carbondale, IL: Southern Illinois University Press.
    Pearson, P.D., and Tierney, R.J. (1984). On becoming a thoughtful reader: Learning to read like a writer. In A.C. Purves and O.S. Niles (Eds.); see note 37.
55. Scardamalia, M., and Bereiter, C. (1986). Research on written composition. In M.C. Wittrock (Ed.), *Handbook of research on teaching* (3rd ed.) (p. 779). New York: Macmillan.
56. Applebee, A.N. (1982). Literature. In H.E. Mitzel (Ed.); see note 5, pp. 1105–1118.
57. Braddock, R. (1969). English composition. In R.E. Ebel (Ed.), *Encyclopedia of educational research: Vol. 4* (4th ed.) (pp. 443–461). New York: Macmillan.
58. Clifford, G.J. (1984). Buch und lesen: Historical perspectives on literacy and schooling. *Review of Educational Research, 54,* 472–500.
59. Commager, H.S. (1962). Introduction. In H.S. Commager (Ed.), *Noah Webster's American spelling book.* New York: Teachers College.
60. Cremin, L.A. (1970). *American education: The colonial experience, 1607–1783.* New York: Harper & Row.
    Cremin, L.A. (1980). *American education: The national experience,*

1783–1876. New York: Harper & Row.

61. Quoted in Gilmore, W.J. (1982). *Elementary literacy on the eve of the Industrial Revolution: Trends in rural New England, 1760–1830* (p. 109). Worcester, MA: American Antiquarian Society.

62. Cohen, S. (Ed.) (1974). *Education in the United States: A documentary history* (p. 497). New York: Random House.

63. Braddock (1969); see note 57.

64. Freeman (1913); see note 38.

65. Griscom, J. (1859). *Memoir of John Griscom, LL.D.* (p. 24). New York: Robert Carter & Brothers.

66. Grant family papers (1841). Unpublished papers, Sophia Smith Collection, Smith College, Northampton, MA.

67. Clifford (1984); see note 58.

68. Ohmann, R. (1986). Reading and writing: Work and leisure. In T. Newkirk (Ed.); see note 22, p. 11.

69. Applebee (1974); see note 11.

70. Berlin, J.A. (1984). *Writing instruction in nineteenth-century American colleges* (p. 34). Carbondale, IL: Southern Illinois University Press.

71. Townsend, L.F. (1986, April). *The gender effect: A comparison of the early curricula of Beloit College and Rockford Female Seminary.* Paper presented at the annual meeting of the American Educational Research Association, San Francisco.

72. Ohmann (1986); see note 68, p. 23.

73. Berlin (1984); see note 70.

74. Ohmann (1986); see note 68.

75. Applebee (1982); see note 56. p. 1106.

76. Braddock (1969); see note 57.

77. Baker (1913); see note 17, p. 166.

78. Church, R.L. (1976). *Education in the United States: An interpretive history.* New York: Free Press.

    Krug, E. (1964). *The shaping of the American high school.* Madison: University of Wisconsin Press.

79. Knott, T.A. (1940). Observations on vocabulary problems. *Elementary English Review, 17,* 63–67, p. 63.

80. NCTE Commission on the English Curriculum (1956). *The English language arts in the secondary school* (p. 161). New York: Appleton-Century-Crofts.

81. Douglas, W.W. (1970). The history of language instruction in the schools. In H.G. Richey (Ed.), *Linguistics in school programs. 69th Yearbook of the National Society for the Study of Education, Part II* (pp. 155–166). Chicago: University of Chicago Press.

82. College Entrance Examination Board Commission on English (1965). *Freedom and discipline in English* (p. 1). Princeton, NJ: College Entrance Examination Board.

83. Hosic, J.F. (Compiler) (1917). *Reorganization of English in secondary schools* (Bulletin 1917, No. 2, p. 11). Washington, DC: United States Bureau of Education.

84. Hosic (1917), p. 7.

85. Hosic (1917), p. 26.

86. Braddock (1969); see note 57, p. 445.

87. NCTE Curriculum Commission (1935). *An experience curriculum in English* (p. ix). New York: Appleton-Century.

88. NCTE (1939). *Conducting experiences in English.* New York: Appleton-Century.

89. NCTE Curriculum Commission (1935); see note 87, p. 1.

90. NCTE Committee on Correlation (1936); see note 2, p. l.

91. NCTE (1936), p. 285.

92. Connors, R.J. (1986). The rhetoric of mechanical correctness. In T. Newkirk (Ed.); see note 22, pp. 27–58.

93. Hyde, W.D. (1894). Educational values as assessed by the Committee of Ten. *School Review, 2,* 628–645, p. 640.

94. Braddock (1969); see note 57, p. 448.

95. Conant, J.B. (1959). *The American high school today.* New York: McGraw-Hill.

96. Berlin (1984); see note 70, p. 72.

97. Connors (1986); see note 92, p. 27.

98. Labov, W. (1969). On the logic of non-standard English. *Georgetown Monographs on Language and Linguistics, 22.* Washington, DC: Georgetown University Press.

99. Edelsky, C. (1986). *Writing in a bilingual program: Habia una vez.* Norwood, NJ: Ablex.

100. Chall, J.S., and Conard, S.S. (1984). Resources and their use for reading instruction. In A.C. Purves and O.S. Niles (Eds.); see note 37, p. 213.

101. Calfee, R., and Drum, P. (1986). Research on teaching reading. In M.C. Wittrock (Ed.); see note 55, pp. 804–849.

102. Carroll, J.B., and Chall, J.S. (Eds.) (1975). *Toward a literate society* (Report of the Committee on Reading of the National Academy of Education) (p. 31). New York: McGraw-Hill.

103. Bledstein, B. (1976). *The culture of professionalism: The middle class and the development of higher education in America.* New York: Norton.
    Schein, E.H. (1972). *Professional education: Some new directions.* New York: McGraw-Hill.

104. Newkirk (1986); see note 22, p. 2.

105. Braddock (1969); see note 57.
    Emig (1982); see note 6.
    NCTE Committee on National Interest (1961). *The national interest and the teaching of English.* Urbana, IL: National Council of Teachers of English.

106. Ohmann (1986); see note 68.

107. Blount (1973); see note 29.
      Hendrix, R. (1981). The status and politics of writing instruction. In M.F. Whiteman (Ed.); see note 22, pp. 53–70.
      Muller (1967); see note 19.

108. Newkirk (1986); see note 22.

109. NCTE Committee on National Interest (1961); see note 105.

110. Moffett (1985); see note 23.

111. Shugrue (1966); see note 21, p. 22.

112. Braddock (1969); see note 57.

113. Project English (1964); see note 3, p. 4.

114. NCTE Commission on the English Curriculum (1952). *The English language arts.* New York: Appleton-Century-Crofts.

115. NCTE Commission on the English Curriculum (1956); see note 80.

116. NCTE Curriculum Commission (1935); see note 87, pp. 4–5.

117. NCTE Task Force on Class Size and Workload in the Secondary School, W.L. Smith (Chair) (1986). *Class size in the secondary school.* Urbana, IL: National Council of Teachers of English.

118. Calfee and Drum (1986); see note 101.

119. Quoted in Squire, J.R. (Ed.) (1966). *A common purpose: The teaching of English in Great Britain, Canada, and the United States* (p. 213). Urbana, IL: National Council of Teachers of English.

120. Quoted in Squire (1966), pp. 219–221.

121. Jensen, J.M. (Ed.) (1983). Language arts at sixty: A retrospective [Special issue]. *Language Arts, 60,* p. 76.

122. Henry, G.H. (1986). What is the nature of English education? *English Education, 18,* 4–41, p. 8.

123. Clifford (1978); see note 26, p. 173.

124. Cuban, L. (1984). *How teachers taught: Constancy and change in American classrooms, 1890–1980.* New York: Longman.

125. Emig (1982); see note 6.

126. Jerrolds, B.W. (1978). *Reading reflections: The history of the International Reading Association.* Newark, DE: International Reading Association.

127. Goodman, K.S. (1984). Unity in reading. In A.C. Purves and O.S. Niles (Eds.); see note 37, p. 79.

128. Herber, H.C. and Nelson-Herber, J. (1984). Planning the reading program. In A.C. Purves and O.S. Niles (Eds.); see note 37, p. 181.

129. Gray, W.S., and Larrick, N. (Eds.) (1956). Better readers for our times. *International Reading Association Conference Proceedings: Vol. I.* New York: Scholastic Magazine.

130. College Board (1965); see note 82, p. 1.

131. Project English (1964); see note 3, p. 3.

132. Muller (1967); see note 19.

133. Frazier (1966); see note 20.
      Strickland, R. (1964). The contributions of structural linguistics to the teaching of reading, writing, and grammar in the elementary school.

Bulletin of the School of Education, Indiana University, 40, 1–39.

    Young, R.E., Becker, A.L., and Pike, K.L. (1970). *Rhetoric: Discovery and change.* New York: Harcourt, Brace, & World.

134. Squire (1969); see note 41, p. 465.

135. Blount (1973); see note 29.

    Shugrue (1966); see note 21.

    NCTE Commission on the English Curriculum (1968). *English curriculum development projects.* Urbana, IL: National Council of Teachers of English.

136. Jenkins (1977); see note 40.

137. Bowen, J.D. (1970). The structure of language. In A. Marckwardt (Ed.), *Linguistics in school programs. 69th Yearbook of the National Society for the Study of Education, Part I* (pp. 36–63). Chicago: University of Chicago Press.

    Sarason, S. (1982). *The culture of the school and the problem of change* (2nd ed.). Boston: Allyn & Bacon.

138. Smith, F. (1977). Making sense of reading—and of reading instruction. *Harvard Educational Review, 47,* 386–395, p. 388.

139. Calhoun, D. (1973). *The intelligence of a people* (p. 38). Princeton, NJ: Princeton University Press.

140. Gilmore (1982); see note 61.

141. Calfee and Drum (1986); see note 101.

    Mathews, M.M. (1966). *Teaching to read, historically considered.* Chicago: University of Chicago Press.

    Read, C. (1981). Writing is not the inverse of reading for young children. In C.H. Frederiksen and J.F. Dominic (Eds.), *Writing: The nature, development and teaching of written communication: Vol. 2. Process development and communication* (pp. 105–118). Hillsdale, NJ: Erlbaum.

142. Clifford (1984); see note 58.

143. Squire (1969); see note 41.

144. Elson, R.M. (1964). *Guardians of tradition: American schoolbooks in the nineteenth century.* Lincoln, NE: University of Nebraska Press.

145. Calhoun (1973); see note 139.

146. Lloyd, S.M. (1979). *A singular school: Abbot Academy, 1828–1973* (p. 56). Hanover, NH: Phillips Academy, Andover.

147. Pearson and Tierney (1984); see note 54.

    Tierney and Leys (1986); see note 34.

148. Anderson, Hiebert, Scott, and Wilkinson (1984); see note 14.

    Robinson (1977); see note 12.

    Smith (1965); see note 46.

149. Hansen, Newkirk, and Graves (1985); see note 13, p. ix.

150. Henry (1986); see note 122.

151. Connors (1986); see note 92.

152. Diederich, P.B. (1966). The use of external tests in public schools in the United States. In J.R. Squire (Ed.); see note 119, pp. 146–152.

153. Scardamalia and Bereiter (1986); see note 55.

154. Diederich (1966); see note 152, p. 151.

155. Squire and Applebee (1968); see note 16.

156. Tierney and Leys (1986); see note 34.

157. Blount (1973); see note 29.
     Purves, A.C. (1977). Evaluating growth in English. In J.R. Squire (Ed.), *The teaching of English. 76th Yearbook of the National Society for the Study of Education* (pp. 231–259). Chicago: University of Chicago Press.

158. Counts, G.S. (1952). *Education and American civilization* (pp. 139–140). New York: Teachers College Press.

159. Calhoun (1973); see note 139.

160. Britton, J. (1977). Language and the nature of learning: An individual perspective. In J.R. Squire (Ed.); see note 40, pp. 1–38.

161. NCTE Commission on the English Curriculum (1956); see note 80, p. 295.

162. LaConte, R.T., and Barber, B.S. (1986). English in the eighties: A midpoint international perspective. *English Journal, 75,* 27–31.
     Wresch, W. (Ed.) (1984). *The computer in composition: A writer's tool.* Urbana, IL: National Council of Teachers of English.

163. Calfee and Drum (1986); see note 101.

164. Coleman, J.S. (1972). The children have outgrown the schools. *Psychology Today, 5,* 72–76, 82, p. 72.

165. LaConte and Barber (1986); see note 162, p. 29.

166. Calhoun (1973); see note 139, p. 73.

167. Brown, E. Eagle. Unpublished papers, Newberry Library, Chicago.

168. Connors (1986); see note 92, p. 27.

169. Scardamalia and Bereiter (1986); see note 55, p. 799.

170. Muller (1967); see note 19, p. 14.

171. Applebee (1974); see note 11.

172. Szwed, J.F. (1981). The ethnography of literacy. In M.F. Whiteman (Ed.); see note 22, p. 19.

173. Freeman (1913); see note 38.

174. Baker (1913); see note 17.

175. NCTE Commission on the English Curriculum (1952); see note 114, p. 326.

176. Meckel (1963); see note 35, p. 969.

177. Shugrue (1966); see note 21, p. 12.

178. Jewett, A. (1959). *English language arts in American high schools* (Bulletin 1958, No. 13). Washington, DC: United States Department of Health, Education, and Welfare.

179. Muller (1967); see note 19, p. 12.

180. Frazier (1966); see note 20, p. 13.

181. Fulwiller, T., and Young, A. (Eds.) (1982). *Language connections: Writing and reading across the curriculum* (p. x). Urbana, IL: National Council of Teachers of English.

182. Cited in Calhoun (1973); see note 139, p. 89.

183. Calhoun (1973); see note 139, p. 89.

184. NCTE Commission on the English Curriculum (1954). *Language arts for today's children* (p. 157). Urbana, IL: National Council of Teachers of English.

185. Suzzallo, H. (1913). Reading, teaching beginners. In P. Monroe (Ed.); see note 17, *Vol. 5*, pp. 118–122.

186. NCTE Commission on the English Curriculum (1954); see note 184, p. 206, also p. 325.

187. Dixon, J. (1967). *Growth through English* (p. 3). Reading, England: National Association for the Teaching of English.
      Ruddell, R.B., and Speaker, R.B. (1985). The interactive reading process: A model. In H. Singer and R.B. Ruddell (Eds.), *Theoretical models and processes of reading* (3rd ed.) (pp. 571–793). Newark, DE: International Reading Association.

188. Dixon (1967); see note 187, p. 107.

189. Dixon, J. (1975). *Growth through English, set in the perspective of the seventies.* Huddersfield, England: National Association for the Teaching of English.

190. Clifford (1984); see note 58.
      Cook-Gumperz, J. (1986). Literacy and schooling: An unchanging equation? In J. Cook-Gumperz (Ed.), *The social construction of literacy* (pp. 16–44). New York: Cambridge University Press.

191. O'Neil, W. (1970). Properly literate. *Harvard Educational Review, 40*, 260–263.

192. Myers, G. (1986). Reality, consensus, and reform in the rhetoric of composition teaching. *College English, 48*, 154–174.

193. Hendrix (1981); see note 107.

194. Levine, K. (1982). Functional literacy: Fond illusions and false economies. *Harvard Educational Review, 52*, 249–266, p. 262.

195. West, W.W. (1971). Teaching of composition. In L.C. Deighton (Ed.); see note 28, *Vol. 2*, p. 365.

196. Moffett (1985); see note 23, p. 52.

3 Writing and Reading in the Community

Planning Group Members

Marcia Farr
Jenny Cook-Gumperz

Introduction

Guadalupe Valdés

If one were to take a poll on existing views about literacy and its importance in this country, I would wager that very few Americans would quarrel with the following statement:

> To be literate in today's society, students must learn not only how to manage the basics of writing (and reading) but also how to use what they already know to shape and rethink their ideas, to acquire new knowledge, and to communicate their ideas to others.[1]

In fact, since so much attention has been given to writing in the last few years, I would also wager that most individuals would have little trouble also agreeing that "writing is essential to maintaining a civilized society." Literacy researchers formerly focused almost exclusively on reading in the common community, so the new attention to writing has been an important development: literacy involves receiving *and* transmitting. I focus here on the recent addition of writing to the concept of a *literate* person.

The claims made about the importance of advanced literacy skills for society and the benefits of these skills for individual development may not be clearly supported by research. But the fact is that both the scholarly literature and the popular literature on writing consider it to be a fundamental skill in a very significant sense. Many people, for example, are convinced that writing has a special role in the development of higher order thinking and reasoning abilities. Other people are equally certain that writing is crucial for a citizenry destined to live a lifetime in an increasingly technological society.

It appears, then, that writing, the teaching of writing, and research on writing have become the new trend in American education, a trend to which much time and attention are being devoted.

In cynical moments, I might be inclined to argue along with Berg that we have little evidence to suggest that the increasing use of technology requires a more literate work force, particularly one capable of communicating information through writing. Nevertheless, I would generally agree that the focus on this topic is timely and important.[2] I do, however, have certain concerns about the impact of this focus on linguistic minority students. Given the history of their problems in American schools, I am not optimistic that the educational system can "teach" these students to write in an acceptable form and style in the foreseeable future, especially considering that to this day language differences are seen as language deficits by many researchers and practitioners and that so little research on writing is being carried out on minority populations. We simply know too little about teaching writing and about how to reshape or reorient what minority children bring with them so that it resembles whatever is being defined as *good writing*.

Unfortunately, that entire concept of good writing is itself a problem. Indeed, as Freedman and colleagues point out, good writing is more difficult to characterize than most people had assumed.[3] In spite of this fact, however, standards based on highly subjective and individual notions of good writing are currently used to screen applicants for college entrance, for graduate school admission, and for many types of employment. Formerly, institutions and employers seemed to rely on a student's past record, grades, and even standardized test scores. Today, however, the tendency is to require a writing sample from each applicant. If writing is important (and the scholarly community has unquestionably said that it *is*), then surely prospective employees or students must be able to demonstrate that they can write and write well. This posture seems logical and, most of all, consistent with current thinking.

Logic and consistency aside, however, the use of writing as a screening device is clearly unfair to those students whom the educational system has not served well. It is especially unfair if the standard for the evaluation of writing samples is both vague and imprecise. But vague and imprecise it is! Casual judgments about people's writing style or ability are made frequently, often with little support. For example, when committees evaluate candidates, taking into account their writing, the process goes something like this: The committee meets to examine applications. Files are read. Grades are computed. Statements of purpose are examined. When the time for a decision approaches, one member of the committee states that candidate Y is unacceptable because he or she cannot write. The committee member may or may not make explicit the standards being applied, but for another committee member to challenge the judgment of the first member and to disagree with the evaluation of the writing sample is clearly difficult and awkward. Unless someone on the committee feels strongly about the candidate and argues that other qualifications should be taken into account as well, the "poor" writer will simply be eliminated. If the committee has no criteria, no definitions of what will be considered good writing to guide it, judgments will be made subjectively and quite possibly unfairly.

In an age when minority students have only recently begun to enter previously inaccessible institutions, the implications of using vague and imprecise judgments about writing are quite serious. It is obvious that entire classes of applicants could be eliminated (fairly or unfairly) using writing as an excuse. Compared with other criteria used for exclusion, however, writing seems even more problematic. Without requesting that their samples be sent to "experts" in the field of writing evaluation, unsuccessful applicants have little ground on which to question a committee's decision or their judgment about the applicants' ability to write.

Writing, then, with an emphasis on using writing in the decision-making process, is for some American minority students yet another shibboleth, another test they cannot pass because of their background and experience.

This chapter is an excellent example of the direction and perspective that future research on writing and, more generally, literacy must take if it is to address the needs of linguistic minority students. In this chapter, Gundlach, Farr, and Cook-Gumperz contribute significantly to developing a framework that has important implications for those concerned about the teaching and learning of writing and reading at school, especially for those concerned about the education of linguistic minority students. As the authors remind us, we are just beginning to discover that much knowledge about literacy is acquired *outside* the formal school context, whether at home, in the community, or in the workplace.

As Gundlach points out, what children bring with them into the classroom is a product of their experiences and interactions with others. The danger, however, as Farr suggests, is that "normal children from nonmainstream cultural groups will be seen as abnormal, language delayed, or disabled because their highly developed linguistic (and cognitive) abilities may not include the ability to speak standard English or to assume comfortably social roles that involve writing and reading activities." She argues that teachers must become "ethnosensitive," rather than ethnocentric, that they must work to develop literacy activities that help children use what they bring in acquiring "mainstream" skills.

Cook-Gumperz, on the other hand, raises important questions about exactly what these mainstream skills actually are in the "real" world. By focusing on literacy in the workplace and showing how literacy in such contexts is often entirely unrelated to the kinds of literacy emphasized in classroom contexts, she calls for instruction that helps students "recognize (and come to value) the knowledge and skills that enable a person to assume the roles of the writer and reader in specific situations." Implicit in her presentation is the notion that definitions of *good writing* must come from the contexts in which writing is actually used, rather than from school perceptions or standards of adequacy.

Notes

1. Berg, I. (1972). *Education and jobs: The great training robbery.* New York: Praeger.
2. Freedman, S., Dyson, A. Haas, Flower, L., and Chafe, W. (1985). Mission statement. In *A proposal to establish a center for the study of writing.* Submitted by the University of California–Berkeley and Carnegie-Mellon University to the National Institute of Education, Washington, DC.
3. Freedman et al. (1985).

Writing and Reading in the Community

Robert Gundlach, Marcia Farr, and Jenny Cook-Gumperz

It is often assumed that school is the place where children learn to write and read and that the main goal of school writing and reading instruction is to prepare students for the literacy demands of adult life, particularly in the workplace. In this view, writing and reading are relatively solitary activities that require the individual to draw upon a number of skills. The job of teachers, then, is to teach these skills and to help the student integrate them into the complex processes of writing and reading entire texts. But recent scholarship has raised doubt about these assumptions. In fact, children in modern literate cultures often begin learning to write and read before they begin school—and continue to use written language and to develop writing and reading abilities in nonschool settings even as they attend school. Often, too, the writing and reading demands of school differ from those of nonschool writing and reading activities. Moreover, the literacy skills emphasized in school do not coincide with those needed or desired in the working world.

In this chapter we review recent scholarship on writing and reading outside of school—that is, in the community, both at home and in the workplace. Through this review, we explore particularly the relatedness of writing and reading as social practices, and we consider the implications of this social view of literacy outside of school for writing and reading instruction in school. Our premise is that learning to write and read involves more than being taught in school, in part because such learning occurs in a range of social contexts. We do not mean to suggest that the role of teachers is insignificant. Rather, our point is that, when teachers of writing and reading consider the broader social dimensions of their work, they may thereby increase their understanding of how to contribute most effectively to their students' learning.

We have chosen to emphasize three particular topics. First, we discuss recent research on young children's early writing and reading, focusing on what some scholars have termed "emergent literacy." This section of the paper, "Children's Writing and Reading in Nonschool Settings," was written by Robert Gundlach. Our second section, "Literacy and Language Variation at Home and at School," written by Marcia Farr, discusses the linguistic patterns that children acquire in their development of spoken language and analyzes the relation of those patterns to the demands of written language activities that children meet in school. If the first section suggests the value of establishing continuities between young children's experience of writing and reading at home and in school, the second section emphasizes ways to approach key contrasts between home and school language expectations. Our third section projects beyond the school years into adult uses of literacy. This section, "Writing and Reading in the Workplace," written by Jenny Cook-Gumperz, considers both similarities and differences between literacy demands in school and at work, offering an analysis of how writing and reading activities are embedded in social relationships in work settings.

In a final section we draw implications from all three discussions for school policy, curriculum development, and teaching practice. Let us now turn to the particulars, beginning with young children's early experience with written language.

Children's Writing and Reading in Nonschool Settings

Roger Brown, writing in 1974 about the surge of scholarly interest in language acquisition during the 1960s and early 1970s, remarked that "all over the world the first sentences of young children are being as painstakingly taped, transcribed, and analyzed as if they were the last sayings of the great sages." This, he added, "is a surprising fate for the likes of 'That doggie,' 'No more milk,' and 'Hit ball.' "[1] More recently still, in the late 1970s and the early 1980s, a similar fate has befallen the first scribbles and seemingly makeshift spellings of slightly older preschool children. Careful analyses have been performed on such texts as EFUKANOPNKAZIWILGEVUAKANOPNR (a five-year-old's rendering of "If you can open cans, I will give you a can opener")[2] and *JJ l'''*, which, as its four-year-old author explained, is a "drawing with rhymes" accompanied by "bullets making gun noises."[3]

This attention to preschool children's earliest steps in learning to write and read has been the dominant focus in recent discussions of children's written language use in nonschool settings. Some studies of preschoolers have started from the premise that a relatively small percentage of children are "early readers"[4] or "young fluent readers."[5]

The goal of these studies has been to determine what can be learned from exceptional children that might be applied to reading instruction for children who are less precocious. But the more common guiding premise in recent research has been that all children growing up in literate societies encounter print before they start school and, just as they learn spoken language in the preschool years, they begin to acquire written language as well. The main focus of recent research has been on the development of literacy in typical children, not just in the exceptional early learners.

How, though, can we determine what is "typical"? Researchers have taken two approaches. The first concentrates on general cognitive strategies. These studies search for common, perhaps even universal, developmental trends in the way children's minds construct a working understanding of the forms and functions of written language. The second approach concentrates on how children learn reading and writing as social practices, as culturally formed ways of doing, knowing, and being. From this point of view, typicality is relative to the habits and values of specific groups. Studies taking this approach seek to explain how children become members of particular communities of readers and writers.

Both approaches suggest a close relationship between writing and reading. The first approach assumes that the child's cognitive reinvention of written language provides the child with the fundamental knowledge, or competence, for both receptive and productive uses of written language—that is, for both writing and reading. The processes of reading and writing may be different, but both draw on common linguistic knowledge and require overlapping cognitive strategies for "meaning-making."

The second approach assumes that a writer and a reader in any given situation must interact on reciprocal terms. They work with a shared understanding of particular conventions of written communication that allow them to proceed with some confidence of success in establishing shared or negotiated meaning, whether the exchange centers on a shopping list, a personal letter, a poem, a novel, or a formal business report. Written texts allow for communication across space and time and permit exchanges among people who otherwise do not know each other and have no other form of contact. Nonetheless, learning to participate in such communicative exchanges is a matter of socialization, a matter of learning to enact particular social roles. The efforts of a writer are always partly governed by the anticipated needs and desires of the reader, and of course a reader's efforts are always partly directed by the purposes and interests of the writer.

Indeed, as Nystrand points out, all written communication depends on some form of reciprocity between writer and reader.[6] To succeed in one role requires some understanding of the other.

What has research conducted from these two points of view taught us? Below we assess what we know about young children's writing and reading in nonschool settings.

We know, first, that many children *do* begin experimenting with writing and reading well before they meet literacy instruction in school, and indeed before they attend school at all. Teale and Sulzby, listing the conclusions they draw from studies to date, state the point in strong terms: "Literacy development begins long before children start formal instruction. Children use legitimate reading and writing behaviors in the informal settings of home and community."[7] The use of the word *legitimate* in this formulation is noteworthy, because it suggests that some observers may not find evidence of reading and writing activity in the behavior of the children Teale and Sulzby refer to here. Surely it is true that scholars, educators, and parents alike may be inclined to discount the young child's "pretend" reading or undecipherable scribbling as evidence of the onset of literacy development.

Such a view has much of the authority of tradition on its side. Writing and reading are viewed by most adults as highly conventionalized acts; unless a reader understands the socially established meanings of the words on the page or unless a writer produces interpretable spellings and sentences, he or she cannot, in the traditional perspective, be said to be truly reading or writing. In this view, literacy learning begins with mastering simple matters first: the formation of the correct shape of letters, the discrimination of sound contrasts in decoding, the comprehension and spelling of simple words and sentences, the use of fundamental punctuation marks, and so on. Mistakes are to be avoided, even at the start; the learner masters the basics first, then moves up to more sophisticated forms.

Although there is some disagreement about precise definitions,[8] recent research on preschool children's early literacy learning is unified by its rejection of this traditional view of the nature of learning to read and write. As Teale and Sulzby put it, those studying emergent literacy in the young child believe that in previous research programs "the search for skills which predict subsequent achievement has been misguided because the onset of literacy has been misconceived."[9] A more accurate picture, they suggest, is one that portrays the young child as an active learner, developing not isolated reading or writing skills, but a coordinated understanding of the uses and forms of written language and a working knowledge of the processes of reading and writing.

This broad understanding develops slowly, and perhaps by stages, but from the start it embraces both purpose and form, intention and structure—reading and writing are learned as complex, meaningful activities, not as aggregates of separate skills. Furthermore, the learning of written language is connected with the learning of spoken language. As Teale and Sulzby assert, "The child develops as a *writer/reader*. The notion of reading preceding writing, or vice versa, is a misconception. Listening, speaking, reading, and writing abilities (as aspects of language—both oral and spoken) develop concurrently and interrelatedly, rather than sequentially."[10]

Research designed to explore and test these claims is quite new, and scholars have only begun to recognize the full complexity of the issues involved. As one observer of recent scholarship on children's "awakening to literacy" suggests, "Many important insights and much data relevant to literacy exist—possibly more than any one individual or even one discipline can be expected to know or to take account of— but there is also a great deal to be learned"; and "Literacy is complex and multifaceted, so it should not be surprising that individuals fail to agree on its nature or on how it should be taught."[11] But Teale and Sulzby are unquestionably right to state in the strongest terms that an understanding of children's long-term development of writing and reading ability must include a recognition of the important literacy learning that most children in a society like ours undertake before they arrive in first grade or even kindergarten. To recognize this early phase of learning is to appreciate the knowledge and abilities many children bring to school with them. It is also to confront the considerable differences in early learning experienced by children in different settings and different families, and hence to acknowledge the varying orientations to writing and reading that even the youngest school-age children bring to the literacy instruction and activities they encounter in the classroom.

Research focused on children's common cognitive strategies in the course of literacy acquisition emphasizes the knowledge and abilities many children develop by the time they go to school. The most extensive research program of this kind has been conducted by Emelia Ferreiro, who has formulated the theoretical problem of studying children's literacy development in terms of Piagetian principles of genetic epistemology. Understanding children's literacy development thus becomes understanding a "complex psychological problem."[12]

Written symbols, Ferreiro notes, "can be regarded as objects of the external world and, as such, may become objects to think about."[13]

The issue for research, then, is how children develop in their thinking about written symbols, how they acquire a working knowledge of the logical system of rules or principles that coordinates the use of written language. Writing and reading may be social practices, varying in cultural meaning and function, but children do not, Ferreiro argues, merely absorb social practices and information passively.[14] Rather, they are active participants in their own learning, employing their own logical guidelines in interpreting the objects and practices they observe in their social worlds. They transform the information they take in so that it conforms to the logical understandings (or schemata) they already have—a process Piaget identified as cognitive assimilation. When children encounter information (principles of orthography, for example) that conflicts with what they know, they either fail to learn the conflicting information, or they modify their current logic to accommodate the new principles.

This cognitive dynamic of learning as the selective transformation of objects and practices encountered in the environment—with the child's mind engaged in a continuous, nonconscious balancing act between assimilation and accommodation—will surely be familiar to readers of Piaget. Ferreiro seeks to use this theoretical framework to uncover a pattern in children's successive understandings of the system of written language that "is not only chronological, but developmentally ordered, and thus constitutes a psycho-genetic progression."[15] She focuses particularly on the earliest phase of literacy learning. She observes, for example, that the "child who makes an approximate correspondence between sounds and letters may have spelling diffi-culties, but he is already functioning within the alphabetic system of writing." On the basis of this observation, she asserts that researchers need "to understand the conceptions that are at work even earlier, such as with those children who use unconventional signs but organize them in a linear order that is very different from the order of elements in a drawing."[16]

Ferreiro's analyses are careful and complex as she presses to elucidate the logic young children use as they cope with the literacy tasks that the investigator has put to them. The following passage suggests both the texture and some of the central themes of Ferreiro's work; it is from an account of her studies of four- and five-year-old Spanish-speaking children:

> To take into account the properties of the text [as it has been read aloud to them] and, at the same time, to adjust the anticipation

of meaning to the hypothesis that only nouns are written, children make various attempts, one of which is to try a one-to-one correspondence between segments of the text and syllables of the word. For instance, for the three segments of *el pato nada*, several children proposed "pa-ti-to" (little duck). When syllables are made to fit segments of the text, all segments are treated as equivalent, regardless of their actual length; the number of letters of a segment is taken into account only when the reference is to words, because for the child, there is a condition that must be fulfilled: a complete word cannot be written with less than a given minimum number of letters—usually three.[17]

Ferreiro offers impressively reasoned analyses that are driven by the larger goal of discovering a predictable, universal progression of formulations in children's tacit knowledge of written language as a "socio-cultural object." It must be said, however, that the realization of this ambitious scholarly goal remains a long way off. And indeed it may turn out that the diversity of the cultural forms and social functions of written language will ultimately render the goal unrealizable. In the meantime, much of value can be found in Ferreiro's research. She points to the abstract system of principles that children learn from the start of their development as writers and readers. In this respect she implies that the activities of writing and reading are both guided by a single abstract understanding of the system of written language, however different the two activities may be as social practices. Furthermore, she argues convincingly that the young preschool child's first steps in literacy development can be viewed, on the one hand, as the natural result of the child's developmental reasoning strategies and, on the other hand, as steps in a difficult cognitive project: "The link between print and oral language is not immediately grasped by any child. Even those who grow up in an environment rich in literacy experiences . . . have considerable trouble understanding the relationships between oral language and the graphic forms."[18]

On the issue of universals in children's literacy development, Ferreiro successfully underscores the commonality not of the content of children's literacy learning, but of the cognitive dynamics that impel and shape the direction of that learning. Concluding her report of a particularly interesting study of Santiago and Mariana, two Spanish-speaking preschool children, she argues that the two children, whose observable paths of learning differ considerably, nonetheless have much in common as they learn to manage the conventional written forms of their names. Both young children "try to reconcile contradictory evidence; both pass through periods of acute [cognitive] conflicts [which, Ferreiro notes, can produce great anxiety for some children];

both select (from the information available) that which they are able to assimilate; both disregard information for very precise reasons; both are not satisfied until they find a general coherent interpretative system."[19]

Clifford Geertz, in his essay "The Way We Think Now: Toward an Ethnography of Modern Thought," pinpoints what he describes as the "animating paradox within the social sciences": We have come to recognize that human thought is "wondrously singular as process" and yet "spectacularly multiple as product."[20] Ferreiro and others following an essentially Piagetian model of cognitive development in their studies of children's literacy acquisition emphasize that remarkable singularity. Yet written language—its uses, its forms, its value—is a product and a tool of human cognition; it is indeed spectacularly multiple. Studies that focus only on common human cognitive strategies cannot adequately acknowledge the great variousness of reading and writing as social practices in different places and among different people. Hymes makes this point forcefully: "Models [of language development] which appeal to a universal, innate, nonhistorical, acultural, socially aspecific goal immediately fail in the presence of writing, which is patently not innate but historically invented and diverse in its cultural forms and social functions."[21]

It is easy to accept this notion in principle and at the same time to retain an intuitive sense that certain kinds of literacy are more "natural" than others. Perhaps one explanation for this may be found in the general image of language ability derived from recent linguistic theory. As Litowitz observes:

> American linguists since Chomsky have been preoccupied with abstract, formal structures that represent the underlying competence of a lone, ideal speaker-hearer. The limitations of a psycholinguistics that relies on this kind of linguistics are profound: an ideal speaker-hearer has neither cultural nor personal history, no family, no . . . inner reality.[22]

But probably the source of this intuitive sense in most instances is less theoretical and more experiential, a form of reflexive ethnocentrism that accords special privilege to our earliest experiences and successes with language. Eudora Welty offers a glimpse of this phenomenon in an observation about her own early reading experience: "It had been startling and disappointing to me to find out that storybooks had been written by *people*, that books were not natural, coming up of themselves like grass."[23] All the more important, then, to acknowledge that, as the aphorism has it, books do not teach the use of books—people do. Writing and reading are cultural, not natural, and the social practices of written language use vary depending on situation and cultural group. In recent years researchers have begun to investigate how the social practices of writing and reading are learned and taught in homes and other settings in which some preschool children become participants in particular communities of writers and readers.[24]

Although much of this work is still exploratory, several themes have already emerged. One recurring theme is that social interaction is probably the key element in the context of children's early experience with written language. Surely it makes a difference that children have particular "print environments" that offer them the data from which they infer general principles of written language form and function. But even more significant are the human relationships in which a child learns not only what written language *is*, but also what it *does*.

Some studies focus on how adults (usually parents) orient preschool children to particular uses of written language by firmly managing children's early experiences with writing and reading. Most frequently studied are the lessons young children learn from the experience of having books read aloud to them. Reviewing a number of studies with this focus, Snow and Ninio suggest that children whose parents read aloud to them are likely to learn a series of "literacy contracts":

1. Books are for reading, not for manipulating.
2. In book reading, the book is in control; the reader is led.
3. Pictures are not things but representations of things.
4. Pictures are for naming.
5. Pictures, though static, can represent events.
6. Book events occur outside real time.
7. Books constitute an autonomous fictional world.[25]

Some children's earliest experiences with writing are also tightly managed by adults. Snow, for example, presents a transcript of a conversation between a mother and her thirty-one-month-old son named Nathaniel, tracing the mother's efforts to get her son to join her in the task of spelling his name. Snow comments that the mother's continual attempts to direct her son's attention to the task represents a striking instance of an adult's speech that is pointedly not semantically contingent—that is, not built upon what the child has said or done, and in that sense not directly responsive. Snow likens the mother's managerial way of speaking in this exchange to her nonverbal behavior during the same episode: "She twice even interrupted [Nathaniel's] concentration on the letters to clean out his ears."[26]

If the work reviewed by Snow and Ninio establishes the theme that parents orient their children to the assumptions and practices of literacy,

Heath's ethnographic studies of particular communities' "ways with words" add three important themes. First, both the adults' style of interaction and the lessons preschool children learn about writing and reading vary from community to community. In one community Heath studied, parents believe that "their task is to praise and practice reading with their children"; parents in another community believe that "the young have to learn to be and do, and if reading is necessary for this learning, that will come."[27]

A second theme emerges from Heath's explanation of this difference: writing and reading activities are embedded in the larger flow of activity in people's lives, including the use of other means of communication. Since patterns of living vary from group to group, so do both the patterns of language use that children might observe and the habitual interactions by which adults orient young children to the possibilities and requirements of literacy. Heath notes that in Roadville and Trackton, two contrasting working-class communities she studied, the residents

> have a variety of literate traditions and in each community these
> are interwoven in different ways with oral uses of language, ways
> of negotiating meaning, deciding on action, and achieving status.
> Patterns of using reading and writing in each community are
> interdependent with ways of using space (having bookshelves,
> decorating walls, displaying telephone numbers) and using time
> (bedtime, meals hours, and homework sessions). Habits of using
> the written word also develop as they help individuals fulfill self-
> perceived roles of caregiving and preparing children for school.[28]

A third theme evident in Heath's studies is that the dynamics of literacy learning in adult-child interactions are complicated indeed. The child plays an active role not only cognitively, inferring general principles from bits of experience, but socially as well. The way children participate in interactions from which they may learn about writing and reading is determined by at least two general motives. On the one hand, children seek to cooperate, to learn how to do what is wanted or expected. This motive no doubt helps to explain the behavior of young children during book-reading activities with their mothers in the community Heath calls "Maintown": Children as young as six months "give attention to books and information derived from books," "acknowledge questions about books," and "accept book and book-related activities as entertainment."[29] On the other hand, children seek to increase their power in human relationships. They aim not only to cooperate but to exert control, to determine the direction of interactions. This motive is abundantly evident in children's attempts to disrupt adult-led activities, including book-reading. But it also impels some children to seek the manager's role of such interactions, as in the case of the three-year-old children of Maintown who, faced with the demand during book-reading to "listen and wait as an audience, . . . often choose to 'read' to adults rather than to be read to."[30]

Studies focused on young children's early writing have given less emphasis to adult-child interaction than those focused mainly on reading. Some studies, such as those by Taylor[31] and Harste, Woodward, and Burke,[32] have emphasized the young child's writing as an expression of his or her developing literacy knowledge and ability. Both of these analyses regard early literacy as culturally specific, derived from family experience and particularly from "demonstrations" of specific written language forms and functions.

Other studies of early writing have emphasized the creative capacities of children experimenting on their own with written language, often in ways mysterious to the adults around them. Here the focus is on the child's linguistic and cognitive resourcefulness, as in Glenda Bissex's *GNYS AT WRK*, a case study of the writing and reading development of her son Paul. The title of Bissex's book is taken from the second half of a sign five-year-old Paul wrote and placed above his desk: DO NAT DSTRB GNYS AT WRK. Bissex uses Paul's text as the occasion for spelling out the implications of her study: "The GNYS (genius) at work is our human capacity for language. DO NAT DSTRB is a caution to observe how it works, for the logic by which we teach is not always the logic by which children learn."[33]

Bissex's comments may be read as support for the more purely cognitive approach to understanding early literacy exemplified by the work of Ferreiro and others. But her remarks also serve as a useful reminder to researchers studying what Cook-Gumperz has called children's "social construction of literacy"[34]—the social processes by which children become participants in particular communities of writers and readers. Bissex's comments remind us that, although children learn the expressive and communicative resources that become available to them as they grow up in specific social settings, they adapt these resources to serve their own developmental and individual purposes. These purposes, though ultimately culturally shaped, are not necessarily similar to the conventional purposes of the adults they interact with or observe. Part of learning to read and write is finding a way to make written language one's own.

In this process of making written language their own, children often incorporate writing and reading activities into their play. They thus create opportunities to explore the potential of writing and reading outside the immediate context of social interaction. This allows them to experiment with the tools of writing and reading and to improvise freely with the writing and reading roles they have been asked to adopt themselves or have seen enacted by important people in their lives. Children sometimes use play activity as an opportunity to explore the reciprocity between writer and reader by shuttling back and forth between writing and reading roles, much as children sometimes play games in which they cast themselves both as parent and child, or as teacher and pupil.

Another dimension of the process by which children begin to take personal control over the social practices of writing and reading is the tendency of some young children to combine the use of writing with the use of other representational systems—speech, drawing, gesture, the creation of physical designs with objects of various kinds.[35] Observing children at play with literacy—and reading the distinctively obscure texts they produce—can lead us to underestimate the social character of both the content and dynamics of children's writing and reading development. But writing and reading do not exist independently of the social contexts in which they gain their meaning. Writing and reading are each, finally, umbrella terms for many specific, culturally bound activities that vary in character, consequence, and significance.

Recognizing the variousness of writing and reading—acknowledging that "the relative importance of [written] language among other modes of communication, its role as resource or danger, art or tool, depends on [what people make] of it"[36]—does not require advocating a school literacy program that gives equal importance to all possible forms of literacy. In fact, the premise that "particular ways of using and interpreting print are not 'natural' but develop as part of early social learning within particular cultures"[37] leads to the recognition that school writing and reading experiences are always organized according to cultural choices and that formal literacy instruction is necessarily an embodiment of the skills, concepts, and attitudes valued by a particular group of people.

Since all literacy is in important respects cultural literacy, the relationship between writing and reading is not inherent in the two activities abstractly considered, but rather is a function of the specific relationships established between the roles of writer and reader in particular communities. Hence one key job for educators is to determine not only the forms of written language that should be taught, but also the writing and reading roles students should be encouraged to adopt in school—to determine, that is, the sort of community of writers and readers a school should be if it is to serve its cultural function well. Another important task for educators is to find ways to offer every child a fair chance to participate successfully as a member of the school community of writers and readers. To do this second job well, educators need to take into account the active and various preschool literacy experiences that many children bring to school with them.

Literacy and Language Variation at Home and at School

As we have illustrated in the previous section, children do not go to school as empty vessels that are to be filled up with "school knowledge." Although there is much for them to learn during their school years, all children already have acquired considerable knowledge about the world and their particular community before they begin formal schooling. They have, in other words, considerable facility with particular cognitive processes.

A major aspect of this cognition concerns the language used in their communities, both its formal structure (grammar) and the culturally based ways it is used in both its oral and written modes. As we also discussed in the previous section, some cognitive processes are shared by all children, whereas some vary sharply from one cultural group to another. In other words, the community in which children are enculturated determines to a great extent what it is that they know.

The knowledge that a person has about his or her language has been referred to as "communicative competence."[38] Communicative competence in this sense involves both the ability to generate, for example, English sentences with words in the right order and the ability to use those sentences appropriately in different contexts to convey slightly different meanings. Although children entering kindergarten have not finished acquiring their native language, much of that process is complete, and they certainly can be considered full-fledged speakers of the language.

Beyond their knowledge of spoken language, most children of preschool age in a highly literate society such as ours also know a great deal about written language. Print surrounds them, from MacDonald's signs to labels on tin cans and cereal boxes. In many homes, moreover, books and magazines abound, and children frequently are read to.

Although generalizations often have been made equating such literacy in the home with middle-class parents, several studies have shown much literacy activity in white, black, and Hispanic working-class homes.[39] So it is important for us to realize that low socioeconomic class does not mean a lack of experience with written language (nor, in fact, as many teachers would attest, can we assume that all middle-class children do have such experiences).

Teachers, then, can assume well-developed linguistic abilities—highly developed oral language as well as some understandings of writing and reading—in elementary school children. Because of the importance of teacher expectations in student achievement, it is crucial for teachers to be aware of such resources in their students. And it is equally crucial for them to realize that these resources can be assumed on the part of *all* normal students, no matter what ethnic or social class background they are from. Excluding a very small percentage of people who have genuine language disabilities, this is true regardless of other varying individual abilities, such as IQ. The danger is that normal children from nonmainstream cultural groups will be seen as abnormal, language-delayed, or disabled because their highly developed linguistic (and cognitive) abilities may not include the ability to speak standard English or to assume comfortably mainstream social roles that involve writing and reading activities.

Viewing nonmainstream children and adolescents as having linguistic or cognitive *deficits*—when in reality their language use is simply *different* from standard English usage—can have serious consequences on their achievement in school. Much research has documented such language differences among various nonmainstream groups, and some findings from this research will be presented below. In spite of this available body of knowledge, however, the notion of such children having linguistic or cognitive deficits has persisted. This may be due, in part, to a lack of understanding of linguistic systems and of linguistic—and cultural—variation.

Variation, of course, is a natural part of all languages and of all language use. All languages, even those with a small number of speakers, have dialects[40]—either regional ones such as southern American English or social ones such as Vernacular Black English. In addition to differences among dialects (for example, in the way a word is pronounced), standard and nonstandard dialect speakers alike use more or less formal language in different contexts, depending upon the person they are speaking with or writing to, the topic being discussed, and so forth.

Another kind of variation exists in the ways that speaking, writing, and reading are *used* in particular communities. Language use—oral as well as written—is always a social practice in a particular community; and as social practices vary from community to community, so does language. Thus social roles in which writing and reading are used can differ distinctly from one community or culture to another. Scollon and Scollon provide us with an example of this.[41]

In their research on Northern Athabaskans in Alaska, the Scollons show how the deep respect for individual differences in this culture leads its members to negotiate meaning jointly, rather than to impose it on listeners (and, by extension, on readers). The making of oral narratives, a frequent occurrence among Athabaskans, emphasizes cooperation between narrator and audience to the extent that stories change according to the needs of a particular audience.

When members of this culture write, we would expect their texts to display the same kind of reliance on audience as their ways of speaking do. If listeners are unknown and, similarly, if the audience for a piece of writing is unknown (as it is, at least ostensibly, for most school writing), the tendency is to remain silent—or to express oneself only tersely. As teachers of other Indian cultures have noted, eliciting prose that exhibits characteristics of the "mainstream" version of academic writing (prose that is explicit and elaborated) can be very difficult. This apparently is because using language (or literacy) in such mainstream ways conflicts with traditional Athabaskan ways.

The Athabaskans are of course not the only people who use language and literacy in culturally specific ways. All ways of using language, oral and written, are embedded in cultural beliefs and conventions,[42] and this is as true for mainstream as for nonmainstream language use. Consequently, the concept of "good writing" that underlies writing instruction in school is embedded in the cultural beliefs and conventions by which "schooled" people live. As members of what Street terms the academic subculture of Western society,[43] schooled people immerse themselves in certain kinds of oral and written language, and they value objectivity and explicitness in it, particularly in writing.

Because school in our society is part of mainstream culture, the language use in school—for writing, reading, and speaking-closely resembles the language use of mainstream culture. For example, in the study we discussed earlier, Heath shows, among other things, how members of the mainstream culture in the community she studied used "expository talk" that was similar to school-taught expository prose on the job (in this study as mill executives and teachers) and at home as parents.[44] In contrast, nonmainstream cultural groups use language in ways that often do not resemble, in fact sometimes conflict with, "school" language. In the next section we will review briefly what we know about speaking, writing, and reading among a variety of nonmainstream groups from research in this area.

Nonmainstream Varieties of English

Ethnic variation in oral language has been investigated in numerous studies during the last two decades. This work has explored a variety of American English dialects, including Vernacular Black English,[45] Puerto Rican English,[46] Appalachian English,[47] varieties of American Indian English,[48] and others.[49] The primary finding of all this work is that nonstandard varieties of English, in fact of any language, are as complex and as regularly patterned as are standard varieties. Moreover, these studies have provided considerable information about the specific linguistic features in different varieties of American English.

In addition to sociolinguistic studies of language structure, other studies have focused on language function, or use. They have taken place both within classrooms[50] and within home and community contexts.[51] This work has found that ways of using language can vary extensively from one cultural group to another and that such differences can cause communication to break down between speakers from different groups. Schools, of course, are one significant place in our society where members of different cultures meet. Once there, however, everyone is expected to interact according to the linguistic patterns of the "school culture."[52]

Studies focused specifically on variation in written language are not as numerous as those focused on variation in oral language. Here, work has investigated the writing of nonstandard dialect speakers[53] or literacy in homes and other nonschool community settings.[54]

The research on language variation and writing has identified particular linguistic features characteristic of the "home language" of various ethnic groups; these features occur in the writing of children, adolescents, and adults from these groups. For example, when a Vernacular Black English (VBE) speaker writes the sentence "Mickey have so many friend," it illustrates two home language features: *have* rather than *has* and *friend* rather than *friends*.[55] Work in this area has identified home language features in the writing of VBE speakers, Hispanic and Indian bilinguals, and deaf users of American Sign Language.

Most of this work on the relation of home language to literacy learning explicitly advocates what Baugh terms "ethnosensitivity" (rather than ethnocentricity) on the part of those teaching such students.[56] In this view, an emphasis is placed on understanding and building on the cultural values and linguistic patterns of the nonmainstream students.

The work on literacy in community settings has found that literacy is not a single entity that occurs in different contexts, but a social practice that varies according to its particular use in each context. Likewise, the cognitive demands of writing (and the cognitive effects of learning to write) also vary according to particular uses.

For example, Scribner and Cole studied writing and reading among the Vai in Liberia, where Vai, Arabic, and English are used both orally and for writing and reading.[57] They found that the performance of the literates was superior to that of the nonliterates on certain cognitive tasks. The specific cognitive tasks, however, were closely related to the specific ways that each group of literates used writing or reading. For example, the practice of letter writing in the Vai script seemed to increase "audience awareness" as a cognitive skill. This study provides, then, additional evidence that, as social (and literacy) practices vary from community to community, so do the characteristic cognitive processes of those who participate in these practices.

The Question of Dialect Interference

The question of whether, or to what extent, a student's home dialect actually interferes with learning to write and read has been controversial, both in research and in the schools. The notion of such "dialect interference" was modeled on that of language interference, which occurs when a speaker who knows two languages uses features from one language while speaking the other language. For example, a native speaker of Spanish may write, in English, a sentence that places an adjective after a noun (as is the rule in Spanish), rather than before the noun (as is the rule in English). Bilingual students who know Spanish and are learning English sometimes do this, and it is an example of interference from Spanish. When these students are made aware of the contrastive differences between Spanish and English in this type of construction, they can learn to edit their writing accordingly. Increased fluency in English (and tacit knowledge of it) may also decrease instances of interference.

Although dialect interference appears to be more or less parallel to *language* interference, the analogy is limited because nonstandard dialect speakers do not change languages when they use either a standard feature such as including the plural -s suffix or a nonstandard feature such as omitting that suffix. Moreover, nonstandard dialect speakers rarely use nonstandard features all of the time. Instead, like all speakers of English, they use such features according to the linguistic context of the particular sentence and the social situation. If, however, they use a nonstandard feature a high percentage of the time, they are more likely to have difficulties in learning to write and read.

A number of studies have investigated the effect of nonstandard dialects on learning to read, and their results are mixed and inconclusive. Hall and Guthrie critically reviewed these studies and concluded that many of them were flawed. The authors called for new studies that would move beyond the experimental situation and focus more on the ways that nonstandard dialects are used in real-life contexts, rather than solely on their linguistic structure.[58] Since then, some researchers, notably Heath,[59] have done just that and found that the way language is used in some communities can conflict sharply with the way children are expected to use it for speaking, writing, and reading in school.

As discussed above, Heath's ethnographic study of two nonmainstream communities described the cultural and linguistic differences that interfered with the children's success in school.[60] Moreover, she worked with local teachers to devise instructional strategies that were sensitive to these differences and that provided the children the meaningful experience with written language needed to learn to write and read. Her book reports in detail on her research and on the successful teaching strategies.[61]

In addition to important studies such as Heath's and in spite of Hall's and Guthrie's criticism of its experimental nature, a study by Labov provides convincing evidence of some dialect interference from linguistic features of VBE in reading standard English. VBE speakers often omit the final -ed suffix of some words in spoken language. Labov's experiment attempted to determine whether such speakers comprehended that -ed when reading, even though they often omitted it when reading aloud. He found that his junior high school subjects comprehended the suffix only 35 to 55 percent of the time, indicating significant interference with comprehension. Further testing indicated that those speakers who omitted the -ed less often comprehended the test sentences more accurately.

While Labov found that linguistic differences between dialects do cause some interference in comprehension, he originally cautioned that he did not see this as the major cause of reading failure among VBE speakers. Rather, he saw that failure as the result of "political and cultural conflict within the classroom," with Black English the symbol of this conflict. More recently, however, Labov has attributed more of the problem to linguistic differences because "we know more about the structural differences between Black English and standard American English than we did ten years ago due largely to research conducted by Black linguists in the 1970s." He continues, however, to affirm the importance of teacher attitudes toward Black English in the cultural conflict within the classroom.[62]

Similarly, a study of dialect interference in the writing of black and white nonstandard dialect speakers showed a significantly higher percentage of suffix omission in the writing of those who omitted the suffix in spoken language.[63] This study looked at *-ed* and *-s* suffixes, as well as at other linguistic features of VBE and revealed a complex picture of dialect interference in writing: though it clearly is not the only explanation for the occurrence of nonstandard features in student writing, there is, nevertheless, evidence that dialect is one contributing factor.

Although several reviews have concluded that dialect interference in writing does not exist, none refutes the existing evidence.[64] Hartwell, moreover, assumes that nonstandard dialect speakers should be able to use their intuitive knowledge of English to edit nonstandard features out of their own writing.[65] This assumption is based on another assumption—that all speakers of English share the same linguistic competence. As we have seen in the review of studies above, this is not the case.

The claim that dialect interference does not exist is often used to buttress arguments against the teaching of "traditional, schoolbook" grammar and for the teaching of more global concerns of writing such as the development of ideas and coherence. Most writing researchers agree strongly with the importance of a primary instructional focus on more global concerns and with the claim that the traditional teaching of grammar does not improve writing.[66] Nevertheless, it does not serve nonstandard dialect speakers well to ignore evidence of the differences between dialects that do exist. The question is not whether to teach mechanics and standard grammar, but how. Farr and Daniels review in detail what we know about nonstandard dialects and suggest how to improve the teaching of writing to speakers of such dialects.[67] Moreover, we know that an understanding of specific differences in linguistic competence and in the ways one's own students use language can help to improve instruction.[68]

Recent research has also shown that discourse patterns (language patterns that link sentences together to form a coherent discourse, rather than a random set of sentences) differ from one cultural group to another. In a series of studies in elementary school classrooms, Michaels identified two discourse patterns used in oral narratives during the classroom event called Sharing Time, or Show and Tell.[69] One of the patterns was used by middle-class, mainstream children in telling their stories, and the other pattern was characteristic of VBE-speaking black children. The mainstream pattern closely resembled the kind of pattern expected in school literacy—in the texts that children read and in the writing they are taught to produce. This pattern emphasizes explicit lexical ties—specific words, that is, to show the connections between thoughts or events (for example, *then, so,* rather than *and*). The VBE pattern, on the other hand, showed a less explicit connectedness; the ties between thoughts and events were there, but more implicitly and were not shown with specific words.

Other research also has yielded similar findings about discourse patterns among VBE-speaking black Americans. Smitherman[70] describes black adult narrative style as "concrete narrative . . . [whose] meandering away from the 'point' takes the listener on episodic journeys."[71] In addition, Erickson, in a study of black adolescents informally discussing politics, found that shifts from one topic to another were not explicitly stated; meanings had to be inferred from a series of concrete anecdotes.[72]

Those students who unconsciously know and use native discourse patterns that do not match those of school literacy presumably have more difficulty becoming literate than those whose patterns do match those of school literacy. As we have pointed out in our discussion of emerging literacy among preschoolers, however, becoming literate is not just a matter of learning new language structures, important though these may be. Interference in this learning process also comes from differences in the ways language—both oral and written—is used in various communities.

Philips studied the language use of Warm Springs Indian children at home and at school.[73] She found that differences in social roles of speakers and listeners between Anglo mainstream teachers and the Warm Springs Indian community accounted for some of the difficulties the Indian children were having in school. Anglo teachers perceived these children as "non-comprehending" because of their characteristic lack of response in certain classroom situations. Philips determined that this lack of immediate response (for example, to teacher questions or directives) was not because the students did not understand the linguistic structures being used, but "because they [did] not share the non-Indian's assumption in such contexts that use of these syntactic forms by definition implies an automatic and immediate response from the person to whom they were addressed."[74] In contrast, the children were responsive in communicative contexts in school when the roles of speakers and listeners resembled those characteristic of language use at home.

To sum up, all the studies of conflicts between ways that different cultural groups use language make it clear that such differences can be extensive and deeply ingrained.[75] Although it is not entirely clear how these differences precisely affect learning to write and to read, it is clear that they do, and more well-designed studies will undoubtedly help us identify more specifically the interaction of cultural and linguistic differences with writing and reading instruction in standard English. In the next section, we will consider the implications of what we now know, including a brief review of two studies that have successfully improved literacy instruction for nonmainstream cultural groups of students.

Implications for the Classroom

The most important implication of all that we now know about language variation in this country is that teachers need to become aware of the specific linguistic and cultural differences among their students. To be effective in teaching writing and reading, teachers need to be "ethnosensitive," rather than ethnocentric. That is, we cannot assume that our own views of the world, or ways of using language in that world, are shared by others. Almost by definition our own cultural orientation will not, in many ways, be shared by students who do not come from mainstream, middle-class families. These students, like all students, bring to school with them much knowledge about the world and about how to use language in that world—knowledge that they have learned from birth in their homes and communities. We need to find out what this knowledge entails so that we can build on it to provide effective instruction. In addition to reading about the results of linguistic and ethnographic research on nonmainstream groups, teachers can identify characteristic patterns in the way their own students use language and view the world. Many teachers do this by engaging in oral and written dialogues with students on topics of interest to, and often chosen by, the students.

Teachers can also improve instruction for nonmainstream students by structuring activities that will provide the kind of intensive, meaningful interaction with written language that is required for anyone learning to read and write. Several studies have shown that, when such experience is provided as a large part of time in school, students make substantial progress in becoming literate. Some of these studies have been done in classrooms of mainstream children,[76] and others in classrooms of nonmainstream children.[77]

The classroom literacy activities in these studies share a common underlying principle that may account for much of their effectiveness with students. The activities do not focus explicitly on teaching the *forms* of school literacy (for example, the discourse structures with lexical connectors or standard English grammatical patterns), even though these forms are abundantly available both orally and in written materials. Students have multiple and redundant opportunities to become familiar with these language resources (in dialogue with the teacher and in reading journals, letters, and books), but these resources are less emphasized than the interaction itself. The interaction, between writers and readers, for example, is functional; it exists for communicating thoughts, ideas, and other information among members of the classroom community. In short, students have plenty of opportunity not only to become experienced with the forms of literacy, but also, and perhaps more importantly, to begin to operate in new social roles as writers and readers.

Staton provides an example of this.[78] In a multicultural section of Los Angeles, she studied the use of dialogue journals in a sixth grade classroom, where the children spoke thirteen different languages. Their teacher, who had been using dialogue journals for seventeen years, asked her students to write daily entries in English, to which she wrote short responses. Even those students who had minimal literacy skills in English were asked to write, as best they could, at least three sentences. The teacher did not evaluate this writing for mechanics, but instead responded to it as a natural form of communication between two people who were writing and reading rather than talking.

Analysis of the journals over the course of a year showed substantial growth in writing,[79] including an increase in quantity, elaboration of student-initiated topics, fluency, and control of English syntax.[80] Moreover, these students experienced, some for the first time, writing and reading for a purpose of their own. They eagerly read the teacher's responses to their own entries and wrote copiously—some even ending the year with several filled notebooks that made up their yearlong dialogue journal.

Heath and Branscombe also showed that structuring activities so as to create a community of writers and readers helps students learn how to use writing and reading in mainstream ways.[81] In this study, Branscombe's ninth grade remedial track English students (primarily nonmainstream blacks and a few nonmainstream whites in a southern city) wrote and read long letters to and from Heath and her family, whom the students did not know. They also corresponded with Branscombe's regular track eleventh grade students.

As in the journals of the Staton study, the letters emphasized communication—the interaction between writers and readers—rather than the direct teaching of literate forms. Over the course of the year, Branscombe's students became comfortable operating in these roles of writer and reader and learned much about school literacy in the process. They learned, for example, that expository writing requires "linguistic devices and background information in explicated form if the addressee is to understand the [writer]."[82]

We have learned from these and other studies that three factors are crucial for effective literacy instruction for culturally nonmainstream students. First, teachers need to be aware that nonstandard dialect features reflect linguistic differences among varieties of language and not linguistic or cognitive deficits in the speakers who use them. When teachers are unaware of this, their expectations of their students' abilities are lowered and so, presumably, are the success rates of their students. Second, schools should provide nonmainstream students with substantial exposure to the linguistic characteristics of literate texts. Third, schools should give students substantial practice operating in social roles that use writing and reading as ways to communicate. Then students who begin school unfamiliar with mainstream ways of writing and reading can acquire the linguistic and cognitive knowledge they need not only to be successful in school, but to operate comfortably with literacy after they leave school.

Writing and Reading in the Workplace

So far we have discussed what is known about how children learn to write and to read, including, in the previous section, how best to facilitate this learning among culturally nonmainstream students. Now we will turn our attention to what is known about writing and reading in the workplace, focusing particularly on writing. We focus on writing because it is often the more neglected half of literacy in the workplace. Within this area, two primary issues of immediate concern to educators emerge:[83]

1. How applicable to work contexts is school writing instruction? Is the writing experience gained at school similar to that gained in the workplace?

2. How important are writing and reading abilities in the work world and in job success?

To explore these general concerns we need to pose more specific questions and assess the available evidence from various work settings. Beginning with the contrast between school literacy instruction and workplace literacy, we will optimistically start with what may be seen as the best of school-based instructional experience. The two instructional studies discussed in the previous section suggest some of the most important characteristics of school writing success.[84] Other studies of effective instruction and the principles underlying it are reviewed in Farr.[85] These principles involve, among other things, what Heath and Branscombe refer to as "a rich responsive context."

In providing this context for mainly nonmainstream black and white students, school instruction focused on learning both through exposure to a variety of texts—from letters to bureaucratic instructions to informal narratives and formal prose—and through repeated trial and error in different writing tasks with teacher-audience feedback. In such responsive contexts, as Heath and Branscombe suggest, students become able "to generate the needed internal rules or knowledge about how to make writing work to communicate their feeling and knowledge."[86] The expression of such knowledge as a coherent text, of course, is the main goal of school writing.

In looking at literacy in the workplace, we see a rather different picture. In several studies Mikulecky found that writing was used as just one part of a chain of activities.[87] He studied forty-three work settings in which writing was used to complete a job task; in 90 percent of those settings several other modalities of communication also were used during the task. In contrast, school writing is a self-contained task on its own and for its own sake. Thus the essential focus of school writing is on the generation of coherent text, whereas the focus in work settings is on the successful completion of a chain of activity.

Odell[88] and Odell and Goswami[89] studied a number of varied work contexts in some detail, including the writing of social caseworkers and clerical and administrative workers in an insurance company. Their general conclusions are that the functions of workplace writing vary distinctly from those taught in writing classes, whether at school or college level. Considering these findings as well as those of Mikulecky and of Jacobs, who both have looked at blue-collar as well as low-level white-collar work settings,[90] we can list in order of importance an overall view of the most frequent functions of writing in the workplace. This list also shows the most likely written medium for each function:

1. To record: for example, to fill in forms, keep notes, write reports
2. To inform: for example, to write memos, letters, notices
3. To instruct: for example, to prepare instruction sheets, booklets, memos

4. To persuade, change opinions: for example, to compose letters, memos, reports

5. To express a personal opinion, feelings: for example, to write reports and evaluations, memos, letters, notes

From this list we can see that some forms, such as letters or memos, perform several functions. Also, as recent research in a large corporation shows, some of the more functionally specific items, such as written technical reports, can be used for more than conveying objective technical information; they can also become an indirect way of expressing personal opinions and feelings.[91] Thus in workplace writing, several different functions overlap; it is this multipurpose, multifunctionality that makes work writing different from school writing. Multifunctionality requires different considerations and expectations on the part of both writers and readers. For example, much business writing does not observe the formal-informal prose distinction, such as that between business correspondence and informal personal letters, usually made in school instruction.

Moreover, as Odell and Goswami point out, the writing and evaluation of written performance may have critical consequences for keeping a job or for promotion.[92] School writing, of course, rarely has such direct penalties or rewards. However, to answer our first general concern we need to look in more detail at whether school-learned skills are of special use in the workplace and whether job-related experience in writing can be gained in the workplace.

In a review of surveys of writing in different settings, Anderson showed that the functions and importance of writing were evaluated differently by college-educated, managerial-personnel and lower-level white- and blue-collar workers.[93] Thus the educational level attained by workers can be of critical importance in evaluating the usefulness of writing techniques on the job. Several recent studies of college graduates have found that they consider writing to be the most important job-related skill they took from college into the work world.[94]

Several studies have explored the writing skills valued in managerial work and found that overall clarity, conciseness, and objectivity are given as most useful before basic mechanics or stylistic concerns. The "model of good writing," then, that emerges from research with managerial employees is one where style and elegance of self-expression are less valued than the clear presentation of facts in a concise and to-the-point form; control over basic mechanics and grammar is taken for granted. Bataille has suggested that preferences for business writing vary according to whether the intended audience consists of superiors, in which case conciseness is seen as most important, or others outside the organization, in which case clarity is paramount. In a study at Exxon, Paradis and co-researchers found that the aims or goals of organizational writing at the management level could be listed as follows: (1) to objectify evidence, (2) to instruct others, (3) to justify, and (4) to plan and organize.[95]

The model of good writing revealed by all these studies stresses communication of information, organization, accuracy, and accountability more than self-expression, which is a part of effective writing instruction in school. However, when it comes to the actual composing process, managers are expected to follow the usual well-taught process of planning, drafting, and revising that characterizes most school and college composition courses.[96]

But do these considerations apply to lower-level white-collar and blue-collar work writing? Detailed studies of clerical and secretarial work have shown that, while the basic writing skills of grammar, mechanics, and spelling are most essential, many secretarial and clerical work tasks involve other skills that are not necessarily taught in school.[97] In detailed studies of government agency clerical work, both Hoagland and Crandall found that clerical workers spent a great deal of time translating written narrative reports into standardized forms. In these tasks, they often were called upon to work with material on subjects with which they were unfamiliar. Thus secretaries had to be able to repair and edit but also to interpret others' written text, skills that include but also go beyond those taught in school writing courses.

Other studies of clerical work in banks, retail sales, and technical service jobs give a different picture. They have found that few writing skills are required, that mostly routine tasks are limited to prepared forms and telegraphic-style communications.[98] Similar findings apply to most blue-collar jobs, where writing needs are very limited. In short, school-taught writing skills are at best a preparation for decoding, or reading, but not always for encoding, or writing, the written materials that are part of many work routines.

Given that so many work writing tasks are different in goals and aims from those of school instruction, we might expect a high level of on-the-job training. In their recent compendium of research on writing in nonacademic settings, Odell and Goswami have shown that while, in the past decade, research into workplace writing has grown, the numbers of specific training courses have not increased greatly.[99]

One reason may be that—as Redish suggested after examining the on-the-job effectiveness of professional writers—workplace learning is essentially a socialization process.[100] In this process, the writer learns through informal feedback and repeated practice on work tasks. She points out that such learning may be cumulative and may result in decreases as well as increases in effectiveness.

The importance of on-the-job learning is also emphasized by Stitcht, who suggests that many lower-level workers need to learn the tasks necessary to operate complex advanced technology systems on the job.[101] Such learning primarily involves reading skills necessary to understand the instructional sequences for complex machines. This suggests a paradox. On the one hand, machines are now being designed to simplify the interaction of human beings with the machines. On the other hand, learning to make full use of even "user-friendly" machines requires specialized literacy techniques for which school writing and reading instruction could help prepare students.[102]

At the college-educated upper managerial level, learning on the job is again seen as very important. More than 70 percent of employees surveyed in one study reported that their writing had improved during their work experiences.[103] Similarly, studies of noncollege-educated workers found that necessary literacy skills also are taught on the job through an informal process of learning from those more experienced in the tasks. These tasks are repeated frequently[104] and require an interaction of different people to produce a finished product.[105]

In fact, one of the most important features of corporate writing, at both the lower and higher clerical-administrative and managerial levels, is that it is collaborative and so necessarily open to job experiential learning.[106] Odell, investigating many different writing tasks in a large insurance corporation, has shown that workplace writing varies over time, becoming more informal as workers become more experienced at judging the specific audiences for different written products.[107] Clearly, such audience-tailored specificity is possible only through on-the-job learning.

We can conclude that writing in the workplace, while building on basic skills learned at school, does have some very different requirements and functions. The main thrust of the best in school writing instruction leads toward self-motivated and self-generated text production. Workplace writing focuses on a very different set of communicative modalities.

In workplace writing the focus is on recording and transferring information; elegant self-expression is usually considered out of place. However, underlying all the stated goals and aims of business writing for a smooth information flow are many stylistic and rhetorical assumptions that risk being overlooked when workplace writing is studied.[108] What Odell and Goswami refer to as the "tacit knowledge" component is a critical part of much work writing and covers a great deal of the worker's knowledge of her or his position in the organization, the audience for the text, and the organizational importance of the communication.[109] This knowledge touches directly upon our second area of concern: How important is literacy in the work world?

To address this concern we must first ask more specifically who the workers are and what jobs they do. Anderson, surveying studies of workplace writing, has pointed out that there is a major division between the college educated and noncollege educated. This division can indicate not only the distinction between technical, managerial positions and lower-level white- and blue-collar jobs, but also a basic difference in the employees' educational experience of literacy. But many of the differences in the importance of literacy skills may be attributable to particular jobs, rather than to pre-employment training. If the needs of different job tasks and the occupational structure in different companies are considered in some detail, it can be seen that jobs with similar descriptions may differ in their actual performance.

We should also ask how the importance of literacy skills can be evaluated. The available evidence suggests that there are at least three ways to consider the importance of writing: (1) the amount of time spent on writing in any setting; (2) the type of writing and its importance within a task analysis of any particular job; and (3) the workers' perception of the importance of writing as a work-related skill, including its place in their chances for advancement. Let us consider each approach in turn.

First, looking at writing as time spent on the task, survey evidence suggests that college-educated workers compared with blue-collar workers spend as much as seven times more of their work time in writing.[110] In a comparison of several very different occupations, government and service agencies required 29 percent of job time to be spent in writing, whereas retail and blue-collar personnel spent about 13 percent of their time in writing tasks. However, these broad categories need to be looked at more carefully, because detailed studies of single industries, such as Jacobs's study of a dairy,[111] indicate clear differences among types of work settings. Moreover, as shown in a study of business management graduates, there are even differences among occupations that are all classified as advanced management and technical. Thus a comparison study found that accountants spent 25 percent of their work time in writing tasks, bankers 15 percent, plant management 14 percent, and office management 9 percent.[112]

Second, the type of literacy tasks and expectations within job categories can vary. Jacobs's detailed ethnographic study shows that the distribution of workers' time did not match usual expectations; that is, office and clerical workers actually spent less time on writing tasks than did blue-collar stock and warehouse workers. Such findings lead us to consider what kinds of writing tasks are being examined by researchers in specific work settings and to analyze job tasks. Comparing managerial and blue-collar job tasks, Mikulecky found that routine writing tasks such as filling in forms, order sheets, and brief reports accounted for 30 to 50 percent of all workers' time.[113] This study also showed that professional and clerical staff spent a higher proportion of their time than did blue-collar workers on such tasks as writing reports and notes.

For this type of work, as noted earlier, detailed studies have shown that clerical workers often must independently compose and translate narrative materials into formal reports, frequently on subjects about which they have no expert knowledge. Thus the perceived importance and difficulty of the writing tasks cannot be known from a general description of work categories or from general survey interviews with employers or management not close to the actual work situations.

This limitation of descriptive and management survey approaches to assessing the importance of literacy on the job suggests a third approach: how employees themselves evaluate the importance of literacy skills in their occupations and in their career success. In a survey of business school graduates employed in managerial positions, Storms found that writing skills were considered very important to job success; more than 74 percent responded that the ability to write was important to their career and of these, 30 percent thought that writing was critically important.[114] Another study of engineers found that 73 percent of science graduates employed in managerial and technical positions said that writing skills had helped their career advancement.[115]

In studies of workers who have not completed college, less attention has been given to how employees evaluate the importance of literacy skills in their work, though prospective employers consider writing part of basic literacy. Studies of office and clerical workers have shown that basic skills of "clear and legible writing and competence in grammar and spelling" are given as major job requirements.[116] Nonetheless, as we have pointed out, in actual tasks performed by many clerical workers and secretaries, writing skills are considerably more advanced, requiring selection and transfer of information that goes beyond repetitious basic tasks. Moreover, at both college- and noncollege-educated levels, literacy skills are confounded with communication skills so that writing and speaking-oral presentation of information become confused.

Overall, literacy skills do help job advancement and conduct, but it is not clear exactly how these skills are evaluated or rewarded as part of employability and career prospects. There seems to be a much better understanding of the literacy skills needed for managerial and advanced technical careers than of those for lower-level white-collar work. At this level, literacy can either be seen as restricted to very basic skills or can be confounded with other behavioral traits such as dependability. Crain conducted a survey of 4,080 personnel managers for the National Institute of Education, focusing on the characteristics sought in young adults for entry-level jobs. While 65 percent of the managers thought that basic literacy skills were important, only 23 percent thought that any advanced skills could be useful; many more stressed dependability and oral skills as important.[117] Thus, although we have some information about literacy in the workplace, no clear picture emerges of the specific literacy skills that could help young people to find entry-level jobs with good prospects.

Having identified some gaps in our knowledge, let us conclude with some suggestions for future research.

Research indicates that many similarly described jobs may differ in the literacy tasks they entail. Detailed, on-site investigations are needed to find out the real extent and nature of the literacy tasks in any single occupational category. For example, not all warehouse workers need the same skills. Some warehouses are computerized at the level of stock retrieval and storage, while others are automated only at the level of office stocktaking. In any analysis of writing and reading requirements, the specific operational tasks need to be examined in context during actual performance. Such inquiry requires detailed ethnographic methods rather than survey methods.

There is also a need to examine both employers' and employees' perceptions of the literacy requirements of different occupational positions, with special attention to how these perceptions meet or differ. Crain's survey of the range of literacy skills that employers consider important or useful rarely mentions writing specifically.[118] Reading and speaking skills are mentioned most often. The writing demands of most jobs, other than those for professional writers, are usually a hidden dimension of occupational tasks. In professional and managerial work, writing skills are taken for granted; in routine clerical, service, and sales positions, writing is viewed as limited to small, preformatted tasks such as filling out forms and orders and filling in service reports in telegraphic style. Little recognition is given to what Odell has called "the tacit component" in business writing: interpreting and reformulating information for formal reports and judging the correct level of specificity and formality of style.[119] How literacy skills, requirements, and talents are judged is often a situated judgment, apart from more formal assessments of job efficiency and occupational needs. Thus we need a better understanding of how both employers and employees perceive the literacy demands of specific tasks.

Given the current concern with target areas of employability, particularly in entry-level jobs, the need to refocus literacy programs must be considered. As is often commented upon, vocational education has failed to target adequately the skills that are at once general enough to allow for employment flexibility and specific enough to relate to actual job needs of contemporary employment situations.[120] This failure points to the need for further research into the ways that literacy instruction can be reshaped for programs that truly focus on literacy in the workplace.

Conclusion

The discussions we have presented suggest broad issues that any program aimed at improving students' writing and reading abilities must take into account. First, we have emphasized the complexity of the developmental character of learning to write and read, noting in our discussion of children's early writing and reading that such development has cognitive, linguistic, and social dimensions. We suggested not only that children's literacy development occurs in various contexts, but also that their literacy learning is significantly influenced by the particular social roles they observe and adopt in those contexts. Second, in our discussion of literacy and language variation, we pointed to the important cultural differences in the patterns of language use and form among the groups that make up the families of the school population in the United States. And third, in our discussion of literacy in the workplace, we drew particular attention to the ways that institutional settings—their structures, the power arrangements in them, the goals they are designed to meet—influence and sometimes determine the literacy abilities that individuals develop and come to value. These issues hold several implications for educators:

1. Recent studies of young children's early literacy development suggest two themes that pertain to the experience of older children and adolescents as well. First, children all along the developmental

continuum demonstrate their use of powerful cognitive strategies in constructing for themselves the underlying principles of written language. Often conducted in the context of play, their experiments with written language provide evidence of their linguistic powers to segment, to categorize, and to represent for themselves several levels of structure. Most of the cognitive work of written language development operates on a nonconscious level, much as similar processes operate nonconsciously in children's spoken language development.

Second, children use these cognitive strategies in specific social practices. There may be universal processes in human cognition, but literacy learning is a matter of learning particular practices that vary from culture to culture and even among social groups within a culture. In this respect, children's learning is usefully understood as a kind of literacy apprenticeship, in which they learn the knowledge, skills, attitudes, and values of the readers and writers with whom they come into contact. This is not to say that children merely imitate the behavior they observe; there is much room for them to improvise and be creative as they adapt the social practices they observe to their own individual interests and needs. But becoming literate is nonetheless always a matter of learning the knowledge and practices of specific communities of writers and readers. The challenge for educators is to establish the school as a productive community of writers and readers while creating circumstances that encourage individual children to fully use their cognitive capacity to make written language their own.

2. Students of any age bring to school the linguistic resources they acquired from families, neighbors, and others associated with their cultural identities. In some cases the cultural "fit" between the already formed linguistic resources of the student and the linguistic and literacy demands of the school is quite close; in other cases it is not. Such mismatches require educators to devise ways for providing every student a full chance to succeed in school writing and reading tasks, and indeed to succeed more generally in all schoolwork, for success in schoolwork is based largely on observing patterns of behavior and thought associated with particular kinds of literate language use.

3. Too often school instruction in writing and reading fails to prepare students for the tasks they will be asked to perform in the workplace. One clear implication is that educational programs aimed explicitly at preparing students for work should provide literacy instruction that anticipates the specific kinds of experience students are likely to encounter on the job. But another implication is that educators need to consider how students' experiences in a more general curriculum,

from elementary school through college, can best help them develop writing and reading abilities they can carry with them to situations beyond the world of school. One approach is to help students understand the roles of readers and writers in particular situations and to show them how role and situation vary, depending on institutional setting, on the purposes of both writer and reader, and on the nature of the larger activity.

Notes

1. Brown, R. (1974). Development of the first language in the human species. In E. Haugen and M. Bloomfield (Eds.), *Language as a human problem* (p. 121). New York: W.W. Norton.
2. Bissex, G.L. (1980). *GNYS AT WRK: A child learns to write and read.* Cambridge, MA: Harvard University Press.
3. Gundlach, R.A., McLane, J.B., Stott, F.M., and McNamee, G.D. (1985). The social foundations of children's early writing development. In M. Farr (Ed.), *Advances in writing research: Vol. 1. Children's early writing development* (pp. 1–58). Norwood, NJ: Ablex.
4. Durkin, D. (1966). *Children who read early.* New York: Teachers College Press.
5. Clark, M. (1976). *Young fluent readers: What they can teach us.* London: Heinemann.
6. Nystrand, M. (1987). *The structure of written communication.* Orlando, FL: Academic Press.
7. Teale, W., and Sulzby, E. (1986). Introduction: Emergent literacy as a perspective for examining how young children become readers and writers. In W. Teale and E. Sulzby (Eds.), *Emergent literacy: Writing and reading* (p. xviii). Norwood, NJ: Ablex.
8. See Snow, C.E. (1983). Literacy and language: Relationships during the preschool years. *Harvard Educational Review, 53,* 165–189.
9. Teale and Sulzby (1986); see note 7, p. xviii.
10. Teale and Sulzby (1986).
11. Goelman, H., Oberg, A., and Smith, F. (Eds.) (1984). *Awakening to literacy* (p. 221). Exeter, NH: Heinemann.
12. Ferreiro, E. (1983). The development of literacy: A complex psychological problem. In F. Coulmas and K. Ehlich (Eds.), *Focus on writing* (pp. 270–299). Berlin: Mouton.
13. Ferreiro (1983), p. 277.
14. Ferreiro, E. (1986). The interplay between information and assimilation in beginning literacy. In W. Teale and E. Sulzby (Eds.); see note 7, pp. 15–49.
15. Ferreiro (1983); see note 12, p. 278.
16. Ferreiro (1983).

17. Ferreiro (1983), p. 280.

18. Ferreiro (1986); see note 14, p. 16.

19. Ferreiro (1986), p. 49.

20. Geertz, C. (1983). *Local knowledge* (p. 151). New York: Basic Books.

21. Hymes, D. (1984). [Review of J.J. Gumperz, *Discourse strategies*]. *American Journal of Sociology, 90*, 469–471, p. 471.

22. Litowitz, B. (1985). The speaking subject in adolescence: Response to Theodore Shapiro's essay. *Adolescent Psychiatry, 12*, 312–326, p. 322.

23. Welty, E. (1984). *One writer's beginning* (p. 6). Cambridge, MA: Harvard University Press.

24. See Gundlach, R.A. (1982). Children as writers: The beginnings of learning to write. In M. Nystrand (Ed.), *What writers know: The language, process, and structure of written discourse.* New York: Academic Press.
    Heath, S.B. (1982a). What no bedtime story means. *Language in Society, 11*, 49–76.
    Heath, S.B. (1983). *Ways with words: Language, life, and work in communities and classrooms.* Cambridge: Cambridge University Press.
    Snow (1983); see note 8.
    Harste, J.C., Woodward, V.A., and Burke, C.L. (1984). *Language stories and literacy lessons.* Portsmouth, NH: Heinemann.
    Gundlach, McLane, Stott, and McNamee (1985); see note 3.
    Shuman, A. (1986). *Storytelling rights: The uses of oral and written texts by urban adolescents.* Cambridge: Cambridge University Press.

25. Snow, C.E., and Ninio, A. (1986). The contracts of literacy: What children learn from learning to read books. In W. Teale and E. Sulzby (Eds.); see note 7, pp. 116–138.

26. Snow (1983); see note 8, p. 170.

27. Heath (1983); see note 24, p. 234.

28. Heath (1983).

29. Heath (1982a); see note 24, pp. 52–53.

30. Heath (1982a), p. 53.

31. Taylor, D. (1983). *Family literacy.* Exeter, NH: Heinemann.

32. Harste, Woodward, and Burke (1984); see note 24.

33. Bissex (1980); see note 2, p. 199.

34. Cook-Gumperz, J. (1986). Literacy and schooling: An unchanging equation? In J. Cook-Gumperz (Ed.), *The social construction of literacy.* Cambridge: Cambridge University Press.

35. See Gundlach (1982); see note 24.
    Harste, Woodward, and Burke (1984); see note 24.
    Gundlach, McLane, Stott, and McNamee (1985); see note 3.
    Litowitz, B., and Gundlach, R.A. (1987). When adolescents write: Semiotic and social dimensions of adolescents' personal writing. *Adolescent Psychiatry, 14*, 82–111.

36. Hymes, D. (1980). *Language in education: Ethnolinguistic essays* (p. 149). Washington, DC: Center for Applied Linguistics.

37. Schieffelin, B.B., and Cochran-Smith, M. (1984). Learning to read culturally: Literacy before schooling. In H. Goelman, A. Oberg, and F. Smith (Eds.); see note 11, p. 5.

38. Hymes, D. (1971). Competence and performance in linguistic theory. In R. Huxley and E. Ingram (Eds.), *Language in acquisition: Models and methods* (pp. 3–28). London: Academic Press.

39. Anderson, A., and Stokes, S. (1984). Social and institutional influences on the development and practice of literacy. In H. Goelman, A. Oberg, and F. Smith (Eds.); see note 11, pp. 24–37.

  Teale, W. (1986). Home background and young children's literacy development. In W. Teale and E. Sulzby (Eds.); see note 7, pp. 173–206.

40. Ferguson, C. (1977). Linguistic theory. In *Bilingual education: Current perspectives* (pp. 43–52). Washington, DC: Center for Applied Linguistics.

41. Scollon, R., and Scollon, S. (1981). *Narrative, literacy and face in interethnic communication.* Norwood, NJ: Ablex.

42. Heath (1983); see note 24.

43. Street, B. (1984). *Literacy in theory and practice.* Cambridge: Cambridge University Press.

44. Heath (1983); see note 24.

45. Labov, W. (1972a). *Language in the inner city: Studies in the Black English vernacular.* Philadelphia: University of Pennsylvania Press.

  Labov, W. (1972b). *Sociolinguistic patterns.* Philadelphia: University of Pennsylvania Press.

  Wolfram, W. (1969). *A sociolinguistic description of Detroit negro speech.* Washington, DC: Center for Applied Linguistics.

  Kochman, T. (Ed.) (1972). *Rappin' and stylin' out: Communication in urban black America.* Urbana, IL: University of Illinois Press.

  Fasold, R. (1972). *Tense marking in Black English.* Washington, DC: Center for Applied Linguistics.

46. Wolfram, W. (1974). *Sociolinguistic aspects of assimilation: Puerto Rican English in New York City.* Washington, DC: Center for Applied Linguistics.

  Zentella, A.C. (1981). Language variety among Puerto Ricans. In C. Ferguson and S.B. Heath (Eds.), *Language in the U.S.A.* (pp. 218–238). Cambridge: Cambridge University Press.

47. Wolfram, W., and Christian, D. (1976). *Appalachian speech.* Washington, DC: Center for Applied Linguistics.

48. Wolfram, W., Christian, D., Potter, L., and Leap, W. (1979). *Variability in the English of two Indian communities and its effects on reading and writing* (Final report to the National Institute of Education, NIE-G-77-0006). Washington, DC: Center for Applied Linguistics.

49. Labov, W. (Ed.) (1980). *Locating language in time and space.* New York: Academic Press.

  Ferguson and Heath (Eds.) (1981); see note 46.

  Amastae, J., and Elias-Olivares, L. (Eds.) (1982). *Spanish in the United States: Sociolinguistic aspects.* Cambridge: Cambridge University Press.

50. Cazden, C., John, V., and Hymes, D. (Eds.) (1972). *Functions of language in the classroom.* New York: Teachers College Press.

  Green, J., and Wallat, C. (Eds.) (1981). *Ethnography and language in educational settings.* Norwood, NJ: Ablex.

Cherry Wilkinson, L. (Ed.) (1982). *Communicating in the classroom.* New York: Academic Press.

Gilmore, P., and Glatthorn, A. (Eds.) (1982). *Children in and out of school: Ethnography and education.* Washington, DC: Center for Applied Linguistics.

51. Bauman, R., and Sherzer, J. (Eds.) (1974). *Explorations in the ethnography of speaking.* Cambridge: Cambridge University Press.

Kochman, T. (1981). *Black and white styles in conflict.* Chicago: University of Chicago Press.

Heath (1983); see note 24.

Gumperz, J.J. (1982a). *Discourse strategies.* Cambridge: Cambridge University Press.

Gumperz, J.J. (Ed.) (1982b). *Language and social identity.* Cambridge: Cambridge University Press.

52. Green, J. (1983). Research on teaching as a linguistic process: A state of the art. In E.W. Gordon (Ed.), *Review of research in education: Vol. 10* (pp. 151–252). Washington, DC: American Educational Research Association.

53. Reed, C. (1981). Teaching teachers about teaching writing to students from varied linguistic social and cultural groups. In M.F. Whiteman (Ed.), *Writing: The nature, development and teaching of written communication: Vol. 1. Variation in writing: Functional and linguistic-cultural differences* (pp. 139–152). Hillsdale, NJ: Erlbaum.

Whiteman, M.F. (1981). Dialect influence in writing. In M.F. Whiteman (Ed.), pp. 153–166.

Valadez, C. (1981). Identity, power and writing skills: The case of the Hispanic bilingual student. In M.F. Whiteman (Ed.), pp. 167–178.

Charrow, V.R. (1981). The written English of deaf adolescents. In M.F. Whiteman (Ed.), pp. 179–196.

Cronnell, B. (Ed.) (1981). *The writing needs of linguistically different students.* Los Alamitos, CA: Southwest Regional Laboratory Education Research and Development.

54. Scribner, S., and Cole, M. (1981). *The psychology of literacy.* Cambridge, MA: Harvard University Press.

Heath (1983); see note 24.

Schieffelin and Cochran-Smith (1984); see note 37.

Teale (1986); see note 39.

Moll, L., and Diaz, R. (1987). Teaching writing as communication: The use of ethnographic findings in classroom practice. In D. Bloome (Ed.), *Literacy, language and schooling.* Norwood, NJ: Ablex.

55. Whiteman (1981); see note 53.

56. Baugh, J. (1981). Design and implementation of writing instruction for speakers of non-standard English: Perspectives for a national neighborhood literacy program. In B. Cronnell (Ed.); see note 53, pp. 17–44.

57. Scribner and Cole (1981); see note 54.

58. Hall, W., and Guthrie, L. (1980). On the question of dialect and reading. In R.J. Spiro, B.C. Bruce, and W.F. Brewer (Eds.), *Theoretical issues in reading comprehension* (pp. 439–452). Hillsdale, NJ: Erlbaum.

59. Heath (1983); see note 24.
60. Heath (1983).
61. Heath (1983).
62. Labov, W. (1970). The logic of non-standard English. In F. Williams (Ed.), *Language and poverty* (pp. 153–189). Chicago: Markham.
    Labov, W. (1983). Recognizing Black English in the classroom. In J. Chambers, Jr. (Ed.), *Black English: Educational equity and the law* (p. 32). Ann Arbor, MI: Karoma.
63. Whiteman (1981); see note 53.
64. Hartwell, P. (1980). Dialect interference in writing: A critical view. *Research in the Teaching of English, 14,* 101–118.
    Hartwell, P. (1985). Grammar, grammars, and the teaching of grammar. *College English, 47,* 105–127.
    Rubin, D. (1979). The myth of dialect interference in written composition. *Arizona English Bulletin, Spring.*
65. Hartwell (1985); see note 64.
66. Hillocks, G. (1986). *Research on written composition: New directions for teaching.* Urbana, IL: National Council of Teachers of English.
67. Farr, M., and Daniels, H. (1986). *Language diversity and writing instruction.* Urbana, IL: National Council of Teachers of English.
68. Baugh (1981); see note 56.
    Heath (1983); see note 24.
69. Michaels, S. (1981). Sharing time: Children's narrative style and differential access to literacy. *Language in Society, 10,* 423–442.
    Michaels, S., and Collins, J. (1984). Oral discourse styles: Classroom interaction and the acquisition of literacy. In D. Tannen (Ed.), *Coherence in spoken and written discourse* (pp. 219–244). Norwood, NJ: Ablex.
    Cazden, C., Michaels, S., and Tabors, P. (1985). Spontaneous repairs in sharing time narratives: The intersection of metalinguistic awareness, speech event, and narrative style. In S.W. Freedman (Ed.), *The acquisition of written language: Response and revision* (pp. 51–64). Norwood, NJ: Ablex.
70. Smitherman, G. (1977). *Talkin' and testifyin': The language of black America.* Boston, MA: Houghton Mifflin.
71. Smitherman (1977), pp. 147–148.
72. Erickson, F. (1984). Rhetoric, anecdote, and rhapsody: Coherence strategies in a conversation among black American adolescents. In D. Tannen (Ed.); see note 69, pp. 81–154.
73. Philips, S.U. (1972). Participant structures and communicative competence: Warm Springs children in community and classroom. In C. Cazden, V. John, and D. Hymes (Eds.); see note 50, pp. 370–394.
    Philips, S.U. (1983). *The invisible culture: Communication in classroom and community on the Warm Springs Indian Reservation.* New York: Longman.
74. Philips (1972); see note 73, p. 392.
75. For a synthesis of research on such differences, see Farr, M. (1986). Language, culture, and writing: Sociolinguistic foundations of research

on writing. In E. Rothkopf (Ed.), *Review of research in education: Vol. 13*. Washington, DC: American Educational Research Association.

76. Graves, D.H. (1982). *A case study observing the development of primary children's composing, spelling and motor behavior during the writing process* (Final Report to the National Institute of Education, NIE-G-78-0174). Durham, NH: University of New Hampshire.

King, M.L., and Rentel, V.M. (1981). *How children learn to write: A longitudinal study* (Final Report to the National Institute of Education, NIE-G-79-0137 and NIE-G-79-0039). Columbus, OH: Ohio State University.

King, M.L., and Rentel, V.M. (1982). *Transition to writing* (Final Report to the National Institute of Education, NIE-G-79-0137 and NIE-G-79-0031). Columbus, OH: Ohio State University.

King, M.L., and Rentel, V.M. (1983). *A longitudinal study of coherence in children's written narratives* (Final Report to the National Institute of Education, NIE-G-81-0063). Columbus, OH: Ohio State University.

77. Edelsky, C. (1986). *Writing in a bilingual program: Habia una vez.* Norwood, NJ: Ablex.

Staton, J. (1982). *Analysis of dialogue journal writing as a communicative event* (Final Report to the National Institute of Education, NIE-G-80-0122). Washington, DC: Center for Applied Linguistics.

Staton, J. (1988). *Dialogue journal writing: Linguistic, cognitive, and social views.* Norwood, NJ: Ablex.

Heath, S.B., and Branscombe, A. (1985). "Intelligent writing" in an audience community: Teacher, students, and researcher. In S.W. Freedman (Ed.); see note 69, pp. 3–32.

78. Staton (1982); see note 77.

79. Staton (1982).

Staton (1988); see note 77.

Farr, M. (1982, March). *Learning to write English: One dialogue journal writer's growth in writing.* Paper presented at the annual meeting of the American Educational Research Association, New York.

80. Kreeft, J.P., Shuy, R.W., Staton, J., Reed, L., and Morroy, R. (1984). *Dialogue writing: Analysis of student-teacher interactive writing in the learning of English as a second language* (Final Report to the National Institute of Education, NIE-G-83-0030). Washington, DC: Center for Applied Linguistics. (ERIC Document Reproduction Service No. ED 252 097)

81. Heath and Branscombe (1985); see note 77.

82. Heath and Branscombe (1985); see note 77, p. 26.

83. Gantry, L. (Ed.) (1982). *Research and instruction in practical writing.* Los Alamitos, CA: Southwest Regional Laboratory Education Research and Development.

Odell, L., and Goswami, D. (1985). Introduction. In L. Odell and D. Goswami (Eds.), *Writing in non-academic settings.* New York and London: Guilford Press.

84. Staton (1988); see note 77.

Heath and Branscombe (1985); see note 77.

85. Farr, M. (1984). Writing growth in young children: What we are learning from research. In C. Thaiss and C. Suhor (Eds.), *Speaking and writing, K-12* (pp. 126–143). Urbana, IL: National Council of Teachers of English.

86. Heath and Branscombe (1985); see note 77, p. 31.

87. Mikulecky, L. (1982a). Functional writing in the workplace. In L. Gantry (Ed.); see note 83, pp. 51–72.

    Mikulecky, L. (1982b). Job literacy: The relationship between school preparation and workplace actuality. *Reading Research Quarterly, 17,* 400–419.

88. Odell, L. (1981). Business writing: Observations and implications for teaching composition. *Theory into Practice, 13,* 225–232.

89. Odell, L., and Goswami, D. (1982). Writing in a non-academic setting. *Research in the Teaching of English, 16,* 201–223.

90. Mikulecky (1982a); see note 87.

    Mikulecky (1982b); see note 87.

    Jacobs, E. (1982). Research on practical writing in business and industry. In L. Gantry (Ed.); see note 83, pp. 37–50.

91. Paradis, J., et al. (1985). Writing at Exxon I.T.D.: Notes on the writing environment of an R & D organization. In L. Odell and D. Goswami (Eds.); see note 83.

92. Odell and Goswami (1985); see note 83.

93. Anderson, P. (1985). What survey research tells us about writing at work. In L. Odell and D. Goswami (Eds.); see note 83.

94. Bataille, R. (1982). Writing in the world of work: What undergraduates report. *College Composition and Communication, 33,* 226–283.

    Flateley, M.E. (1982). A comparative analysis of the written communication of managers of various organizational levels in the private business sector. *Journal of Business Communication, 19,* 35–49.

    Storms, C.G. (1983). What business school graduates say about the writing they do at work: Implications for the business communication course. *ACBA Bulletin, 46,* 13–18.

95. Paradis et al. (1985); see note 91.

96. Paradis et al. (1985).

    Roundy, N., and Mair, D. (1982). The composing process of technical writers. *Journal of Advanced Composition, 3,* 89–101.

97. Crandall, J. (1981). *A sociolinguistic investigation of the literacy demands of clerical workers.* Unpublished doctoral dissertation, Georgetown University, Washington, DC.

    Hall, O., and Carlton, R. (1977). *Basic skills at home and work.* Toronto: Ontario Economic Council.

    Hoagland, N. (1982). A report on the occupational writing of developmental English students. In D. Gallehr, R. Gilstrap, A. Legge, M. Mohr, and M. Wilson-Nelson (Eds.), *The writing process of college students.* Fairfax, VA: George Mason University.

98. Farning, M., Boyce, E., and Mahnke, R. (1975). *Developing a list of competencies for the communication skills area of vocational-technical post-secondary education.* (ERIC Document Reproduction Service No. ED 112 194)

99. Odell and Goswami (1985); see note 83.

100. Redish, J. (1985). *Adult writers: Using and learning job-related skills.* Unpublished manuscript.

101. Stitcht, T. (1980). *Literacy and vocational competence.* Columbus, OH: National Center for Research in Vocational Education.

102. Suchman, L. (1985). *Plans and situated actions: The problem of human-machine communication* (Research document). Palo Alto, CA: Xerox Parc.

103. Anderson (1985); see note 93.

104. Jacobs (1982); see note 90.

105. Farning, Boyce, and Mahnke (1975); see note 98.

106. Mitchell, R. (1982). Negative entropy at work: A theory of practical writing. In L. Gantry (Ed.); see note 83, pp. 9–36.

107. Odell (1981); see note 88.

108. Odell and Goswami (1982); see note 89.
    Odell, L., Goswami, D., and Herrington, A. (1983). The discourse-based interview: A procedure for exploring the tacit knowledge of writers in nonacademic settings. In P. Mosenthal, L. Tamar, and S. Walmsley (Eds.), *Research on writing: Principles and methods* (pp. 220–235). London and New York: Longman.

109. Odell and Goswami (1985); see note 83.

110. Faigley, L., Miller, T.P., Meyer, P.R., and Witte, S.P. (1981). *Writing after college: A stratified survey of the writing of college-trained people.* Austin: University of Texas.

111. Jacobs (1982); see note 90.

112. Radar, M., and Wunsch, A. (1980). A survey of communicative practices of business school graduates by job category and undergraduate major. *Journal of Business Communication, 17,* 33–41.

113. Mikulecky (1982a); see note 87.
    Mikulecky (1982b); see note 87.

114. Storms (1983); see note 94.

115. Anderson (1985); see note 93.

116. Hall and Carlton (1977); see note 97.

117. Crain, R. (1984). *The quality of American high school graduates: What personnel officers say and do about it* (Final Report to the National Institute of Education). Washington, DC: Office of Educational Research and Improvement, U.S. Office of Education.

118. Crain (1984).

119. Odell (1981); see note 88.

120. Grubb, N. (1984). The bandwagon once more: Vocational preparation for high tech occupations. *Harvard Educational Review, 54,* 429–451.

4 The Problem-Solving Processes of Writers and Readers

Planning Group Members

Linda Flower, Cochair
Bertram Bruce, Cochair
Mary Sue Ammon
Paul Ammon
Wallace Chafe
Herbert D. Simons

Introduction

Sandra Murphy

Our curriculum is fragmented. Think about it. We may teach reading from 8:30 to 9:45 and writing from 10:00 to 11:00. We may teach writing, reading, and even literature as if they were components that operate independently from one another. What may be worse, we often teach writing and reading as if they were the sums of separately taught subskills (for example, "This exercise will help you get your verb tenses right. Here is an example of how to do it." Or "This exercise will help you find the main idea. Here is an example of how to do it.").

Part of the reason for this fragmented curriculum lies in some very common conceptions (or to put it bluntly—misconceptions) about writing and reading. In the past, reading theory largely treated the process of reading solely as information retrieval; the underlying assumption was that the text carried meaning, and the reader's job was to retrieve it. From that perspective, reading was viewed as a process of translation of text meaning. Writing, on the other hand, was largely viewed as a product, or at most as something one does after all the thinking has been done—"like the dishes that have to be washed after the guests have left," in Peter Elbow's words (personal communication).

The authors of this chapter echo recent changes in theoretical perspectives on writing and reading. They make it clear that reading is not merely the retrieval of information, but a constructive thinking process, and that writing is not a process that occurs after the thinking has been done, but a process that contributes to thinking and learning. What is even more important, from my point of view, is that the authors of this chapter situate the processes of individual writers and readers in school contexts, where the processes of the individual language user are mediated by the processes of both peers and teachers. Further, the authors project a view of school writing and reading that

133

involves more than simply students demonstrating their knowledge and skill to the teacher.

Why do I think this is important? Because it can make a difference in how effective we are as teachers. The authors illustrate how a sense of purpose and audience can powerfully influence both process and outcome in writing and reading. Scenarios developed in this chapter illustrate how cognitive strategies can be functional or not, depending upon how the task is framed for and by the writer-reader. They illustrate how writing and reading processes can aid one another—or be short-circuited when students are left to guess the intentions of teachers. And they illustrate how teachers can support students as those students set goals for themselves that may be, for the moment, slightly beyond their abilities. They invite us, in short, to reflect upon the things we could do as teachers to foster the development of growing writers and readers. They illustrate how writing and reading, when viewed as purposeful, communicative activities, can foster the development of thinking, as well as the development of skill in writing and reading.

The approach the authors adopt is unusual. They rely on "cases" developed from a synthesis of research—exemplars, so to speak, of what research has to tell us about the processes of writing and reading at different levels of development. As such, these "cases" provide us with telling examples of diversity within a common thread of development, from simple, less sophisticated approaches to more sophisticated ones. As students develop, they more consciously define the communicative purposes they set for themselves in writing—and the ways they analyze what they have read—within the context of classroom assignments. The authors provide us with examples of where we want our students to go, of the kinds of things we want our students to be able to do. They also provide us with examples of where the processes may go awry—both the processes of individual writers and readers and the processes of instruction. And finally, at the same time, the authors convey a sense of the intensely individual and constructive natures of writing and reading processes.

By placing individual processes within classroom contexts, the authors remind us of an important link between writing and reading— the communicative purpose that shapes both of these activities. They remind us that reading is not just the garnering of information, but also the construction of an understanding of the author's communicative purpose and the linking of that information to the individual's own knowledge of the world. At the same time, they remind us that writing skill depends in part upon the ability to formulate and carry out purposes for writing and that development can be characterized by the student's attempts at increasingly complex purposes.

What a different view of development this is—and what a challenge for teachers. The emphasis is on the individual learner, the situation, and what is emerging in the process of development, not on a set of writing skills or types of writing to be taught in sequence. The challenge for teachers will be to devise ways—as Mr. Oakes does for Anita and as Ms. Plourde does for Kenny in the following chapter—that support and guide students at those critical points when they are attempting something they have not attempted before.

The Problem-Solving Processes
of Writers and Readers

Ann S. Rosebery, Linda Flower, Beth Warren, Betsy Bowen,
Bertram Bruce, Margaret Kantz, and Ann M. Penrose

A revolution has occurred in the way we think about writing and reading. We have moved from a focus on the product—the text—to a focus on the process—writing and reading as dynamic acts of thought and communication. This shift in emphasis has been productive in shaping new attitudes and practices, but *process* has not meant the same thing to everyone. Some of us picture the process that goes on in a classroom in which students read, write, and discuss texts. Process from this perspective is a school-based activity supported by teachers, curricula, and assignments (see chapter 5). Others of us picture the process as reflecting participation in a community with its norms, beliefs, and values influencing the literacy transactions that occur (see chapter 3). And for others, the notion of process conjures up an intimate picture of an individual student reflecting on what he or she is writing or reading. From this perspective, one sees a writer thinking about her purpose for writing and her audience, developing a plan for what she wants to communicate. Or one sees a reader trying to understand an author's message, using background knowledge to situate the text's meaning in relation to what he already knows.

In this chapter we focus on this last interpretation of process, in particular on writing and reading as forms of problem solving that are shaped by communicative purpose. We examine the kinds of problems that arise as writers and readers attempt to communicate with one another and the strategies they draw upon to resolve those problems. We explore how, for example, a writer attempts to solve the problem of writing to a specific audience by setting and refining goals, for-mulating plans, and tailoring content. We also explore the kinds of problem-solving strategies that a reader invokes in trying to interpret an author's meaning.

We have chosen a problem-solving framework because it emphasizes the dynamic, constructive nature of the thinking processes that underlie both writing and reading. From this perspective, writers and readers are said to be faced with the "problem" of constructing meaning for some purpose. To solve this problem, we see them call on their knowledge to define their goals or situate a problem; we see them build representations of meaning; and we see them monitor, evaluate, and revise their emerging understanding.

To elucidate the problem-solving character of writing and reading, we offer three sets of vignettes that show students at different stages of schooling as they write and read.[1] We begin our exploration of mature problem solving in writing and reading by looking at the mental activity of two highly skilled college students whose problem solving is rooted in a deep understanding of the constructive, purposeful nature of writing and reading. In particular, we see them tackle challenging assignments involving analysis and interpretation of a rhetorically complex text. In the process, we see them as they work at constructing a coherent understanding of what they are reading and what they want to write, and we see them confront their misunderstandings and reshape their purposes as their understanding evolves. This first set, then, illustrates the kind of writing and reading processes that we hold as goals for our students.

The second set of vignettes places these processes in context by considering some of the factors that influence students' problem solving as they write and read in response to typical school assignments. We explore a range of responses that students adopt, focusing on how students' understanding of writing and reading and of an assignment can influence both their problem-solving activity and the quality of what they learn.

The third section explores the problem-solving skills that young students—children learning to write and read and adolescents expanding their writing and reading abilities—bring to their school assignments. Here we see young students exercising and expanding the kinds of problem-solving skills that are the foundation of highly skilled writing and reading. In particular, we see them using purpose to guide their meaning-making and we see them struggling to expand their skills as their goals for their writing and reading become more demanding.

The decision to synthesize the current research in the form of vignettes is itself the solution to an interesting problem that arose in the initial group-planning session for this book. As we began to talk about ways to pull together the research on writing, reading, and cognition, it became clear that we all valued two aspects of this research. One was the theory-building thrust of research—the attempt to distill the results of numerous individual studies into some more general principles and ideas and to integrate those ideas into a broader, coherent picture in which individual differences are part of a meaningful whole.

However, the other aspect of research we wanted this chapter to convey concentrates on difference, diversity, and the constructive experience of individual writers and readers. The broader principles research seeks to uncover matter only if they can explain what actual people do. Moreover, when those principles are acted out in real situations, when they are contextualized, they take on an importantly different shape in each context. The "meaning," then, of the research we hoped to synthesize was in both the abstract and the concrete, in the general principles and the specific contextualization of those principles.

Our hope was to capture some sense of this interaction by showing how the claims and findings from research in this area play themselves out in different contexts. The scenarios we have created to contextualize this research are hypothetical. This allowed us to base them point for point on what we saw as the robust findings and claims from the research (though we must admit to a little poetic license in presenting conversations). In many cases the vignettes are drawn directly from the data of studies cited or the observations of teachers. We have tried, then, to construct a sharply focused *theory-driven picture* of how writing, reading, and cognition operate in some of their contexts.

On the other hand—and this is a crucial point—these vignettes and the findings they dramatize represent only *one of many ways* in which these more general reading and writing processes can be embodied in the performance of real students. Learning by writing, for instance, can take many forms, though we describe only one. We also wish to emphasize the descriptive nature of this chapter. Our purpose is not to prescribe "correct" problem-solving activity, but to illustrate a view of writing and reading that, we feel, has some important implications for teaching and learning. When we talk about sophisticated writers and readers, we are describing goals for students' writing and reading that derive from a problem-solving perspective. When we investigate the classroom context, we are looking at some of the factors that can influence the attainment of these goals. And when we describe developing writing and reading skill, our aim is to establish a sense of the continuity that naturally holds between the problem solving of children and that of mature adults.

The Nature of Problem Solving in Skilled Reading and Writing

Max is a college undergraduate majoring in English literature. He is working on an assignment for a seminar. His task is to read Jonathan Swift's *A Modest Proposal*, a classic satire, and be prepared to discuss it in class.[2] While this assignment is extremely open-ended, it is not uncommon in high school and college English classes.

As we first look in on Max, he is thinking about the author and the text, his knowledge of them and the relation of that knowledge to the assignment. He knows, for example, that Swift was a political writer whose major works were published in the eighteenth century and who lived in Ireland for much of his life. Ireland was at that time a poor country, economically dependent on England. Thinking in this way (often referred to as activating prior knowledge) helps Max establish a general, historical context for understanding the text.[3]

In the same way, he draws on his knowledge of text structure to establish a preliminary framework for understanding the rhetorical structure of the text. He knows from the professor's introduction that *A Modest Proposal* is a political tract and that such tracts were used to make ideas public in the seventeenth and eighteenth centuries. He considers their structure in more detail: typically, a problem is identified and analyzed and a solution offered and evaluated, perhaps with regard to alternative solutions. In a sense, Max thinks he knows what kind of structure to expect from the text and will use these expectations to guide his understanding.[4]

Knowledge is not just used to situate a text. It is used in all phases of reading, from thinking about a text or a topic before reading to evaluating its central theme or argument during or after reading. Readers continually look for connections between the ideas in the text and their prior knowledge.[5] Prior knowledge can in this way help readers draw inferences about an author's intentions and beliefs and can serve as a basis for acquiring knowledge.[6]

As Max begins reading, he finds that the full title of the work, *"A Modest Proposal for Preventing the Children of Poor People from Being a Burthen to Their Parents or the Country, and for Making Them Beneficial to the Public,"* reinforces his expectations concerning the text's genre. From it, he infers that Swift will address problems associated with poverty and, in particular, the difficulties associated with raising children in poverty. The solution to these problems appears to be the "modest proposal" itself. At this point, Max believes that the tract is a straightforward use of the genre and that he has identified the structure of the argument that Swift will set forth. As he reads on, this initial understanding will serve as a framework for integrating and evaluating the rest of the text.

But as Max uncovers the true nature of Swift's "modest proposal," namely, that the children of the poor be bred, slaughtered, and sold for human consumption, he will begin to realize that an adequate understanding of Swift's meaning will require more than a simple mapping between an expected text structure and the words of the text. To understand Swift's meaning fully, he will have to recognize the discrepancy between his expectations for the text and the meaning Swift intended for the reader to construct, a meaning that is couched in a complicated narrative structure.[7] This recognition will lead him to revise his understanding so that it distinguishes between the surface (or apparent) meaning of the text and its deeper, satiric meaning, in which the author's intentions are unmasked and their effect on the meaning of the narration explained.

To effect this restructuring of his understanding, Max will draw on several problem-solving strategies. He will question the assumptions that are implicit in the understanding he has built; he will reread the text for specific kinds of evidence; and he will formulate and revise hypotheses regarding the author's intended meaning.[8] His question-asking, for example, will lead him to abandon many of his original assumptions about the essay's purpose. He will also reread portions of the text, looking for clues that support an ironic interpretation. As he uncovers these clues, he will construct a revised understanding of the text that represents more than its content; he will revise his understanding so that it *explains* the content with respect to his understanding of the author's true beliefs and intended meaning.[9] That is, rather than simply connecting the events or ideas in the text into a coherent, sequential structure (for example, a rendition of a text's plot or surface meaning), Max will build an interpretation that attempts to explain the author's communicative purpose ("What did the author really mean?").

With this picture of the reading process in mind, we now turn to a consideration of writing as a similarly complex problem-solving process that involves interactions among an author, a reader (or readers), and an evolving text.

Emily is in Max's English class. Each week the class is required to write a short, three-to-five-page essay on any topic related to the week's readings. In these essays, the professor expects the students to write a critical analysis of some topic or issue related to the major themes of the course. For this week's essay, Emily has decided to focus on *A Modest Proposal*. Our exploration of her problem-solving process begins with her attempt to define more precisely her topic and goals for the essay, in other words, the problem she will try to solve in writing.

The initial problem confronting Emily—to write a short paper that is related to the week's reading—is an extreme (although not atypical) example of an ill-defined problem. It is explicit only with respect to the scope of "possible texts" and the paper's length. It is silent on such important dimensions as specific goals of the assignment, topic, and focus. Many of the problems Emily faces therefore derive from the nature of the assignment itself, namely, what goals and topics to pursue, what focus to adopt.

How does a writer define the problem she wants to solve? What aspects of a rhetorical problem does she consider? These are important questions because research has shown that a major difference between skilled and less skilled writers is in the ways they define the rhetorical problems they encounter.[10] The process of defining and exploring a problem is a critical part of what makes writing a creative act.[11]

Thinking about *A Modest Proposal* and what she might write, Emily begins with a conventional formulation of the general problem she faces. She will write on some issue related to Swift's work, maybe on satire (perhaps as a literary and political tool) or on Irish-English relations past and present. By formulating the assignment in this way, she has adopted a conventional representation for the assignment "Write an essay on. . . ." Experienced writers have many such representations for familiar writing problems, from those for writing a vacation postcard to those for writing student recommendations.[12] What makes such representations so useful to the writer is that they essentially dictate a solution for a particular, well-defined writing problem, specifying the situation, the audience, and the purpose for writing, even in some cases providing explicit suggestions for tone and wording.[13]

Many writing problems, however, do not have a conventional solution. And even those that do are open to alternative solutions, depending on the situation and the writer's skill, energy, and imagination. As Emily, for instance, begins to consider the consequences of her choice of topic, she finds that one idea leads to another, but nothing coherent or compelling emerges from the chain reaction. She begins to ask herself how she can make the assignment more interesting to herself and her reader. In the process, she realizes that what interests her most about Swift's work is his use of irony to convey his indignation toward those of his countrymen who exploit the poor. From this realization, she begins to formulate a vague but suggestive goal, namely, to demonstrate the power of Swift's irony in a novel way.

As Emily pursues this line of thinking, an approach begins to take shape. She will rewrite the work, or some portion of it, stripping it of its ironic tone and substance. But to satisfy what she understands to be her professor's requirements, she decides in addition to examine the effects of her revision on the force of Swift's argument. Precisely how she will do this is as yet unclear, although writing a short, academic critique that accompanies the revised text or annotating her text seem to be good possibilities. The outline of a plan for writing has thus emerged.

In defining a rhetorical problem, skilled writers actively consider a number of elements. As Flower and Hayes have suggested, these include the rhetorical situation itself (the givens of assignment and audience) and the writer's purpose and goals (those affecting the reader, the writer's voice, the content and form of the text).[14] Emily initially considered the rhetorical situation in conventional terms and began to generate possible themes on that basis. Subsequently, she felt dissatisfied with the results of this process and redefined the problem by moving beyond the conventional representation with which she started, a leap that novice writers rarely make.

As part of this problem redefinition, Emily revised her image of the assignment by questioning her original assumptions about its purpose and character and by redirecting her attention to her own interests and goals.[15] In addition, she elaborated her problem representation to include her audience's requirements and expectations, a process that will continue as she develops her plan and text more fully. Less skilled writers do not typically devote much attention to how their writing will affect the reader. Instead, they tend to focus almost exclusively on their topic and on telling what they know about it, a process referred to as knowledge-telling.[16]

Emily's new problem representation also involved a redefinition of her goals for the meaning she would create and the form it would take. Rather than defining a broad goal (for example, to discuss Swift's use of irony) and generating a network of ideas related to it, she defined a goal that would allow her to use her knowledge creatively. And she made some decisions about the form of her text in relation to the set of goals—goals for reader, self, and text—that she had considered in defining her problem. The result of all this active, reflective problem-solving activity was an elaborated image of the problem she would attempt to solve in writing and the sketch of a plan for how she might go about solving it.

Emily's "discovery" of her writing problem should not be mistaken for inspiration. Nor should it be equated with the conventional activity of formal outlining as a way of getting started in writing. It was, to the contrary, the result of reflective, at times unpredictable, cognitive activity on her part.[17] In identifying her interests and the nature of the problem to be solved, Emily engaged in a very flexible kind of planning, sometimes referred to as "constructive planning," that (1) encourages discovery through the interaction of different modes of thinking (for example, deliberate, associative, incidental), (2) does not lock students into premature outlines that emphasize content over such things as goal definition and planning, and (3) offers a way to think through one's goals and play with ideas and structures before trying to produce prose. This is a vision of the planning process that is much closer to planning as people really do it—the planning and debate that go on in one's head in the shower, the notes and sketchy outlines on the back of a handy envelope, and the conversations and bits of draft text in which ideas get tried out, refined, or discarded. Planning is, by definition, a way to try out ideas in a form that is easy to build and easy to change.[18]

Thinking she has a good idea of what she wants to do, Emily decides to see how hard it will be to rewrite Swift. She picks up the text, pen in hand, but immediately comes up against a problem. How is she to decide how much and what part of the selection to rewrite? Her angle is a good one, she feels sure, but it is not yet precise enough to guide her in making these kinds of decisions. A little disappointed, she spends some time going over the text, thinking about specific ways in which Swift makes the irony felt, jotting down some notes, occasionally trying her hand at some rewriting, worrying that she won't meet the assignment deadline. What Emily has discovered is that there are many ways to realize her abstract plan and that the process of finding the one that suits her and the situation will entail a good deal of hard thinking and a more fully articulated, or concrete, plan for realizing her goals.

Emily's current problem, then, is to develop a more fully articulated plan and to realize that plan even more concretely in prose. This process, sometimes called "instantiation," in which a writer moves from images and plans to the special demands of prose, helps explain why writing can call for such active problem solving, even when the writer has a good but still abstract plan or a rich store of knowledge from which to write.[19] By thinking about her goals, plan, and audience, Emily will gradually generate the ideas and focus from which her paper will flow. As she plans, composes, and revises her text, she will not simply be calling up what she already knows. Rather, she will be developing a set of increasingly well-articulated goals and building new meaning representations.

A problem-solving perspective on writing and reading helps make clear how, for any given problem, there are potentially many solutions. As we have seen, a given writing plan is open to multiple textual realizations; a given text is open to multiple interpretations. Through Emily and Max, we have tried to illustrate that the problem solving of highly skilled writers and readers is directed at crafting solutions that satisfy their goals and purposes. In attempting to interpret or create a text, these writers and readers determine, among other things, the nature of the problem to be solved, the kinds of knowledge they need to activate, and the appropriate strategies for organizing and monitoring their problem solving.

Moreover, their problem solving is grounded in the belief that writing and reading are based on a communicative interaction, that is, the interaction of a writer, a reader, and a text.[20] The writer plans, composes, and revises with some idea in mind of what her readers are likely to know and believe, and she uses this knowledge to write in ways that will evoke relevant aspects of the reader's knowledge and beliefs (for example, Swift's labeling as "modest" a morally unacceptable proposal). The reader in turn uses his knowledge and problem-solving skill to solve the problem of intended meaning (for example, "What does the author really mean when she says . . . ?").

Max and Emily represent the long-range goals we have for students' problem solving in writing and reading. With this in mind, we now examine the kinds of problem-solving strategies that students may actually use to complete their school assignments.

Investigating Writing and Reading in Context

Shirley, an above-average student in her first year of college, applies herself conscientiously to her work. When she was a high school student, the study skills she learned (for example, finding the main idea, remembering facts, summarizing) and the writing patterns and strategies she developed (agreeing-disagreeing, comparing-contrasting, relating theory to practice, expressing opinions, describing impressions) helped her successfully complete most of the assignments she was given. To her surprise, she is not doing as well in her college studies.

As we look in on her, Shirley is thinking about a term paper she wrote for a course in English history. She chose the Battle of Agincourt as her topic. For her research, she located half a dozen sources, each describing the circumstances of the battle in a few pages. Although the topic was unfamiliar to her, her sources provided a lot of detail, and she quickly understood the course of events that had taken place.

Because Shirley has been taught that histories are narratives that tell the truth, she conceived her function as an historian-researcher to be to synthesize the various accounts into one "completely truthful" account. Therefore, as she prepared her paper, she used her well-learned high school strategies to compile the facts from her sources into a coherent story with a beginning, a middle, and an end.[21] In writing the paper, she adopted the narrative style that predominated in her sources.[22] The result was a coherent description of the major events and participants in the Battle of Agincourt.[23] Shirley felt that her paper met the assignment criterion of originality. As she saw it, her originality came not from the factual material, which could not be changed or disputed, but from her presentation, which she thought was more accurate than any one of her sources because it was more complete. She was genuinely surprised when her paper was returned with a grade of C.

What are the sources of Shirley's difficulties? One major source can be traced to a naïve understanding of the role of rhetorical purpose in writing and reading.[24] Understanding purpose is basic to constructing meaning; without it, text loses its communicative function. Writers, for example, cannot formulate effective plans unless they understand their purposes for writing.[25] Likewise, building an argument becomes an impossible task if a writer does not have in mind a clear understanding of her purpose for writing—that is, not just what she was arguing, but why. In much the same way, readers need to understand the purposes and perspectives of authors. They need to realize, in particular, that authors have beliefs and intentions and that these influence the meanings of texts, as Swift's text so clearly demonstrates.[26]

Feeling upset about her C, Shirley consulted her friend Alice, who had received an A− on the assignment. Not surprisingly, Alice had defined the assignment differently than Shirley had. The strategies that she had used to guide her research and writing followed directly from her defined purpose. The differences in approach that each took in completing the assignment can be seen in Alice's comments:

> We were supposed to research a topic and then write a paper that expressed an original idea or point of view. OK. Who were your sources? Winston Churchill, right? A Victorian lady, a French

couple—Guizot and Guizot—and a few others. And they didn't
agree about certain facts, like the sizes of the armies, right? Didn't
you wonder why? You could have asked whether the English and
French writers were representing the battle to favor their national
interests and then looked to see if the factual differences actually
supported your idea. Or you could have thought about how a
book entitled *The Romance of Chivalry* might present a different
view of the battle than a book entitled *A History of the English-
Speaking Peoples*. You could even have talked about *Henry V*—
which I know you've read—and looked at how Shakespeare
presents the battle. You would have had an angle, a problem.
Professor Boyer would have loved it.

Alice is suggesting that Shirley invent a purpose or original problem
for her paper and then develop an argument to support it, in much
the same way that Emily did when she wrote about Swift's *A Modest
Proposal*.[27] Alice's representation of the assignment is, to be sure, more
difficult to plan and complete than is Shirley's.[28] Among other things,
it would require that Shirley select and evaluate her material in light
of a problem and then organize it in such a way that a convincing
argument can be developed.[29]

Clearly, Alice and Shirley approached this assignment from very
different perspectives and with qualitatively different knowledge about
the role that purpose plays in academic writing and reading. Alice, on
the one hand, appears more consciously aware that texts have rhetorical
purposes, and she uses this knowledge to inform her writing and
reading. Shirley, on the other hand, is still learning what it means for
texts to have rhetorical force and communicative purpose. She has not
yet fully realized, for example, that an essential part of reading includes
interpreting content in relation to an author's purpose and knowing
or inferring something about the audience to whom the author is
writing. Nor has she realized the extent to which understanding one's
purpose in writing can affect the quality of the texts one writes because
different types of texts carry with them different conventions and
purposes.[30] This kind of knowledge, often referred to as "rhetorical
knowledge," is essential to understanding a text within its larger context,
whether it be social, political, historical, literary, or otherwise.

Alice's suggestions for a paper would require a radically different
composing process than the one Shirley used, one more akin to the
constructive process Emily used in writing her paper on Swift. It would
include, among other things, articulating an original purpose, elaborating a writing plan that is sensitive to the rhetorical situation, and
identifying a point of view and using it as a focus for developing a
forceful argument.[31] Alice's suggestion, in short, would require Shirley

to evaluate her reading and, in turn, to use that evaluation to build an argument that would reflect her ideas about the material rather than simply knowledge-telling or organizing the ideas of others into a narrative.[32] To construct texts that are appropriate for the academic context in which she is writing, Shirley will have to learn to see her writing as purposeful and to use that sense of purpose more constructively to guide her writing and reading.[33]

Here we have seen the role of problem solving in building academic arguments, but students face many other kinds of writing tasks as well. The sense of purpose that distinguishes Alice's thinking from Shirley's is equally important in other writing contexts. Let's look now at how two high school students, Danielle and Ed, approach a typical "writing to learn" task in their earth science class.

Their teacher, Mr. Burns, has given them a fairly typical assignment. The students are to read a textbook chapter on hurricane formation and write an essay that summarizes its key points. Mr. Burns has two major goals in mind for his students with regard to this assignment. First, he wants them to acquire background knowledge about hurricanes that will help them better understand the unit they are about to study. Second, he hopes that the writing assignment will force them to learn the material more thoroughly than if they had only read it. From Mr. Burns's perspective, the assignment is an opportunity for students to draw connections among the various facts in the reading and to place this new information in the context of other weather phenomena that have been discussed in class.

He would no doubt be surprised to see the different ways that his students interpret this seemingly straightforward assignment and how this, in turn, affects their problem solving and learning.[34] Let's look at how Danielle and Ed go about completing the assignment.

Danielle is an average student who thinks of herself as a good writer and reader. She sees this assignment as routine, not unlike the questions she answered after reading a story in grade school or the "Who–What–Where–When–Why" book reports she wrote in junior high. Over the years, she has encountered many such assignments, and in each case she has had a "formula" or "recipe" that has helped structure her problem solving.

As Danielle understands it, her assignment is to write a summary of the chapter on hurricanes. Accordingly, she invokes her "summary" strategy, a routine that defines her writing task as one of translating or paraphrasing the text into her own words. To write her summary, Danielle sits down with the text, pen in hand, ready to begin reading and writing. She reads and rereads the title and the first few paragraphs of the text until she feels she understands them. Then she writes, translating those segments of text that seem important into her own words and deleting those she perceives as less important. She reads what she has written, making sure that her text makes sense, and then turns to the next few paragraphs and repeats the procedure. When Danielle has gone through the entire article in this way, she rereads her summary, checking its coherence and correcting grammar and spelling errors.[35]

Although Danielle will produce a "summary" that contains some of the important ideas in the chapter, her interpretation of the assignment and her problem solving significantly influence what she will learn as she reads and writes. For example, she does not gain as much as she could from her reading because she defines her task according to a formula that emphasizes sequential translation over conceptual integration. Instead of building an integrated representation of the main concepts, Danielle focuses on understanding concepts in isolation from one another, more as a list of ideas than an explanation.[36] Moreover, her method leaves little opportunity for reflection, in particular on how any newly acquired knowledge might relate to what she already knows about hurricanes or weather in general.[37]

Danielle's understanding of the assignment and problem-solving routine also influence what she learns from her writing. Although essay writing has been demonstrated to be a more effective learning activity than more restrictive tasks such as answering study questions, students often fail to use writing to best advantage as a means for learning.[38] Because Danielle represents the assignment as one of translation, she does not take the opportunity to reflect on or restructure the reading material in her own mind for her own purposes. She does not in any sense "transform" the material she has read into usable knowledge, knowledge that is related somehow to what she knows about the physical world. Transforming knowledge in this way is a crucial aspect of learning from writing.[39] Nor does her strategy allow for any constructive planning as she writes; her writing is entirely determined by the order of presentation in the chapter itself.[40]

From this perspective, it becomes clear that Danielle did not engage in the kind of learning that Mr. Burns had in mind when he gave the assignment. She has not explored or created connections among facts in the reading, nor has she thought about how this new information relates to other concepts that have been discussed in class.

In contrast, Ed takes a different approach to the hurricane assignment. Also a good writer and reader, Ed quickly sizes up the task: Mr. Burns wants an essay that highlights the principal causes of hurricane formation. Before he begins reading, Ed reviews what he knows about hurricanes, anticipating the contents of the chapter. He hypothesizes that it will cover the causes and consequences of hurricanes and perhaps refer to other ocean storms such as squalls and tidal waves, which the class has been studying. He knows that his essay is supposed to include a causal description of hurricane formation, so he is on the lookout for such material. As he reads, he makes notes about those things he wants to include in his essay. In this way, he uses his writing goals to guide his reading and note-taking.[41]

When he has finished reading, Ed draws up a plan for writing. He looks over his notes, elaborating those ideas he wants to include and bracketing, for the moment at least, those that seem less relevant. He decides to draw most of his information from the assigned reading and to augment it with information he has learned from other sources. He notes these additional ideas and their connections to the reading material and then begins to think about a rhetorical structure that will suit the material and assignment.

As Ed composes, he refers frequently to his writing plan, in which he has laid out the causal sequence of the events that produce hurricanes. He uses his plan as both a source of ideas and a framework for organizing his prose. He revises or entirely deletes text that does not fit his purpose. When he completes the assignment, he will have a well-structured, comprehensive essay that fully meets Mr. Burns's expectations.

Why do Danielle and Ed take such different approaches to this assignment? In part, it is because the assignment does not *require* the students to engage in the kinds of problem solving and learning that Mr. Burns wants but has not articulated, either for himself or for his students. As Shirley, Danielle, and Ed are meant to illustrate, inattention to the problem solving that underlies different kinds of learning experiences has consequences for all students, regardless of their ability. Too often the ways that students are asked to use writing and reading do not help them understand these processes as constructive acts of thought and communication or do not afford the time or support that would enable them to exercise the problem-solving strategies in their repertoire. As teachers, we must think carefully about the learning experiences we offer students and what it is that we want them to give to and take away from these experiences.

But the assignment is only part of the story. Whether or not students adopt a purposeful, constructive approach to a given writing assignment is not simply a matter of how they interpret that assignment, although interpretation is a critical factor, as Danielle and Ed are meant to illustrate. The way students handle a given task will also be influenced by their skill and fluency as writers and readers, their knowledge of the topic and related topics, as well as their understanding of the purpose of the assignment and the potential purposes of writing and reading in general.[42]

We should not assume that only highly skilled students like Max and Emily are capable of understanding writing and reading as purposeful activities. Students at all levels can adopt this perspective, as the cases of Alice and Ed illustrate. Very young children, moreover, *expect* writing and reading to be purposeful, communicative experiences. Writing and reading are for them engaging activities in which experimentation, discovery, and communication predominate, supported by peers and adults alike. In this final section, we consider the kinds of constructive problem solving that younger students, those in junior high and elementary school, can bring to their writing and reading. We also look at some of the ways that their problem solving changes as their purposes for writing and reading expand.

Problem Solving of Young Writers and Readers

Anita is in seventh grade. It is Sunday afternoon and she is preparing her "You choose!" talk for English. The "You choose!" assignment is one of the best reasons to be in Mr. Oakes's class. Each week a student describes his or her favorite book. He or she can use hand-drawn illustrations, dress up in costume, read an excerpt from the book, or act out a scene or two. The purpose of the talk is to entice other students into reading the book.

Anita has decided to talk about one of her favorite pieces of fiction, a diary kept by the mother of a teenage suicide named Lizzie. The diary describes the lives of Lizzie and her family as they try to cope with the adolescent's unhappiness. Anita likes the book because she feels that it addresses many of the problems that kids her age really face. Moreover, she feels that the emotions and actions of the characters—especially those of Lizzie and her mother—are true to life.

As Anita plans her talk, however, she discovers that the book is not easy to describe. At the outset, Anita thought she had a good understanding of the book. But in trying to describe Lizzie to her imagined audience, the class, she realizes she was a little confused. She is not sure how Lizzie felt sometimes or why she acted as she did.

This assignment is challenging Anita to reflect on her understanding of the book. By thinking about what her audience will need to understand the main character, she has hit upon some confusions in her own understanding. In this way, she is motivated to articulate more fully what it is that she does and does not understand.[43] From those insights, she can try to identify the sources of her misunderstanding. To clarify her confusions, Anita will return to the text. She will carefully reread those parts that contain the sources of her confusion. Her reflections will eventually lead her to substantially revise her understanding of the book. Anita is, in short, becoming aware of the need to monitor her understanding, a critical component of skilled reading.[44]

In some instances, students recognize the need to monitor their meaning-making activities in writing and reading on their own. Writers, for example, begin to see that if they are to shape their writing for an imagined audience and particular purpose, they need to look over and evaluate a number of options.[45] They also begin to see that, to write the piece they want to write, they need to make plans that outline their goals and purposes for writing.[46] Readers like Anita begin to see that understanding a text can involve not only thinking about the text, but also thinking about one's understanding of it.[47] At other times, however, as we shall see, students need outside support to help them recognize the need to monitor and revise their understandings.[48]

A few weeks later, we see Anita and her English teacher, Mr. Oakes, meeting together after school. The principal has received complaints about the book Anita described in her "You choose!" talk. Some parents feel that it is not appropriate for their adolescent children. In particular, they feel that a book about suicide can bring more harm than good and that its language is offensive.

The principal has asked Mr. Oakes and Anita to tell her why the book should remain in the school library. Anita is writing a letter that explains her thoughts. She wants to argue that the book is valuable and that students her age are mature enough to handle its content and language. She begins writing her first draft immediately. It is easy for her to describe what she liked about the book, and she writes several pages before stopping.

"Mr. Oakes, what do you think? This is my letter to the principal."

When Mr. Oakes reads the letter, he can see that Anita has had a hard time doing what she set out to do. The letter is an enthusiastic description of the book, not an argument against critics who want it banned.

"Anita, do you know why some parents have objected to this book?"

"Yeah, they think kids shouldn't read about someone committing suicide. They think it might give us the idea. But we *know* about it already. A book like this explains it so that kids don't feel like they're weird for thinking about it. It shows how there are things kids can do when they're in trouble, like talk to someone. Lizzie just couldn't see them."

"'So you think this book might even help some kids, then?"

"Yeah, it's really more about *not* committing suicide."

"What about the language in the book? You know some parents object strongly to it."

"Everyone already knows the words. And what else would you say if you felt that bad?"

"You've really thought about this book, haven't you? How do you think you could use some of that in your letter?"

Mr. Oakes is helping Anita see that to write a strong letter she will have to do more than describe the book or explain why she enjoyed it. She will have to think carefully about her purpose for writing and her audience. She will have to consider her text rhetorically and write from a point of view. And she will have to monitor her writing, making sure that the meaning she is constructing is the meaning she wants to communicate.

To do this, Anita will have to set aside her knowledge-telling strategy and adopt a more purposeful one. She will have to decide why she is writing, and what it is she wants to say. This means that she will have to establish goals for her writing and develop a plan for meeting those goals. In her role as mediator, she will also have to visualize her audience, namely, angry parents and the principal, with their needs and beliefs. It also means that she will need to anticipate their reactions to her message. And, as Anita translates her plans into text, she will need to monitor the meaning she is constructing in light of her communicative intent. She will have to judge the appropriateness of its content, tone, and language with respect to her goals and audience, revising both her plans and drafts as the need arises.

Like the "You choose!" talk, this task, coupled with Mr. Oakes's constructive intervention, is challenging Anita to expand her problem-solving skills. It is helping her to gain an appreciation for the importance of purpose and planning in her writing. It is also helping her to become aware of the need to shape and monitor the meaning she is constructing for a particular audience. When she began her letter, Anita did not spontaneously consider the importance of these issues. With Mr. Oakes's assistance, she was able to see that her letter was not meeting the goals she had set for herself.

To focus her letter-writing effort, therefore, Anita clearly needed Mr. Oakes's help. This stands in contrast to the awareness of audience that emerged independently as she prepared her "You choose!" talk. It is interesting to note that students can use sophisticated strategies in familiar contexts or for highly motivating tasks or on topics they know well. This does not mean, however, that they are able to apply that skill to a new or difficult task. In these cases, they often need support from an outside source such as a teacher or fellow student to get their writing and reading back on track, especially when their goals, at least momentarily, exceed their abilities.[49]

With support and guidance, Anita's problem-solving skill will continue to evolve. She will learn to monitor her problem solving independently of any outside agent. She will begin to engage in high-level planning as she writes and in critical and interpretative thinking as she reads over an expanding range of tasks and contexts. As her skills and self-knowledge expand, she will be able to assume greater control over her problem solving. Through this control, Anita will be able to exercise increasing power over the meanings she is constructing as she writes and reads.

Even very young children are able to engage in constructive problem solving. Preschoolers, for example, demonstrate that they know writing is purposeful when they scribble on paper, walls, and furniture to express their emotions and ideas. Likewise, they demonstrate that they know reading is purposeful when, as prereaders, they sit with a book and tell themselves a story or pretend to read aloud. Some children experiment with more conventional forms of writing, producing invented spellings, writing their names, and labeling their drawings.[50] Other youngsters learn that individual letters represent particular sounds or that particular groups of letters stand for specific concepts.[51] Still others show that they have knowledge about story content, structure, and characterization.[52]

To explore the kinds of problem solving of which emerging writers and readers are capable, imagine a first grade classroom. As we enter the room, we see Kenny and Susan at the Share Table. Kenny is responding to Susan's story about her rabbits. He is telling Susan what he likes about her story and asks questions about what he does not understand.

Kenny and Susan are engaged in collaborative problem solving.[53] Together, they are thinking critically about the meaning of Susan's text and about the process of writing itself. These interactions let them discuss and develop ideas and plans for writing and give them a chance to look at text through the eyes of both writer and reader. In a sense, this kind of collaborative problem solving supports the development of the self-evaluative strategies that experienced writers more spontaneously apply to their own work.[54]

Although Kenny is only seven, he is learning how to respond constructively to writing. When he first read other children's writing, he responded only to the events they described or to surface features such as spelling and handwriting.[55] During the year, however, Kenny has acquired strategies for delving more deeply into a text's content and coherence. In writing conferences, for example, his teacher, Ms. Plourde, has modeled for Kenny the kinds of questions she wants him to ask of his own writing—questions about the problem-solving process as well as about the text (for example, "Do you have more to tell?" "Are you telling the story you want to tell?"). These questions help Kenny focus on his purposes for writing and think about what it is he wants to say.[56] As he continues to write, he will become increasingly independent, asking these questions on his own and applying them to his writing as well as to that of others.

In the back of the room, we see a small group of children participating in a "read-aloud" with Ms. Plourde. They are reading Judy Blume's *Freckle Juice*. The book is about Andrew, an unhappy boy, who believes that his problems will disappear if he can only acquire freckles. Sharon, a classmate whom Andrew dislikes, agrees to sell him "freckle juice." The story unfolds as Andrew deals with his misgivings about Sharon, his doubts about the freckle juice, and his desire to end his troubles.

As Ms. Plourde reads the story aloud to them, the children become deeply involved in constructing a meaning for the story. In fact, as we look on, we see them engage in activities that are quite similar to those used by older, more sophisticated readers like Max. For example, they use prior knowledge to tackle a problem of character motivation,[57] generating a wide range of hypotheses as to why Andrew might want freckles: "He thinks that freckles hide dirt so you don't have to wash. But my little brother has them and he gets a bath every night." "He thinks they're lucky." "They're icky—I don't think he *really* wants them."

Similarly, they use their understanding of the story in conjunction with prior knowledge to speculate about what might happen when Andrew drinks the freckle juice:[58] "He might get freckles, but the kids will still be mean to him." "Sharon is just tricking him so nothing will happen" and "His mother will still make him take a bath."

Like Anita, beginning readers often need support to accomplish their goals. For example, they may need to be reminded to use prior knowledge to solve problems of meaning. Teachers can provide direct support that helps students monitor what they know and integrate prior knowledge with information in a text.[59] Young children can also be taught explicit strategies such as question-asking that prompt them to use prior knowledge during story comprehension.[60] With support from parents, teachers, and fellow students, young children can learn to use prior knowledge to solve increasingly complex problems of meaning.

Later in the day, we see Rachel sitting in the center of the room trying to write a story. Until about a month ago she had written easily, finding lots of topics to write about and reading what she had written to her friends. Today she has started a story three times, writing a few words, crossing them out, crumpling up the paper, and starting again. Ms. Plourde watches as Rachel gives up in frustration and begins fidgeting with her sock. She pulls her stool over to Rachel's desk.

"Tell me what you're writing about, Rachel. You're having a hard time, aren't you?"

"Um. I want to tell how we went out crabbing with my dad, and I caught a crab that was bigger than my brother's. I can't write it, though. Every time I try to tell what happened, it sounds stupid. Then I have to start again."

Rachel is frustrated because her writing abilities are expanding. She is becoming more aware of the demands of her teacher and peer audience. Her newfound concern for her readers makes it hard for her to write. When Rachel began writing in school, she wrote primarily to please herself. She seldom changed her pieces, nor was she concerned when other children found them confusing. Now, however, she wants her story to interest her friends, and she worries when she thinks it is not good enough. Rachel's school writing is evolving from knowledge-telling to a more rhetorical approach in which she gives consideration to her audience and purposes for writing.[61]

The tension that she is feeling will eventually push Rachel toward revising her work rather than abandoning her drafts. To do this, her notions of time, space, and awareness of audience will have to change.[62] She will have to learn, for example, that text is flexible and temporary before she will be willing to change it. And she will have to learn that when a text lacks important information, it is confusing. In short, Rachel will have to think about particular needs of her audience in relation to her purposes for writing as she formulates what she wants to say. As her ability to reflect on audience and purpose develops, she will in turn spend more time and effort planning the ideas and structures that best communicate her meaning. She will, in short, become a more flexible planner, one who is able to generate original plans for a wide range of writing problems.

Conclusion

Through Anita and Rachel, we see that students who are learning to write and read have models of those processes that are, in many ways, close approximations to the mature models held by Emily and Max. While the young children's models are not as elaborated as those of the older students, they share an important belief, namely, that writing and reading are fundamentally purposeful acts of communication. This belief is essential to expertise in writing and reading; it is the engine that drives constructive problem solving.

Indeed, it is precisely this belief that is absent from the learning experiences of Shirley and Danielle. The models of writing and reading that they adopt to complete their assignments, which are in some sense adequate for the task, have no purpose or function beyond satisfaction of the assignment. Much of the responsibility for this falls, as we have said, to the assignment itself, which may unwittingly reinforce a belief in writing and reading as school routines rather than as functionally meaningful tools of communication and learning. This is not in any way to suggest that summarization or any other problem-solving strategy is in and of itself useless. To the contrary, strategies such as summarization and self-questioning, to name only two, are critical components of expertise in both writing and reading.[63] However, it is critical that these skills not become disconnected from the larger communicative, meaning-construction process. If they do, then their function within that process will not be well understood and their power as problem-solving and learning tools will not be fully exploited.

One result of this decontextualization is that students' models of writing and reading may become limited and their original feeling for purpose diminished. This, in turn, has consequences for their ability to meet the demands of open-ended assignments such as the one that Shirley faced. The ability to respond constructively to an open-ended assignment in the way that Max and Emily did grows out of a long experience with writing and reading as problem-solving processes; that is, with defining original purposes and problems, setting goals, formulating plans, constructing meaning, and so on. In their problem solving, students like Max and Emily demonstrate their belief that, as writers and readers, they are linked in a communicative interaction.

Younger students like Anita, Rachel, and Kenny show that they too approach writing and reading as communicative acts. Like Max and Emily, their writing and reading have purpose and function. In fact, they frequently define purposes that, for the moment, exceed their writing and reading abilities. But it is precisely in the attempt to fulfill such goals that they expand their problem-solving skill.

The critical question, then, is how to sustain and further develop the potential evident in the problem solving of young writers and readers. A number of very important steps in this direction have been taken with elementary school children[64] low achievers in middle school,[65] and college students[66]—steps such as the provision of flexibly structured opportunities for teachers and students to exchange views about both their own and professional texts. As illustrated in chapter 6 of this volume, these efforts have in common a focus on having students solve problems within a community of learners so that members of the community—students and teachers alike—support the individual's writing and reading efforts. In each of these cooperative approaches, moreover, problem solving is situated in a context that emphasizes the purposeful construction of meaning. Efforts such as these are more than experimental in nature. They are helping to cultivate students' understanding of writing and reading as purposeful acts of communication and to transform the contexts in which writing and reading occur.

Notes

1. The students described in this chapter have been created to illustrate particular aspects of the problem-solving process in writing and reading; they are fictional "composites" of students we have met in our research and teaching.
2. Swift, J. (1984). A modest proposal. In A. Ross and D. Woolley (Eds.), *Jonathan Swift* (pp. 492–499). Oxford: Oxford University Press. (Original work published 1792)
3. Bransford, J.D., and Johnson, M.K. (1972). Contextual prerequisites for understanding. Some investigations of comprehension and recall. *Journal of Verbal Learning and Verbal Behavior, 11,* 717–726.
   Anderson, R.C., Pichert, J.W., Goetz, E.T., Schallert, D.L., Stevens, K.V., and Trollip, S.R. (1976). Instantiation of general terms. *Journal of Verbal Learning and Verbal Behavior, 15,* 667–679.
   Spilich, G.J., Vesonder, G.T., Chiesi, H.L., and Voss, J.F. (1979). Text processing of domain-related information for individuals with high and low domain knowledge. *Journal of Verbal Learning and Verbal Behavior, 18,* 275–290.
   Haas, C., and Flower, L. (1988). Rhetorical reading and the construction of meaning. *College Composition and Communication, 39,* 167–183.
4. Adams, M.J., and Bruce, B. (1982). Background knowledge and reading comprehension. In J. Langer and T. Smith-Burke (Eds.), *Reader meets author/bridging the gap: A psycholinguistic and sociolinguistic perspective*

(pp. 2–25). Newark, DE: International Reading Association.

Stein, N., and Glenn, C.G. (1979). An analysis of story comprehension in elementary school children. In R. Freedle (Ed.), *New directions in discourse processing* (pp. 53–120). Norwood, NJ: Ablex.

Rumelhart, D. (1975). Notes on a schema for stories. In D. Bobrow and A. Collins (Eds.), *Representation and understanding: Studies in cognitive science* (pp. 211–236). New York: Academic Press.

5. Perfetti, C.A., Bransford, J.D., and Franks, J.J. (1983). Constraints on access in a problem-solving context. *Memory and Cognition, 11,* 24–31.

Rumelhart, D., and Ortony, A. (1977). The representation of knowledge in memory. In R.C. Anderson, R.J. Spiro, and W.E. Montague (Eds.), *Schooling and the acquisition of knowledge* (pp. 99–136). Hillsdale, NJ: Erlbaum.

6. Franks, J., Vye, N., Auble, P., Mezynski, K., Perfetti, C.A., Bransford, J., and Littlefield, J. (1982). Learning from explicit vs. implicit text. *Journal of Experimental Psychology: General, 111,* 414–422.

Newman, D., and Bruce, B. (1986). Interpretation and manipulation in human plans. *Discourse Process, 9,* 167–195.

Kintsch, W., and van Dijk, T.A. (1978). Toward a model of text comprehension and production. *Psychological Review, 85,* 363–394.

7. Baker, L., and Brown, A. (1984). Metacognitive skills and reading. In D. Pearson, M.L. Kamil, R. Barr, and P. Mosenthal (Eds.), *Handbook of reading research* (pp. 353–394). New York: Longman.

Brown, A., Armbruster, B., and Baker, L. (1986). The role of metacognition in reading and studying. In J. Orasanu (Ed.), *Reading comprehension: From research to practice* (pp. 49–76). Hillsdale, NJ: Erlbaum.

Bruce, B. (1981). A social interaction model of reading. *Discourse Process, 4,* 273–311.

8. Collins, A., Brown, J.S., and Larkin, K.M. (1980). Inference in text understanding. In R.J. Spiro, B.C. Bruce, and W.F. Brewer (Eds.), *Theoretical issues in reading comprehension* (pp. 385–410). Hillsdale, NJ: Erlbaum.

9. Newman, D. (1986). The role of mutual belief in the development of perspective-taking. *Developmental Review, 6,* 122–145.

Newman and Bruce (1986); see note 6.

10. Flower, L., and Hayes, J.R. (1981b). The pregnant pause: An inquiry into the nature of planning. *Research in the Teaching of English, 15,* 229–243.

11. Flower, L., and Hayes, J.R. (1980). The cognition of discovery: Defining a rhetorical problem. *College Composition and Communication, 33,* 21–32.

12. Jeffery, C. (1981). Teachers' and students' perceptions of the writing process. *Research in the Teaching of English, 15,* 215–228.

Flower, L., Hayes, J.R., Carey, L., Schriver, K., and Stratman, J. (1986). Detection, diagnosis, and the strategies of revision. *College Composition and Communication, 37,* 16–56. 13. Haas and Flower (1988); see note 3.

14. Flower and Hayes (1980); see note 11.

15. Flower, L., and Hayes, J.R. (1984). Images, plans, and prose: The representation of meaning in writing. *Written Communication, 1,* 120–160.

16. Scardamalia, M., and Bereiter, C. (1982). Assimilative processes in composition planning. *Educational Psychologist, 17,* 165–171.

    Bereiter, C., and Scardamalia, M. (1985). Cognitive coping strategies and the problem of "inert knowledge." In S. Chipman, J. Segal, and R. Glaser (Eds.), *Thinking and learning skills: Vol. 2* (pp. 65–80). Hillsdale, NJ: Erlbaum.

17. Flower, L., and Hayes, J.R. (1981a). Plans that guide the composing process. In C.H. Frederiksen and J.F. Dominic (Eds.), *Writing: The nature, development, and teaching of written communication: Vol. 2. Process, development, and communication* (pp. 39–58). Hillsdale, NJ: Erlbaum.

18. Flower, L. (1985). *Problem-solving strategies in writing.* San Diego, CA: Harcourt Brace Jovanovich.

19. Flower and Hayes (1984); see note 15.

20. Bruce (1981); see note 7.

    Rosenblatt, L. (1978). *The reader, the text, the poem.* Carbondale, IL: Southern Illinois University Press.

21. Spivey, N. (1983). *Discourse synthesis: Constructing texts in reading and writing.* Austin: University of Texas Press.

    Flower, L. (1979). Writer-based prose: A cognitive basis for problems in writing. *College English, 41,* 19–37.

22. Mandler, J.M., and DeForest, M. (1979). Is there more than one way to recall a story? *Child Development, 50,* 886–889.

23. Zeller, R. (1985). *Developing the inferential reasoning abilities of basic writers.* Paper presented at the Penn State Conference on Rhetoric and Composition.

24. Brown, A. (1980). Metacognitive development and reading. In R.J. Spiro, B.C. Bruce, and W.F. Brewer (Eds.); see note 8, pp. 453–482.

25. Flower, L. (1980). Planning to be creative. *Composition and Teaching, 2,* 61–67.

26. Adams and Bruce (1982); see note 4.

    Newman and Bruce (1986); see note 6.

27. Atlas, M. (1979, April). *Expert–novice differences in the writing process.* Paper presented at the American Educational Research Association, San Francisco. (Educational Document Reproduction Service No. ED 170 769)

    Kennedy, M.L. (1985). The composing processes of college students writing from sources. *Written Communication, 2,* 434–456.

28. Durst, R.K. (1986). The cognitive and linguistic dimensions of analytic writing. *Dissertation Abstracts International, 46,* 12A. (University Microfilms No. DA 8602471)

29. Scardamalia and Bereiter (1982); see note 16.

30. Haas and Flower (1988); see note 3.

    Meyer, B.J.F., Brandt, D.M., and Bluth, G.J. (1980). Use of top-level structure in text: Key for reading comprehension of ninth-grade students. *Reading Research Quarterly, 16,* 72–103.

31. Flower and Hayes (1980); see note 11.

    Higgins, L. (1986). *Inference and argument: An exploratory study.* Unpublished manuscript, Carnegie-Mellon University, Pittsburgh, PA.

32. Scardamalia and Bereiter (1982); see note 16.

33. Kaufer, D., Geisler, C., and Neuwirth, C. (in press). *The architecture of argument: A cross-disciplinary rhetoric.* San Diego, CA: Harcourt Brace Jovanovich.

   Scardamalia, M., and Bereiter, C. (1987). Knowledge telling and knowledge transforming in written composition. In S. Rosenberg (Ed.), *Advances in applied psycholinguistics: Vol. 1* (pp. 142–175). Cambridge: Cambridge University Press.

34. Penrose, A. (1986). What do we know about writing as a way to learn? *English Record, 37,* 10–13.

   Marshall, J.D. (1984). *The effects of writing on students' understanding of literary texts.* Paper presented at the annual meeting of the National Council of Teachers of English, Detroit, MI. (ERIC Document Reproduction Service No. ED 252 842)

   Langer, J.A. (1986a). Learning through writing: Study skills in the content areas. *Journal of Reading, 29,* 400–406.

   Langer, J.A., and Applebee, A. (1987). *How writing shapes thinking: A study of teaching and learning.* (Res. Rep. No. 22Z). Urbana, IL: National Council of Teachers of English.

35. Bridwell, L. (1980). Revising strategies in twelfth grade students' transactional writing. *Research in the Teaching of English, 14,* 197–222.

36. Brown, A., and Day, J. (1983). Macrorules for summarizing texts: The development of expertise. *Journal of Verbal Learning and Verbal Behavior, 22,* 1–14.

   Brown, A., and Smiley, S. (1977). Rating the importance of structural units of prose passages: A problem of metacognitive development. *Child Development, 48,* 1–8.

   Winograd, P.N. (1984). Strategic difficulties in summarizing texts. *Reading Research Quarterly, 19,* 404–425.

37. Kennedy (1985); see note 27.

38. Copeland, K.A. (1984). *The effect of writing upon good and poor writers' learning from prose.* Unpublished doctoral dissertation, University of Texas at Austin.

   Newell, G.E. (1984). Learning from writing in two content areas: A case study/protocol analysis. *Research in the Teaching of English, 18,* 265–287.

39. Scardamalia and Bereiter (1982); see note 16.

40. Flower and Hayes (1980); see note 11.

41. Flower and Hayes (1981a); see note 17.

42. Spivey (1983); see note 21.

   Langer, J.A. (1984). The effects of available information on responses to school writing tasks. *Research in the Teaching of English, 18,* 27–44.

43. Markman, E. (1981). Comprehension monitoring. In W.P. Dickinson (Ed.), *Children's oral communication skills* (pp. 61–84). New York: Academic Press.

   Markman, E. (1985). Comprehension monitoring: Developmental and educational issues. In S.F. Chipman, J.W. Segal, and R. Glaser (Eds.),

Thinking and learning skills: Vol. 2 (pp. 275–292). Hillsdale, NJ: Erlbaum. Baker and Brown (1984); see note 7.

44. Baker and Brown (1984); see note 7.

45. Kroll, B.M. (1984). Audience adaptation in children's persuasive letters. *Written Communication*, 1, 407–428.

46. Burtis, P.J., Bereiter, C., Scardamalia, M., and Tetroe, J. (1983). The development of planning in writing. In C.J. Wells and B.M. Kroll (Eds.), *Explorations in the development of writing: Theory, research, and practice* (pp. 153–174). Chichester, England: Wiley.
    Tetroe, J. (1981, April). *The effect of planning on children's writing.* Paper presented at the American Educational Research Association, Los Angeles.

47. Markman (1981); see note 43.
    Markman (1985); see note 43.
    Baker and Brown (1984); see note 7.

48. Brown, A., and Palinscar, A.S. (1985). *Reciprocal teaching of comprehension strategies: A natural history of one program for enhancing learning* (Tech. Rep. No. 334). Urbana–Champaign, IL: University of Illinois, Center for the Study of Reading.
    Graves, D.H. (1983). *Writing: Teachers and children at work.* Exeter, NH: Heinemann.
    Scardamalia, M., Bereiter, C., and Sternbach, R. (1984). Teachability of reflective processes in written composition. *Cognitive Science, 8,* 173–190.

49. Ninio, A., and Bruner, J. (1978). The achievement and antecedents of labelling. *Journal of Child Language, 5,* 1–5.
    Graves (1983); see note 48.
    Short, E.J., and Ryan, E.B. (1984). Metacognitive differences between skilled and less skilled readers: Remediating deficits through story grammar and attribution training. *Journal of Educational Psychology, 76,* 225–235.
    Flower (1985); see note 18.
    Palinscar, A.S., and Brown, A. (1984). Reciprocal teaching of comprehension-fostering and monitoring activities. *Cognition and Instruction, 1,* 117–175.

50. Bissex, G. (1980). *GNYS AT WRK: A child learns to write and read.* Cambridge, MA: Harvard University Press.
    Read, C. (1971). Preschool children's knowledge of English phonology. *Harvard Educational Review, 41,* 1–34.
    Chomsky, C. (1979). Approaching reading through invented spelling. In L. Resnick and P. Weaver (Eds.), *Theory and practice of early reading: Vol. 2* (pp. 43–66). Hillsdale, NJ: Erlbaum.

51. Dyson, A. Haas. (1984a). Emerging alphabetic literacy in school contexts: Towards defining the gap between school curriculum and child mind. *Written Communication*, 1, 5–55.

52. Whyte, J. (1980). Stories for young children: An evaluation. *International Journal of Early Childhood, 12,* 23–26.
    Mandler, J.M., Scribner, S., Cole, M., and DeForest, M. (1980). Cross-

cultural invariance in story recall. *Child Development, 51,* 19–26.

Green, G.M., and Laff, M.O. (1981). *Five-year-olds' recognition of authorship by literary style* (Tech. Rep. No. 181). Urbana–Champaign, IL: University of Illinois, Center for the Study of Reading.

Newman, D. (1981). *Children's understanding of strategic interaction.* Unpublished doctoral dissertation, City University of New York.

53. Hillocks, G. (1984). What works in teaching composition: A meta-analysis of experimental treatment studies. *American Journal of Education, 93,* 133–170.

Bruffee, K. (1984). Collaborative learning and the "conversation of mankind." *College English, 46,* 635–652.

54. Ninio and Bruner (1978); see note 49.

Graves (1983); see note 48.

Short and Ryan (1984); see note 49.

Palinscar and Brown (1984); see note 49.

55. Newkirk, T. (1982). Young writers as critical readers. In T. Newkirk and N. Atwell (Eds.), *Understanding writing: Ways of observing, learning, and teaching* (pp. 106–113). Chelmsford, MA: Northeast Regional Exchange.

56. Sowers, S. (1982). Reflect, expand, and select: Three responses in the writing conference. In T. Newkirk and N. Atwell (Eds.); see note 55, pp. 76–90.

57. Newman (1981); see note 52.

Brewer, W. F., and Hay, A. (1981, April). *Children's understanding of the author's point of view in stories.* Paper presented at the meeting of the Society for Research in Child Development, Boston.

Liebling, C. (1989). *Children's comprehension of inside view and character plans in fiction: A pilot investigation.* (Tech. Rep. No. 459). Urbana–Champaign, IL: University of Illinois, Center for the Study of Reading.

58. Liebling (in press); see note 57.

Newman (1981); see note 52.

59. Palinscar and Brown (1984); see note 49.

Langer (1984); see note 42.

Smith-Burke, T., and Ringler, L. (1986). STAR: Teaching reading and writing. In J. Orasanu (Ed.); see note 7, pp. 215–234.

60. Hansen, J. (1981). The effects of inference training and practice on young children's reading comprehension. *Reading Research Quarterly, 16,* 391–417.

Hansen, J., and Pearson, P.D. (1983). An instructional study: Improving the inferential comprehension of 4th grade and poor readers. *Journal of Educational Psychology, 79,* 821–829.

61. Rose, M. (1980). Rigid rules, inflexible plans, and the stifling of language: A cognitivist analysis of writer's block. *College Composition and Communication, 31,* 389–401.

Calkins, L.M. (1980). Children's rewriting strategies. *Research in the Teaching of English, 14,* 331–341.

Flower (1979); see note 21.

Scardamalia and Bereiter (1987); see note 33.

Bereiter and Scardamalia (1985); see note 16.

62. Graves (1983); see note 48.
    Calkins (1980); see note 61.

63. Brown and Smiley (1977); see note 36.
    Brown and Day (1983); see note 36.
    Palinscar and Brown (1984); see note 49.

64. Graves (1983); see note 48.
    Hillocks (1984); see note 53.
    Applebee, A.N. (1986). Problems in process approaches: Toward a reconceptualization of process instruction. In A. Petrosky and D. Bartholomae (Eds.), *The teaching of writing. 85th Yearbook of the National Society for the Study of Education* (pp. 95–113). Chicago: University of Chicago Press.
    Langer (1986a); see note 34.
    Calkins (1980); see note 61.
    Scardamalia and Bereiter (1982); see note 16.

65. Palinscar and Brown (1984); see note 49.
    Smith-Burke and Ringler (1986); see note 59.

66. Flower (1985); see note 18.

5 Writing and Reading Working Together

Planning Group Members

Robert J. Tierney, Chair
Paul Ammon
Rebekah Caplan
Linnea C. Ehri
Mary K. Healy
Mary K. Hurdlow
Judith Langer
Robert Ruddell

Introduction

Wallace Chafe

The chapter that follows illustrates with numerous examples the beneficial effects that can be achieved when teachers bring together the traditionally separated activities of writing and reading. Drawing on their manifold experiences in both primary and secondary classrooms, the authors show how the integration of writing and reading activities can enhance learning in a variety of ways.

They have seen, for example, students become more motivated not just toward writing and reading per se, but also toward any content areas taught with writing and reading as a unified part of the instruction. They have found, too, that a significant admixture of reading has furthered the learning of specific writing skills, all the way from the learning of sound-letter correspondences in the earliest grades to an appreciation of the subtle aspects of genres and styles at the high school level. Conversely, the authors have seen that incorporating writing into the teaching of reading has fostered a critical and more evaluative approach to what has been read. And through this writing-reading integration students have grown in their abilities to clarify, elaborate, and adapt their own ideas, while at the same time learning to profit more substantially from the ideas of others.

On the face of it, it is odd that writing and reading should ever have been separated, either in the classroom or in the world of educational research. Nevertheless, within both those environments they have traditionally been handled as distinct and separable endeavors. It is as if a child's ability to speak had been thought of as totally independent of the ability to listen. For in one sense writing and reading are the written language equivalents of speaking and listening. Literate people are accustomed to using language in all four of these ways—speaking, listening, writing, and reading—whose interdependence, once one stops to think about it, is beyond question.

Although the authors do not make a point of it, I was struck by how often their examples involved classroom *discussion* of writing samples. It is quite apparent that the gains in students' motivations, writing skills, critical attitudes, and abilities to manipulate ideas were promoted to a large extent by these oral discussions, which at the same time added to the social and personal growth of the students by giving them opportunities to articulate their ideas in a sharing, interactive way. Classroom discussion plays such a major role in the examples provided here that the chapter could justifiably be titled "Reading, Writing, Listening, and Speaking, All Working Together."

The specific teaching techniques illustrated here typically involve discussions of students' own work and comparisons of it with the writings of well-known authors. To cite just one example, a well-known technique that seems to combine these ingredients in an especially happy way is the assignment to write about a topic (for example, "the living room was romantic"), then to discuss what various students have done with it, and finally to read what an established writer (in this case F. Scott Fitzgerald) did with the same topic. It is easy to see how the students were more highly motivated to read Fitzgerald and why they completed the assignment with more understanding after writing on the same subject themselves and talking together about what they had produced. One can appreciate how the specific literary devices exploited by the author were more readily assimilated and more critically evaluated after students had themselves been involved in searching for such devices.

If one may extract a general principle from the examples in this chapter, it is that students more easily learn to do something when they have already tried it themselves, when they have seen what kinds of problems arise, and when they have seen how someone more experienced has handled those problems. Not surprisingly, learning in a meaningful context is bound to be more successful than learning in a vacuum.

In the end, that is what is meant by writing and reading working together. Writing profits from being taught against a meaningful background of reading and vice versa. I would only add that both writing and reading become more meaningful still when they are placed in a still larger context of overall language use (a concept to be elaborated upon by the author of chapter 6).

Writing and Reading
Working Together

Robert Tierney, Rebekah Caplan, Linnea Ehri,
Mary K. Healy, and Mary Hurdlow

Over the past several years, the authors of this chapter have spent a
great deal of time working with teachers and students in their efforts
to improve literacy by teaching writing and reading in tandem. Early
in 1986 a conference sponsored by the Center for the Study of Writing
and the Center for the Study of Reading brought us together to plan
a chapter on how writing and reading can be intertwined in the
classroom. The authors agreed that the chapter should be approached
collaboratively. At subsequent meetings and through the mail, each of
the authors shared examples of classroom episodes involving various
combinations of writing and reading activities. Some classroom episodes
were drawn from our own experiences; others were drawn from
colleagues. Together, they allowed us, as a group, to reflect upon the
nature of these activities, especially their benefits.

As we examined classroom episodes in which writing and reading
were working together, we were struck by the extent to which student
learning and development could be enhanced. Repeatedly we were
impressed with these results: (1) the social and personal growth of
students who explored their own work in the context of sharing their
writing and reading with others; (2) the growth in learning as students
integrated what they read with what they knew and would discover
as pen was put to paper; (3) the establishment of a framework in
which students read more critically whether they were reading their
own writing or the writing of others; and (4) improvements in their
reading and writing skills as students explored an author's craft, for
example, the use of letter-sound relationships for spelling or the use
of techniques to invite predictions or create suspense for readers. This
chapter tries to capture these episodes and our consideration of them,
together with research that relates to these efforts.

In the everyday world, writing and reading are naturally intertwined.
A mechanic might jot down marginal notes while studying a manual

or textbook. A journalist might frequently refer to various books while developing an essay. A person might constantly refer to a friend's letter while writing a response. When completing an application form, a prospective employee reads directions and generates written responses. Even when a writer creates a text without appearing to do any reading, he or she is repeatedly reading that text.

What occurs in the everyday world is in sharp contrast with what has been happening in classrooms. In the world of classrooms, writing and reading tend to be kept apart. In their reading programs, teachers sometimes rationalize not giving students writing assignments because they distract from reading. Writing periods are the reverse: teachers often admonish students to clear the desk of any books in case their reading should interfere with their writing. Even in those classrooms purported to represent an integrated approach to teaching writing and reading, the two have often cohabited rather than worked together. Whatever the reason, in many classrooms, it has only been in recent years that teachers have embraced the marriage of writing and reading. (See chapter 2 for a discussion of the history of writing-reading relationships and possible reasons for that history.)

The question we would like to address is: What if writing and reading are working together? We would like to invite you to explore analyses of such marriages. Our analyses are based upon research and classroom examples representing a variety of working relationships in different settings. We begin with primary classrooms.

What If Writing and Reading Are Working Together in the Elementary School?

As far back as 1908, Edmond Huey reported the use of the sentence method, which enlisted students' writing as the basis for learning to read.[1] Since that time, various educators have advocated numerous practices in which writing and reading are interrelated. For example, they have urged integrating writing and reading through the "language experience" approach as well as selected "creative writing" approaches.[2] Support for these approaches often came from the long-standing professional belief in the worth of interrelating the language arts (see chapter 2), as well as from teachers' testimonials about the benefits of doing so. Research support tended to be limited to large-scale survey-like comparisons of methods. Nonetheless, these studies did show that students improved in concept development, word recognition, vocabulary, and comprehension.[3]

More recent analyses of the attitudes, strategies, and understandings of children during their first five years have substantiated these notions and given them further impetus as well as new directions (see, for example, Bissex; Chomsky; Dyson; Ferreiro and Teberosky; Harste, Woodward, and Burke; Read).[4] Writing samples collected from very young children have shown how various writing experiences such as creating notes, stories, signs, and picture captions give children the opportunity to develop, test, reinforce, and extend their understandings about written language. As Harste, Woodward, and Burke stated, writing allows children the opportunity to test their "growing under-standing of storiness, of wordiness, of how one keeps ideas apart in writing, of how the sounds of language are mapped into written letters, of how one was writing to mean and more."[5]

On the basis of their analyses of the writing samples of young children, Carol Chomsky and Charles Read, who introduced us to the notion of "invented spellings," have argued strongly for early writing in conjunction with learning to read.[6] As Chomsky states:

> Children who have been writing [alphabetically] for months are in a very favorable position when they undertake learning to read. They have at their command considerable phonetic infor-mation about English, practice in phonemic segmentation, and experience with alphabetic representation. These are some of the technical abilities that they need to get started. They have, in addition, an expectation of going ahead on their own. They are prepared to make sense of the print by figuring it out or by asking questions. They expect it to make sense, and their purpose is to derive a message from the print, not just to pronounce the words.[7]

The notion that writing supports young readers' efforts "to make sense" has also emerged from the recent widespread advocacy for process-oriented writing experiences. For example, Atwell, Calkins, Giaccobbe, Graves, and Hansen, among others, suggest that students involved in a rich writing curriculum develop a keen sense of authorship and readership.[8] These educators report that children understand why something they are reading was written, as well as what its strengths and weaknesses might be. During discussions about various texts in elementary classrooms where children wrote extensively, Calkins re-corded child-initiated questions such as "[I wonder] why the author chose the lead he did?" and "I wonder if these characters come from the author's life?"[9]

To extend our consideration of these notions, we would like to invite you to explore with us selected teachers' attempts to tie together writing and reading. In a growing number of elementary classrooms, teachers

are exploring the power of creating interrelated writing-reading experiences as vehicles for learning more about topics, as well as to learn
more about how to write and read. Our examples in this section are
drawn from kindergarten through third grade in U.S. settings ranging
from the far West to the Northeast.

Our first illustration suggests that writing-reading experiences can
create opportunities even for very young children to explore ideas
(their own and others') and to develop their writing and reading skills.
In this example a kindergarten teacher in the Midwest shared with
her class a book containing both pictures and text (*The Dead Bird,* by
Margaret Wise Brown and Remy Charlip). She then invited the children
to write their own stories to accompany the pictures in the book
(adapted and photocopied onto a worksheet). The story that Kammi
wrote is presented in Figure 1.[10]

About a week later a classmate read the story and commented on
how she liked it. The teacher overheard Kammi say that she no longer
liked her story because she failed to tell what the people were thinking.
Upon the teacher's invitation, Kammi rewrote her story (Figure 2).

Providing Kammi with the opportunity to develop her own story
allowed her to express herself, re-create another person's story, and
revisit her own story. Kammi was thus able to explore her understanding
of written text—including the structure of a story, the use of dialogue,
sentence form, the relation between pictures and text, and letter-sound
correspondence. Interestingly, across just a single week Kammi's spelling improved. Across the two drafts she included 92 words, of which
52 were different. Among the 20 words in common, 50 percent were
spelled conventionally, 15 percent moved toward conventionality, 15
percent became conventional.

What role did reading play in this child's writing? In Kammi's
classroom, the book shared by the teacher was the stimulus for Kammi's
own story rendition. It provided a source of ideas and a basis for
comparison. In addition, Kammi's reading of her own text and her
classmates' reading and reaction prompted her to reconsider and
subsequently revise that text.

Other classroom episodes provide further glimpses of the relationship
among reading, writing, and student learning. In a second grade
classroom, teacher Mary Hurdlow shared with her students *My Friend
John,* a story by Charlotte Zolotow. One of the excerpts from the story
follows:

> John is my best friend and I'm his. . . .
> We know where the secret places are in each other's house.[11]

Figure 1. Kammi's initial response to *The Dead Bird*.

After hearing the story and being interviewed by a classmate about best friends, six-year-old Jesse wrote:

I like my friend and he likes me.
He knows where my toys are
and I know where his toys are.

Figure 2. Kammi's revised response to *The Dead Bird.* (Illustrations are based on those in *The Dead Bird,* by Margaret Wise Brown and Remy Charlip. Illustrations Copyright © 1958 by Remy Charlip. Used by permission of Harper & Row.)

Here the story and the interview provided a framework by which Jesse could share his own sense of friendship in writing. In echoing the author's style, and assuming what appeared to be his ownership of it, Jesse was learning how his own ideas might be expressed. It was as if he were reading as a writer would—recognizing and then borrowing a turn of phrase, learning how to provide descriptive detail.

In this same classroom the teacher read *Higglety Pigglety Pop!* by Maurice Sendak.[12] In this book, Jennie, the dog heroine, runs away from her comfortable home to become a star in the World Mother Goose Theatre. The teacher shared with the class that Maurice Sendak wrote this book when his own dog Jennie became ill and died. One student, Sarah, asked to read the book during the sustained silent reading period. When it was time to check out a book to take home overnight, she chose *Higglety Pigglety Pop!* The teacher knew one of the reasons for this book's special appeal to Sarah. Having waited several years for a cat of her own, Sarah was suffering greatly because her new kitten, a Christmas present, had recently run away. Sarah seemed to find comfort in Sendak's melancholy but humorous tale of a beloved pet's adventure after running away from home.

On Thursday of the same week, Sarah sat in front of the class to read to her teacher and classmates her recently completed book entitled "The Cat That Ran Away." In Sendak's book, Jennie writes to her old master, "I am even a star." Sarah writes about her cat, "He met a family that made him a star." Sarah's text and, for ease of reading, her teacher's conventionalized version are presented in Figure 3.

In this same classroom a different adult author was featured each month. In October Arnold Lobel was "author of the month." The teacher read his books daily to the class, and the Frog and Toad stories were immediate favorites. The simple, straightforward sentences describing the very human adventures of Frog and Toad seemed to attract the second graders. Randa, a second grader, wrote her own book, "Frog and Toad at San Francisco," and read it to the class. The following is her complete story, retaining her invented spellings and punctuation.

> One day Frog and toad were sitting at home. they were thinking of sump thing to Do toDay when all of the Suden Frog sed lets go for a walk . . . no sed toad weve all rety Don tht. Let's go to Safranciscoff! Ya! sed Forg Lets go! So they got there good shoos and coat and hat then they went outide. So Frog and toad walkedto SanFrancisco. When they got to SanFrancisco they rode the Cabelcar up the hill. an then it stopd. when itstoped they got off and then they Bote some stickers and pensels and then they got back on the cabelcar. and then they went to petzza for lunch. and then they went back home. When they got home they sed good by and frog left. The End

Following the reading, the class told Randa specifically what they liked about her book. Then they asked her questions. Allen asked her

The Cat That Ran Away

written and illustrated by Sarah
dedicated to my dear family

One fine day on an early spring morning a cat called Spot
ran away. For one month or two or three the owner of the cat was
very unhappy. She was crying.
Meanwhile about the cat. Well he ran all of the way to
Hollywood. When he got there he was tired. He met a family that
made him a star. His first movie was Super Cat. His second
movie was The Ewok Cat. Then his owner came to Hollywood for a
vacation. She saw her cat playing Super Cat. She said in her
mind, "That looks like my cat." When it was over she went to
visit him. When she did she told his X-owner that it was her
cat. The X-owner said, "Oh well, here's your cat back." After
that she was happy.

Figure 3. Sarah's story ("The Cat That Ran Away"), followed by the teacher's
conventionalized version.

where she got the idea for the book. Randa replied, "From Arnold Lobel, of course. And when I went to San Francisco I rode the cable cars, ate pizza for lunch, and bought stickers and pencils, so I thought it would be fun to make Frog and Toad do that too."

As this example demonstrates, sometimes the books written by students are a direct reflection of the books they have read or listened to. Sometimes a single book will be the impetus for a student's story. Sometimes students synthesize ideas and characters from two or more books when they write their own. The following are some titles of books authored by the students in this class. Their titles are followed, in parenthesis, by titles and authors of the books that inspired them.

> Garfield Meats Frog and Toad (The Garfield cartoon books and Arnold Lobel's Frog and Toad books).
>
> Commander Hurdlow and the Planet of the Kids! (*Commander Toad and the Planet of the Grapes* by Jane Yolen).
>
> The Trumpet of the Bears (*The Trumpet of the Swan* by E.B. White and various books about bears).
>
> Arthur's Teeth (*Arthur's Eyes* by Marc Brown).
>
> Not Again Pinkerton! (*Pinkerton Behave* by Steven Kellogg).[13]

Students' relationship with authors is developed in a number of ways when writing and reading are interrelated. Class discussions might center on who wrote a story and why. After discussing Arnold Lobel's work, some of the students in Hurdlow's class wanted to write to the author. Diane, for example, wrote:

> I have two of your books and I am going to get a new one and then I will have all of them. It is the book of *Frog and Toad All Year.* What is the book you are working on now? I like how you draw your pictures. How did you get the idea of putting a frog in the book? I feel sorry for you because you were sick for along time when you were little. [The class had seen a filmstrip about Arnold Lobel, mentioning his illness.] I like the way you right your words.

Kelly wrote:

> Dear Arnold, I like your book *Frog and Toad are Friends.* What kind of book are you doing now? I like to write books to. I like your books they are the best! I hope you are writing a book right now!

The types of outcomes that emerged in Hurdlow's classroom are not exceptional. Indeed, in other classrooms where writing and reading are interrelated, similar developments occur. Furthermore, students who are involved in such experiences for several years can become quite sophisticated readers and writers. For example, in a third grade classroom, teacher Marilyn Boutwell worked with a number of students who had had rich experiences with writing since first grade. In addition to maintaining those experiences, she focused upon relating the writing and reading.

On a semiformal basis, Boutwell encouraged her students to compare their writing with their reading. She found that they not only used ideas from stories they had read, but also used techniques they had noticed. Melissa, for example, developed a character called Natasha in conjunction with her book, "Natasha Koren and Her Runaway Imagination." Her story was rich with descriptive language and powerful dialogue; it even included a preface to introduce her readers to the story and a moral to ensure they understood her point. Melissa was asked about the source of her ideas and techniques:

> *Interviewer:* I noticed at the beginning of chapter 5 [you wrote] "meanwhile at home." How did you know how to do that?
>
> *Melissa:* I have seen it in other books.
>
> *Interviewer:* What are some of the other things that you use?
>
> *Melissa:* Words and dedications, dialogue, ways to show people that you are going back to something else.

In a class discussion of how writers revealed their characters to readers, Melissa's third grade classmates compared her character development in "Natasha Koren and Her Runaway Imagination" with Robert Peck's in *Soup*.[14] They discussed how Melissa used dialogue and events to reveal her character. In turn, they used Melissa's and Peck's techniques and those of other classmates as a basis for their own attempts to reveal their characters to their readers. There is no reason that students' own stories cannot serve the same functions as texts written by professional authors. Indeed, students will sometimes be more apt to experiment with their classmates' ideas and techniques than with those of professional authors.

Writing and reading may also work together on a less formal basis. Sometimes reading a note from the teacher or another student prompts students to write. Melissa wrote to her teacher about her enjoyment of a classmate's story. She discussed how the author makes the characters "so alive." In response, her teacher shared aspects of her own reading experience and suggested that Melissa might compliment her classmate for his story. In Hurdlow's first grade, Courtney wrote his friend Bobby's name twice, once across the "tummy" of a drawing of Bobby. The teacher wrote, "What do you and Bobby do?" Courtney responded, in the first written sentence of his school life, "Me and Bob make cars, by Courtney."

In the same class, the teacher wrote a note to Ryan, asking, "Will you play Little League this year?" Ryan responded, "I'm going to play Pee Wee Baseball. I played last year my friend was there." And when Karl wrote, "Spot is a nice dog. A dog nice enough for me," the teacher replied, "Do you like dogs better than cats?" Karl wrote back, "Yes I do like dogs better than cats. I don't know why, I just do like them better."

To return to our initial question: What if writing and reading are working together in primary classrooms? Our examples illustrate that writing and reading can work together in primary classrooms, and when they do, certain learning outcomes are supported.

First, our examples suggest that when writing and reading work together certain skills are enhanced. For instance, in Hurdlow's class writing and reading contributed to an understanding of sound-symbol correspondence. By being given opportunities to write, students were able to explore and test their knowledge of this correspondence. More specifically, writing draws learners' attention to sounds in words and to letters that might symbolize those sounds. Students may thus form expectations about how spellings might be structured and become more interested in specific spellings as well as in how the spelling system works as a whole. Reading exposes learners to the conventional spellings of words and declares which of the various possibilities are "correct." Reading provides the input learners need to store the correct spellings of specific words in memory and also to figure out how the general system works. Thus reading directs writing toward more conventional forms, and writing enhances readers' interest in and grasp of the alphabetic structure of print.

Consider the changes that occurred in the spelling patterns of a child in Hurdlow's class. Over a two-year period from the beginning of first grade to the end of second grade, Hurdlow dictated a twenty-word spelling test to her students five times. These words were never taught directly to the students. The spellings of one child who was an average reader-speller are reproduced in Table 1; correct spellings are italicized. At the time of the first test, this child was able to read only a few words presented in isolation. At the time of the final test, he was reading words at grade level. The number of correctly spelled words increased from the first to the fifth test, slowly at first and then dramatically at the end: 0, 1, 1, 6, and 16 words, respectively. One feature of the spellings is especially noteworthy. Although few words were spelled correctly during the first three tests, the *quality* of the spellings changed markedly, from forms that bore little resemblance to the words to forms that symbolized a number of sounds in the words. Many teachers are reluctant to adopt a reading-writing program like Hurdlow's because of children's spelling difficulty. We have therefore elaborated on the connection between learning to read and learning to spell in an appendix to this chapter.

In addition to supporting students' understanding of our spelling system, writing and reading have an impact upon students' understanding of genre and stylistics. In Boutwell's class, students began to understand and experiment with dialogue, descriptive techniques, and transitions. Boutwell's experiences are consistent with the findings of Barbara Eckhoff, who compared the written texts of two groups of first graders after they were exposed to very different writing styles

Table 1

One Student's Responses to Spelling Test Administered in First and Second Grade

Test words	Test number (grade level)				
	1 (1.3)	2 (1.6)	3 (1.9)	4 (2.3)	5 (2.8)
rag	1	RG	*rag*	*rag*	*rag*
buzz	BP	BZ	Boz	buz	*buzz*
lid	E	LD	lad	*lid*	*lid*
six	6	SS	sis	siks	*six*
game		GEM	gam	gars	*game*
nice	SAT	Nis	nis	nis	*nice*
doctor	DA	DOD	did	doktdr	*doctor*
view	Y	vyou	vo	vu	*view*
yellow		yellw	yao	*yellow*	*yellow*
kiss	C	kits	kis	*kiss*	kis
camp	MP	CAP	cap	kap	*camp*
zero	O	ZW	zio	ziro	*zero*
hill		*Hill*	ole	hil	*hill*
tack	P	TAK	tac	tac	*tack*
five	5	FAV	fi	*five*	*five*
pickle	PO	PL	pal	pikl	pikel
muffin	KO	MN	mufn	mufin	muffen
wife	1	yuf	wif	wif	*wife*
job		JB	jig	*job*	*job*
quick	Ka	KWK	cwy	kwic	quice

Note: Correct spellings are in italics.

in their basal reading programs.[15] One of the basals tended to include short and choppy sentences characteristic of controlled vocabulary and sentence length; the other basal was written in a more natural style. The students assigned to the former basal tended to write using a similar pattern of short and simple sentences; the students assigned to the latter basal wrote more complex sentences after the style of those materials. When the students were encouraged to compare their style with the style of others, they appeared willing not only to adopt but also to experiment with various stylistic techniques.

A second outcome of writing and reading working together is the enhancement of motivation. Kammi, the kindergartner described earlier, revised her text after her classmate read and responded to it. In Hurdlow's class, students were motivated to initiate letters to the teacher and to authors. Moreover, they continued writing and reading outside of school. In Boutwell's class, motivation to learn was apparent in some of the students' comments. One explained:

> I like to challenge myself. I do a report that I don't know a lot about and then do research on it, and if I am doing a story and I don't know what to write, I just conference with others to get ideas. After writing about what I've read I can go back and see what I've learned.

In response to the hypothetical situation of being stranded on an island without books, television, or radio, another student replied: "I would be fine. I would find a stick and write in the sand."

Third, many of our examples illustrate how writing and reading can work together to enhance the clarification, elaboration, and adaptation of ideas. Kammi, the kindergartner, redeveloped her text to incorporate what the children in her story were thinking. In Hurdlow's class, we saw evidence of students taking events and characters from stories written by peers and professional authors and placing them in their own. As Hurdlow pointed out, "Students would synthesize ideas and characters from two or more books." She described how one student took several books about bears, together with E.B. White's *The Trumpet of the Swan*, to write "The Trumpet of the Bears." The students in Boutwell's class displayed similar tendencies, as when Melissa explained the origins of her book, "Natasha Koren and Her Runaway Imagination":

> Well, I read this other book and it was about this girl's imagination but I just thought about that book and I thought it would be a good title . . . to have a runaway imagination. . . . It [the other book] wasn't the same . . . she looks at pictures and stuff and imagines they are moving and stuff like that.

Her own book is about a girl who leaves home because she is upset with her brother. The girl's imagination carries her into strange and wondrous experiences.

Fourth, the classroom examples suggest that writing and reading can work together to help students appreciate authorship and readership, as well as to read critically one's own writing and the writing of others. In both Hurdlow's first grade class and Boutwell's third grade, the students had a clear sense of who wrote what and of where the ideas may have come from, and they could often offer some reasons that the book they were reading was written. Likewise, students, especially in Boutwell's class, had a sense of how others might react to what they had written and were often able to use these understandings to refine their craft. For example, one of Boutwell's students offered these comments about a piece he was writing:

> Well, on the second page it says "Brad Wilson was walking down a dirt road" and they [the readers] have a dirt road in their mind, but when they say "which is really a mud road because of a good day's rain," they have a clue and they keep it in their heads.

What If Writing and Reading Are Working Together in the Secondary School?

Data from the National Assessment of Educational Progress paint a bleak picture of our high school students' writing and reading activities.[16] Most high school students are relatively incapable of writing an effective persuasive essay, responding critically to essays written by others, or generating an analytical response to what they have read. For those familiar with classroom observations of writing and reading in schools, these data are not surprising. Past surveys of teaching practices suggest that students have not often been expected to write extensively.[17] Furthermore, even in those classrooms where students have been expected to do a lot of writing and reading, their writing has rarely served to critically examine or extend their reading. In essence, writing was often viewed as an activity that detracted from reading; reading was viewed as an activity that confounded writing.

In recent years a number of educators have proposed a marriage between writing and reading as a partial solution to the problem in high schools. As has been stated in national reports on education:

> It cannot be emphasized too strongly that reading is one of the language arts. . . . Writing activities in particular should be integrated into the reading period.[18]

Reading and writing hold strong positions in American school life today. But our task force concurs that the two have been kept apart, with both losing strength.[19]

The question we would like to explore next is: What if there is a marriage between writing and reading in high school classrooms? To explore this question, we reviewed the research on integrating writing and reading with high school and college students and also took several examples from high school classrooms as a basis for elaborating upon some of these issues. First, we present examples from two English classrooms, together with research pertaining to the role of writing and reading in teaching literature. One of our examples is from an advanced high school English classroom in California. The writing-reading activities there represent attempts to heighten students' sensitivity to what they read and what they write by making them aware of variations in style, elements of plot, and their own ideas. The other example is drawn from an English class in an inner-city middle school in the Midwest. This example illustrates how writing and reading might work together to enhance critical thinking, especially understanding of theme, as well as selected writing and reading skills. Second, we present selected examples from several content area classrooms—a history, a biology, and a science classroom—together with research in writing and reading in content areas.

Writing and Reading in English Classrooms?*

In most high schools, literature serves as the cornerstone of the English program. Short stories, novels, and poems are used as the basis for exploring various issues and themes, as well as for developing literacy skills. Our examples of classroom practice demonstrate the potential power of students writing as well as reading literature. Writing and reading in tandem gives the students a chance to engage with literature, to develop as authors, and to compare their own efforts with the work of their peers and professional authors.

In her advanced high school English classroom, teacher Rebekah Caplan uses writing activities to ensure student engagement with their reading, and in turn she uses their reading to empower their writing development. She feels that, prompted to visually substantiate their own thoughts, her students become actively involved as participants in, as well as observers of, their own craft of meaning-making. Having

---

* Parts of this section appeared in *Writers in Training*, by Rebekah Caplan, published in 1984 by Dale Seymour Publications, Palo Alto, California. We are grateful to the publisher for allowing Rebekah Caplan to use some of her original work, in slightly altered form, in this new publication.

to invent their own vision, students are more likely to take an interest in seeing how others, including professional writers, create similar moods, plots, characters, and settings.

Caplan often asks her students to write in preparation for reading. For example, they might expand a scenario such as "the living room was romantic." During a brief discussion, students may evaluate the vividness of each other's examples. One student, Sylvia, read her response to the class:

The Living Room Was Romantic

by

Sylvia

She patiently waited for the arrival of her boyfriend. It was their six month anniversary and she had so carefully planned the evening and menu. There was fresh-fallen snow three feet deep outside the glass doors, and the moon gave a glistening glow into the room. The crackling, burning fire in the fire-place gave the room a soothing warmth as it flickered almost simultaneously with the candlelight. Chilled champagne rested impatiently in the ice bucket which sat in the shadow of the vase of red roses. The soft, flowing sound of Air Supply drifted from the high-tech stereo and the bear skin rug seemed almost to smile from the pleasant music. The doorbell rings. It was sure to be a memorable night.

The class appreciated the many details that filled Sylvia's description: snow outside contrasting with the warmth from within; moonlight to provide an inner glow to the room; candlelight, champagne, roses, a bearskin rug as typical romantic touches. They especially enjoyed her use of the popular group Air Supply and of the word "high-tech." They considered these details especially helpful in making the scene more contemporary and less traditional. They appreciated that a living room could be romantic with modern influences as well as the old standbys of candlelight, champagne, and roses.

Roger shared his scenario:

The Living Room Was Romantic

by

Roger

The sun, rising over the lake, created a rosy glow in the living room as it shone through the window, and the unseasoned wood in the fire gave the room a musky smell as Christy sat down on the couch. She snuggled closer to her husband, that word was going to take some getting used to, and took a sip of coffee. A honeymoon to her family's cabin in the Sierras was a wonderful idea, and now as she fell deeper into the cushions of the couch and her daydreams she could hear the ticking of the cuckoo clock on the wall, her grandfather's gift to her mother and father on their wedding day. So many memories, so much of a future.

The class liked Roger's phrase "that word was going to take some getting used to" in reference to the word "husband." They thought Roger clever in the way he wove in that comment, showing the shyness of the recent bride. They also thought the cuckoo clock had a nice original touch; they enjoyed the idea of tradition being passed from one generation to another—tradition, they said, is usually romantic.

Finally, Julia shared her scenario:

The Living Room Was Romantic

by

Julia

Margarite gasped as she entered the room Tony had told her to wait in. Stravinsky floated through the air and a hissing sound emerged from the brilliant fire of orange and red in the fireplace that threw light on the dark blue walls of which were dotted with Renoirs and Monets. A matching love seat of the same blue stood not far from the fire and a chilled bottle of champagne waited near by. Valentino could have done no better.

The class thought Julia's version "the most sophisticated." Some students questioned who Stravinsky, Renoir, Monet, and Valentino were, but they knew enough to understand they were famous artists. If someone could afford Renoir and Monet originals and have a decor similar to Valentino's, he must have a great deal of money. In this version of a romantic living room, then, the expensiveness and elegance of the surroundings contributed to the romantic vision.

The students were then introduced to an excerpt from F. Scott Fitzgerald's book *The Great Gatsby*, describing the same scenario:

We walked through a high hallway into a bright rosy-colored space, fragilely bound into the house by French windows at either end. The windows were ajar and gleaming white against the fresh grass outside that seemed to grow a little way into the house. A breeze blew through the room, blew curtains in at one end and out the other like pale flags, twisting them up toward the frosted wedding-cake of the ceiling, and then rippled over the wine-colored rug, making a shadow on it as wind does on the sea.

The only completely stationary object in the room was an enormous couch on which two young women were buoyed up as though upon an anchored balloon. They were both in white, and their dresses were rippling and fluttering as if they had just been blown back in after a short flight around the house. I must have stood for a few minutes listening to the whip and snap of the curtains and the groan of a picture on the wall. Then there was a boom as Tom Buchanan shut the rear windows and the caught wind died out about the room, and the curtains and the rugs and the two young women ballooned slowly to the floor.[20]

Caplan assures us that such comparisons are not intended to suggest that Fitzgerald's version is better than the students' or that the students should be writing as Fitzgerald did in order to be successful writers. Rather, the exercise is meant to help students notice alternatives, to perhaps come to realize that a romantic setting can be achieved beyond the traditional uses of champagne, candlelight (or firelight), roses, and sentimental music, and can be created in ways they might not have considered.

Indeed, when looking back to their own versions of the romantic living room, some students preferred their own writing to Fitzgerald's. They felt their descriptions were more "direct" and not clouded in "difficult metaphors which were hard to understand." On the other hand, many students were favorably impressed with Fitzgerald's talent. When they looked back to their own writings, they suggested that candlelight, champagne, and roses seemed mundane by comparison.

At times the discussion centered upon what makes particular writing styles appealing or unappealing and at other times upon specific images. For example, some students admired how Fitzgerald captured the exquisiteness of the room through imagery. They liked the way the breeze "ripples over the wine-colored rug, making a shadow on it as wind does on the sea." The students remarked that the rug comparison gave the reader the impression of a rug so thick and luxurious, a rug so deeply piled, it moved in waves as the wind moved over it. Also, "wine-colored rug" was quite different from, let's say, a "maroon-colored" rug. A "wine-colored rug" was also a more "original" way to weave in the old "champagne" cliché.

Some students offered the phrase "curtains twisting up toward the frosted wedding-cake of the ceiling" as an appealing line; but others protested, complaining they did not understand what the phrase meant. However, one student who understood it commented that the frosted wedding-cake reminded him of the ornate "sculptings" of fancy, palatial ceilings. His insight thus became a learning experience for those who did not understand. When asked why the writer chose "wedding-cake" as the term for comparison, the students said that a wedding-cake is frosted, is "sculpted" in a way similar to the ceiling with all the little swirls of decoration. Also "wedding-cake" itself implied a kind of romantic vision of perfection—the courtship culminating on the marriage day; and so the house's image became the "dream" house, the ideal form. Students saw the use of "wedding-cake of the ceiling" as more subtle than "two lovers on a loveseat" as in previous student versions.

Sometimes in the course of dealing with a novel Caplan will pursue an even closer examination of a writer's style. For example, to sensitize students to the subtleness of Fitzgerald's style, she had them develop parallel versions of excerpts from *The Great Gatsby* and then discuss them. The following student text parallels the Gatsby excerpt presented above:

> I ran along the dirt path through short scratchy weeds, fiercely grabbing at my legs around bare ankles on both sides. My shoes were new and sparkling clean on the dry dirt below that swirled to form a miniature cyclone of a cloud. A breeze blew through my hair, flung strands across one eye and then the other like a tattered blindfold, tangling it into the hideous snarl of a labyrinth, and then flowed down the back of my neck, creating a coolness on my skin as an oasis does in the desert.
>
> The only really recognizable sound in my ears was my beating heart that quite painfully knocked against my ribs as if it were a caged bird. It was in my throat, and its presence was frightening and weakening as though it was just about to explode at any minute if it continued work so hard. I must have run for a few minutes listening to the whimper and roar of my breathing and the pounding of my shoes on the path. Then there was a cheer as I neared the finish line and some last energy propelled me towards the crowd, and my heart and my breathing and the heat mattered not at all.

In Caplan's experience, when students parallel and later evaluate the distinguishing styles of major authors, not only may they come to appreciate the talent and craft of the writer, they may also learn new rhetorical devices for delivering ideas. They may consider the varying impact of different sentence lengths, of descriptive and nondescriptive language, of direct and indirect narrators. In short, they may learn to tell their stories in new and different voices.

At the same time, Caplan claims that students may acquire a feel for a writer that enables them to appreciate how style contributes to the story. Once they are attuned to an author's style, they may spontaneously comment on his or her use of certain techniques. For example, having emulated Fitzgerald's move from idealism to reality, many students were quick to identify other Fitzgerald paragraphs that repeated this tendency.

Sometimes Caplan will pursue goals that are less directed toward preparing the students for dealing with an author's stylistic idiosyncrasies and more centered upon having students pull together their own ideas. For example, when the students had read *The Great Gatsby* in its entirety, they were asked to compare Jay Gatsby's quest for Daisy Buchanan to the quest for the American dream. Here is an excerpt from one student's response:

Two Dreams

by

Anne

When the founders of this country came to the new world, they were looking for a fresh start. They were looking for the fulfillment of a dream; searching for a place where they could start a new life and shape a better future. Their ideals were high, and they were spiritually enriched by the promise that this new land, America, seemed to hold for them. Gatsby, too, is like these early explorers. Just as the "green beast of the new world" promised new hope for the explorers, so does the "single green light, minute and far away" promise to Gatsby that he may obtain his dream.

So Gatsby's dream to win the love of his fantasy girl, starts out fresh and pure like the dream of the new explorers. However, Gatsby becomes enamored with the idea that the money will win her love, and from this point on, his dreams will begin to decay and eventually crumble. . . .

In these views, Gatsby is demonstrating the characteristics of the American dream. Obsessed with materialism, Americans now believe money can buy love, happiness, and can forever capture youth and beauty. . . .

Ironically, Gatsby's obsession with materialism eventually destroys him. His car, "a rich cream color, bright with nickel, and swollen here and there in its monstrous length with hat-boxes and supper-boxes," is the ultimate American status symbol of money and affluence. It eventually causes his death. . . .

This parallels the moral decay and destruction of American society because of the obsession with money. . . .

In writing this novel, F. Scott Fitzgerald chose Gatsby to symbolize the American experience. Gatsby's dream, starting out as a spiritual quest, "the following of a Grail," and its subsequent corruption, is the personification of the course of the American dream. Fitzgerald wishes to show to us the decline of America, from the fresh "green beast of the new world," to, because of gross materialism, nothing more than a "valley of Ashes."

In this essay Anne explains, first, the similarity between both dreams. Both begin as a search for a better life—Gatsby will be happier with Daisy; Americans crave comfort and security. "Just as the 'green beast of the new world' promised new hope for the explorers, so does the 'single green light, minute and far away' promise to Gatsby that he may obtain his dream [winning Daisy]." Next, in separate paragraphs she details the course of each dream. Gatsby thinks he needs money to impress Daisy, so he becomes obsessed with getting enough to win her approval. Similarly, Americans think money will buy them the happiness and security they long for.

In an additional set of paragraphs, this student interprets the consequences of each obsession. For Gatsby, money had indirectly caused the death of Myrtle and George Wilson as well as his own, symbolizing the destructive powers of materialism. For Americans, Anne said, dependence on money for happiness had indirectly allowed "spiritual goals and morals [to] disintegrate in the race to 'keep up with the Joneses.' " Finally, Anne integrates these likenesses, suggesting how a personal vision might be derived from a larger, collective one— that the corruption of one man's dream is the corruption of all.

As each of the examples from this class illustrates, Caplan believes that a marriage between writing and reading sets a number of powerful forces into motion. She feels that these activities are conscious attempts to join one process to another—the writing assignments (to facilitate increased understanding of text, as in a critical essay in response to a controversial article, analysis and imitation of presented prose models, peer reading, evaluation, and response to each others' writing) and students' analysis of their own writing. The fact that Caplan does not leave this to chance is well documented by these classroom episodes.

In Columbus, Ohio, middle school and high school teachers have developed a variety of writing-reading activities for use in conjunction with the literature program. Their goal was to tie writing and reading strategies together to enhance writing, reading, and critical thinking abilities. In a cycle of writing and reading activities, the exploration of themes from literature (for example, fear and courage) are tied in with a study of an author's craft (for example, character development and plot). Writing activities are intended to prompt students to share their own experiences that are relevant to certain themes and to explore how those themes are crafted by authors. By reading one another's texts along with those of professional authors, students can compare experiences and examine the techniques used to present those experiences. Examining the techniques might involve studying the author's use of plot, setting, character development, and language.

One set of activities involved Edgar Allan Poe's short story "The Tell-Tale Heart."[21] This story served as the cornerstone for exploring the theme "irritation" and how an author's choice of words can enhance an understanding of a character's actions. Students first discussed various people and circumstances that aroused feelings of irritation. They were then asked to write a description of these irritating circumstances, capturing the flavor of their response. Students next discussed how they might convey to readers the intensity of their reaction. They commented on the need to choose words that relay the irritation. Then, after writing for five minutes or so, some students shared their developing text, and the class discussed their reactions and the techniques the author used.

One student, Jerome, shared his irritation with his brother's early morning regimen:

> Every morning at 6:30 sharp, he rises. At 6:35 he has a shower, 6:45 he dresses and at 7:00 he eats breakfast. He finishes breakfast at 7:10, brushes his teeth at 7:12, grabs his books and leaves at 7:18.

The class commented that they could appreciate Jerome's irritation and felt that his description captured the tedium of the regimen. They all felt that mentioning specific times made the point well.

Another student, Debbie, described her irritation with a shop clerk:

> I wasn't stealing it. I was just showing my girlfriend. This can't be happening. I could have guessed it would. That lady had had it in for me from the moment I entered the store.

Debbie's text grabbed her classmates' attention immediately. They wanted to know more, especially about the lady and what happened. They liked Debbie's choice of topics and especially her statement "had it in for me."

After two more students shared their texts, the teacher asked the class to read and discuss "The Tell-Tale Heart." The students read silently and, once finished, spontaneously shared how much they enjoyed the story and admired Poe's craft. When directed to discuss how Poe gave the reader an appreciation for the irritation being felt, they readily generated examples of descriptive language. However, while they did like Poe's story, some students preferred their own, claiming they were "more realistic." Finally, on returning to their own texts, most students revised them, using more descriptive language to illuminate their irritation. For example, Jerome added information about how neat and tidy his brother tended to be and about how his brother "fuzzed at his [Jerome's] easy-going, slothful habits." Debbie gave a detailed description of the "cold eyes of the lady who scrutinized her every step."

The Columbus teachers have commented that writing and reading together create a cycle. The writing sparks the students' desire to read and the reading empowers the students' writing. Furthermore, the teachers suggested that even the reluctant students became more interested in what they were asked to write and read. The students generally seemed more engaged with what they were doing. In addition, their engagement involved reflection, self-assessment, and interaction among self, the text they had read, and the one they were writing. As one Columbus student stated when asked about how writing influenced reading and reading influenced writing:

> I think that writing a rough draft helped me to have a better understanding of the story. As soon as I started reading the story, I could see how it related to the topic I was writing about. I had a better understanding of the story because I was familiar with the theme of the story before I started reading it. Also, I feel that I was more interested in the story because I could relate to the characters better. Reading the short story helped me get some ideas on how to improve my rough draft. Writing my first rough draft was kind of difficult because I didn't have any of my ideas organized. After I finished reading the short story I felt more confident with my writing. My second draft was much easier to write because reading the other story helped me to better understand my topic. While I was revising, I also found that it was easier for me to spot my mistakes in my writing because I could compare it with the short story to see if I was doing anything wrong.

In Caplan's literature class, similar outcomes were apparent. Writing and reading motivated discussions among students about their own work. Comparing their work with that of professional authors also prompted energetic discussions. As one student commented:

> I don't see reading and writing as work but as fun. It's a way of growing, expanding oneself through voicing one's thoughts [writing] and listening to others' thoughts [reading].

The experiences of Caplan and the teachers in Columbus are not extraordinary. There are many testimonials regarding the power of writing to ignite students' engagement with and reflection about literature. In addition, when the effects of writing and reading have been examined in formal research studies, similar outcomes have emerged: understandings are enhanced; meaning-making skills and an appreciation of an author's craft are heightened; and attitudes and approaches to learning are improved.

Consider the following studies. Salvatori used a thoughtfully developed sequence of reading, writing, and discussion activities to demonstrate that students' approach to exploring personal experiences and to reading assignments changed from one that was passive to one that was actively questioning and evaluative.[22] Colvin-Murphy compared how reading comprehension is affected by extended writing activities, by worksheet activities, and by reading alone. She found that students who wrote remembered more, were more engaged in thinking about what they were reading, and were more sensitive to the author's craft.[23] McGinley, and Denner and McGinley explored the use of writing as a prereading activity. Compared with students not engaged in a prereading activity or engaged in a prereading activity with no writing, the students in the writing group recalled more; further, they seemed more engaged in the story itself.[24]

Marshall examined the effects of using different types of writing experiences in conjunction with doing a unit on J.D. Salinger.[25] During the unit, students read Salinger's short stories with no teacher-sponsored discussion and wrote in one of three modes: (1) restricted writing—stated but did not elaborate upon their descriptions, interpretations, and generalizations about a story; (2) personal writing—explained and elaborated upon their individual responses to the story, drawing on their own values and previous experiences; and (3) formal writing—interpreted the story in extended fashion, drawing inferences mainly from the text alone. Marshall found that, compared with restricted writing, formal and personal writing gave students a substantial advantage in understanding Salinger's stories and his craft and in how they approached the text.

Some researchers have examined writing and reading as ways of enhancing students' understanding of certain features of literature. For example, in a series of experiments Bereiter and Scardamalia investigated the knowledge gained by students from exposure to single examples of literary types (suspense fiction, restaurant review, and an invented fictional genre defined as "concrete fiction").[26] In one experiment, some students were explicitly taught features of the genres, while others simply read and wrote in those genres. In another experiment, students read an example of a genre type (concrete fiction), wrote their own rendition, and then indicated what they deemed to be the features of that literary type. Across all experiments, writing in conjunction with reading a single text proved to be a powerful vehicle for learning. Students demonstrated that they had not only acquired a sense of the genres' features, but had also developed a sense of possible variations of the genres.

In summary, our classroom episodes suggest—and research confirms—that when writing and reading are used to explore topics in literature, a number of benefits accrue: understandings are enhanced; meaning-making skills and appreciation of an author's craft are heightened; and attitudes and approaches to learning are improved. The question that we next address is: How generalizable are these findings to other fields of study?

Writing and Reading in Content Area Classrooms

In the 1970s many of us were very excited by the publication of *The Foxfire Books*, which represented the research of high school students from Appalachia.[27] The books were filled with a rich assortment of folklore, historical facts, and advice. The content was interesting, but what was most impressive was that the books had been developed by students considered reluctant readers and writers. *The Foxfire Books* represented students' writing and reading "real" texts about "real-world" experiences. At the same time, the books served as a stimulus for learning. As students explored their research questions, they fine-tuned their problem-solving skills and became immersed in local history and crafts.

Two essential purposes drove the development of *The Foxfire Books*: (1) learning in the content areas and (2) developing communication tools. By learning in the content areas, we mean exploring various issues and topics in different fields of study, as well as acquiring the necessary problem-solving skills for continuing to do so on one's own initiative. For example, in history we want students to explore various historical concerns while developing research skills. In science we want them to understand key concepts and the procedures of scientific inquiry. By communication tools, we mean the ability to enlist writing, reading, speaking, and listening skills as tools for learning. For example, scientists pursuing answers to questions interact with others through written communication and through face-to-face or telephone conversations. Business persons pursuing investment opportunities and sales are involved in an assortment of interactions with others through memos, face-to-face or telephone conversations. Business persons pursuing investment opportunities and sales are involved in an assortment of interactions with others through memos, face-to-face conversations, and other forms of communication. With learning and communication as goals, then, writing and reading in the content areas emerge as more than tools to evaluate and maintain records. Instead, they become vehicles to explore issues, solve problems, interact with others, and discover new questions. The flavor of this sentiment was captured by a recent panel of United States educators commenting on a biologist's use of writing and reading:

> A learner is only a partial biologist, for instance, if he cannot read or write to discover information and meaning in biology. When a student takes the results of his or her observations about lobsters, reads, writes a draft, talks, reads, then writes again, he or she learns what it is to think critically.[28]

Unfortunately, observations of content area teaching suggest that the use of writing and reading for these purposes is more the exception than the rule. Most teachers require students to complete reading assignments in content area textbooks and to respond with a word or two to predetermined questions, but not much more. In the following section, we would like to examine some exceptions.

In Caplan's high school class, students often used explorations of literature as a basis for writing and reading on topics in the sciences. For example, some of her students were being introduced to investigative reporting. They chose various topics to research using field notes, interviews, and other research techniques. En route to doing their own final reports, the students were asked to examine the reporting style in books such as Tom Wolfe's *The Right Stuff* to watch how he artfully weaves together interviews, on-site investigations, and outside research.[29] Here is one student's, Wendy's, analysis of some passages she selected from the book:

> One passage I found memorable was near the end, when Yeager is flying the NF-104 and he goes up to tip downwards because of aerodynamic pressure. He, Tom Wolfe, writes the passage in sentences linked together with three dots, "He's weightless, coming over the top of the arc . . . 104,000 feet . . . It's absolutely silent . . . Twenty miles up . . ." He does this to show how Chuck Yeager is thinking. He's in space and millions of things are going through his mind and Tom Wolfe lets one get the feel of it by having these bits and pieces of thought flying around between three dots, like Chuck in space. Chuck is probably hyped up now and his adrenaline is pumping and he's thinking in fragments, Tom Wolfe shows this. My report is taking the driving test, and this strategy may be useful to me. I'll be driving for another stranger who will be grading me and I'll probably be mega-nervous and things will probably run through my head like Chuck Yeager's. My adrenaline will be pumping a mile a minute and I'll think in fragments and use Tom Wolfe's technique. For example, "the blinker's off . . . the light is green . . . the car ahead of me is moving . . . press the gas pedal . . . not too fast . . . not too slow . . ." I think that it will show how I'm thinking at that moment, in bits and fragments. It will show what happens in my driving test without repetitiously using "I", eg., "I saw the green light. I saw the car ahead of me move. I pressed the gas pedal. I made sure I didn't speed, or go too slow." It breaks the monotony of starting all the sentences with "I."
>
> The other passage I found memorable is when Pete Conrad is having his barium examination by the radiologist and after he's done he has to walk to a john two floors below the one he is presently on and he had to hold the balloon, which keeps the barium in place, and he has to hunch over and walk "with his

tail in the breeze" (p. 76) in a public corridor. Tom Wolfe has interviewed Pete Conrad but he doesn't describe it like an interview, he writes it out as if he could see Pete Conrad then. He doesn't write "and Pete Conrad said, "My tail was in the breeze," as he walked down the corridor. He incorporates it into the third person form and shows what Pete Conrad has told him, without using direct quotes, and quotation marks. I think this will come in handy for me when I interview people and they tell me how their driving tests went. For example, if a person told me he forgot to stop at a stop sign, instead of writing "And Jim said, 'and I realized I had passed it just as I passed it. That's what made me flunk.' " I could write instead, "After realizing he had just passed a stop sign, Jim continued on, knowing he had flunked the test." This will become useful so I don't have to keep on writing, "he said" or "And she said." It also lends a certain continuity to the paper without the constant breaking in of quotes and quotation marks which tend to alienate the reader from the writer's work and who said what.

As Wendy's comments suggest, in the context of developing her own report—involving a variety of other writing and reading activities—writing and reading served as tools for learning and communicating not only with others, but also with herself. More specifically, writing and reading served as vehicles for Wendy to reflect upon what she found memorable ("Yeager flying NF-104" and "Conrad having his barium examination"), issues related to style ("He incorporated it into the third person . . . without using direct quotes"), and possible options for her own reports ("This will become useful so I don't have to keep on writing 'he said' or 'And she said.' It also lends a certain continuity to the paper").

Another example of writing and reading being used effectively to fuel learning comes from a biology classroom."[30] Students in a middle school biology class were asked to write self-reports in conjunction with reading their textbooks. Specifically, they were asked to read selected pages and then write down what they had learned and their reactions to that learning. The teacher explained her rationale thus:

They're not going to learn something until it really becomes part of them and they can use it. I think the idea of the responses is making a bit of knowledge a part of themselves so they can use it. The responses seem to me a much better way of getting them to think about what they've read and make it a part of their own body of knowledge than anything else I've used. I do want them to be able to put it [the reading] in their own words and fit together the ideas from the reading. I feel that's part of the mastery of the material, but I love it more if they would also comment on it. Because I think that's taking it one step more. You sort of can fit it all together but then if you can take it out of the page and the context of the class and comment on it from your own experience, then that's sort of one more step of learning.

The following are the reading responses of two of this teacher's seventh grade biology students to a three-page textbook reading on diffusion and osmosis:

When I read these pages I gained an understanding for the following ideas: Diffusion: when any substance from its starting point spreads out evenly to cover the whole space it is given. Osmosis: When water diffuses through a membrane. The section with the lesser amount of water will be filled by the other section which has a higher concentration. The substance will diffuse through a membrane making both sections equal. Turgor: Is the stiffness of a cell due to osmotic prssure (turgor) will rise. Plasmolysis: Is when water diffuses out of the cell causing it to be limp. This reading was too short! I enjoyed it thoroughly.

—*An eleven-year-old girl*

In reading this section I thought of the lab that I did on diffusion. I knew something about diffusion, but I didn't know *it*. I thought of how neat it was that these molecules seem to have a *brain*. It's like they *knew* and have always known what to do. How to diffuse.

—*An eleven-year-old boy*

In this part I read about the different parts of the circulatory system. The vains; [*sic*] and arteries serve as sort of subway tunnels used to transport blood to the different parts of the body. The valves in the veins and/or heart, are very important in terms of which way the blood is to flow. I learned about the difference in veins and arteries which I thought was pretty neat.

—*An eleven-year-old boy*

Despite the variations in response, the writing together with the reading served similar purposes. In particular, these responses enabled the students to identify what they saw as key issues or main ideas and to share their reactions with their teacher. From the teacher's perspective, the responses also served some diagnostic functions. The teacher could tell what students were keying upon and to what extent they were integrating what they knew with what they read. In the first response, the student is making notes for herself on the subject matter of the reading; her personal response is rather limited. The second reading response is the opposite—all personal connection and little commentary on the information in the chapter. The third student's response represents more of a balance between the information in the chapter and his personal response.

In this same biology class, the teacher asked the students to write a story or a narrative as a means of coming to understand selected textbook material. Barbara, age eleven, wrote the following on the circulation of red and white blood cells:

> I am Barbara, one of the billion red blood cells in Barbara's body. As I go on my journey through the circulatory system, I will explain it. Right now I'm entering the right ornament at the normal pace without any oxygen on my back besides the hemoglobin. Now I'm going through the left ventricle and I wait there while it pumps me up into the pulmonary artery. As the crowds start to go every other one, each to each lung, I find I will go into the right lung. As I go through, I suddenly turn and lots of little chemicals called carbon dioxide go through your esophagus. When that's over, I go back to the left ventricle which pumps it up to the aorta. This time I'm going to head in line and after that start all over.

Barbara's story caused a great deal of reaction. Her classmates immediately began to question her on the accuracy of the account:

> *Student 1:* [to Barbara] The only thing is yours. . . . Is that the right way? I thought it goes I thought it had to go . . . OK, it went into the left atrium . . . OK, then it went into the left, well, I mean the right, it went into the right ventricle . . . ?
>
> *Student 2:* Yeah, I was looking at the sheet-thing too.

Other students took out their single-sheet descriptions of the circulatory system. As they continued talking, their voices became indistinguishable from each other as they reflected upon Barbara's description.

> Well, I started out . . .
>
> You go there . . .
>
> I started in the pulmonary vein.
>
> OK, anyway, you start in the right atrium—the right ventricle?
>
> No, the pulmonary vein and then . . .
>
> OK, the pulmonary vein . . .
>
> You can start right there, too . . . You pass through there . . .
>
> Down through the atrium . . . then up there and then . . .
>
> It's . . . *this* atrium and go down and you're supposed to in through there and then you come up and you go into . . .
>
> The lungs . . .
>
> Right atrium . . . and the right ventricle . . .
>
> Uh huh . . .
>
> Are we supposed to use . . .

> The esophagus ... and then you came back to the pulmonary
> vein and then to the left ornament ...
> Atrium ...
> Atrium ... and to the left ventricle and then to the ...
> Aorta ...

During this rapid-fire exchange, the students concentrated with unbroken intensity on the material they had learned about the circulatory system. Moving from the textbook to the single-sheet diagram, they reviewed the material, corrected each other's narratives. When the comments on her paper began to subside, Barbara brought the group back to their focus on her paper:

> *Barbara:* [to everyone in the group] I don't understand what you want me to do.
>
> *Emily:* Look in the book. See? [pointing to a section of the textbook] Look ... Look, all you do is look under "red blood cells" and then there's all of this [turning pages in the book].
>
> *Barbara:* I think I'm going to write mine more like a story and add stuff like [to Emily] you did in the beginning. I've got to explain all the things that he does. But I did explain, I thought.

Thus writing and reading by a single student spurred further writing and reading together with a discussion that resulted in the students reviewing their understanding of the circulatory system. From their initial focus on their own written narratives, they became absorbed in one another's ideas, referred to diagrams, notes, and the textbook in their search for the correct route of the red blood cell—and used most of their small group time to clarify for themselves and each other their understanding of the process of blood circulation.

Our next example comes from an American history class, where the topic was civil rights. To initiate their exploration of the topic, students were presented a hypothetical situation: a decision to prohibit students from congregating in school halls and the school playground. To respond to the situation, students were asked to adopt different perspectives (teacher, school administrator, parent) and stances (pro, con, mixed) in conjunction with developing position statements. Some students adopted the perspective of a teacher in support of the students' right to congregate, other students adopted a parent's perspective, and so on.

As they developed their arguments, the students were exposed to writings and films on civil rights, including textbook accounts of the civil rights movement, newspaper articles on this topic, and famous speeches. After writing their position statements, the students held a panel discussion, with audience participation, to represent the various opinions. Afterwards, the students were invited to redevelop their positon statements. Some of the students commented on their exploration of the topic. Two offered the following remarks:

> I now have a clearer view of how I think and a better sense of others. I did not appreciate what the arguments were until I began writing my opinion and reading the textbook and some of the other material.
>
> I changed my opinion. Yes, I changed my ideas several times. Writing and reading gave me a sense of what I really wanted to say and how.

The results from these classrooms parallel the findings from research on the effects of writing and reading in the physical and social sciences. Writing and reading experiences described in the classrooms appeared to prompt not just what students learned, but also how they learned. Students gleaned ideas, discovered ways to formulate, and became actively involved in questioning and thinking evaluatively about the topic.

Research suggests that outcomes such as these do not emerge by chance, but are reasonably predictable, given the type of writing and reading activities in which the students are engaged. For example, Rob Tierney demonstrated that the amount his biology students learned was influenced by combining reading with writing activities such as logs, notes, essays, summaries, and group writing.[31] Gould, Haas, and Marino examined the effects on the amount that students recalled when they were given writing assignments related to reading about historical settings.[32]

Studies have also shown that students who engage in particular kinds of combined writing and reading activities not only learn more, but also think more critically about what they are studying. Newell demonstrated that students who wrote essays, especially those students who had limited knowledge of a topic, learned more than did equivalent students who either took notes or responded to study-guide questions. Further, an analysis of think-aloud protocols collected while students were writing essays indicated that the students engaged in more planning, self-questioning, and reviewing.[33]

Tierney, Soter, O'Flahavan, and McGinley examined the effects of traversing different social studies topics with specific kinds of reading, writing, and questioning activities and combinations of these activities (for example, reading plus writing, reading alone, writing alone). They found that the students who engaged in the writing activities before reading approached their exploration of the topic evaluatively, pursuing ideas and answers to questions, judging their own ideas and the author's, reworking these ideas, and sometimes even shifting perspectives. The students who did not engage in the writing activities before reading appeared to read for purposes of remembering ideas. Further, they were more concerned with editing their own written presentation of those ideas than with reworking or rethinking them.[34]

We return here to our question: What if writing and reading are working together in the content areas? Although the research and our classroom examples represent a small sample of what can happen when writing and reading work together, a consistent pattern of outcomes is apparent. Writing and reading activities structured to engage students creatively and critically with varied topics enhance knowledge acquisition, strategy usage, and critical thinking.

Discussion

So then, what if writing and reading are working together in ways that we have illustrated? Let us reexamine the learning outcomes that are served when writing and reading work together. Our review of research and extrapolations from classsrooms suggest that benefits are likely to accrue in four areas:

1. Acquisition of certain skills, including letter-sound correspondence, knowledge of genre and stylistic features, as well as other literacy skills
2. Motivation to engage in learning activities
3. Acquisition, clarification, elaboration, and discovery of ideas
4. Development of a sense of authorship, readership, and critical thinking abilities

What is important to note is that writing and reading may offer more together than apart. As Tierney and McGinley recently suggested:

> Writing and reading are sufficiently overlapping activities that they support a symbiosis in which the impact of the two together becomes greater than the sum of their separate impacts. As they traverse back and forth across the landscape of various domains, reading and writing prompt shifts in perspective which support not just the emergence of new . . . understandings and perspectives, but also the emergence of a new dialectic. And, it is this dialectic which can prompt critical thought—an understanding of understandings or the accruing of a perspective(s) on one's perspectives. . . . It is as if reading and writing foster an attitude of exploring the topic akin to that of being both a "producer" and

a "consumer" of texts. As productive consumers, we become involved in a dialogue with authors as well as with what Murray (1982) terms our "otherselves."[35]

In closing, we would hypothesize that when students crisscross their explorations of topics with writing and reading, they will oftentimes be motivated to learn, be mobilized to access their own thoughts, and be in a position to discover and evaluate what they themselves understand. We offer this conclusion, notwithstanding the fact that we recognize the following:

1. Writing and reading are not the only modes or vehicles by which the aforementioned learning goals are achieved.

2. Individual differences exist in students' ability to coordinate the use of writing and reading.

3. Various facets of classroom life support the outcomes we have described. Indeed, most of the examples included in this chapter involve writing and reading supported by a rich classroom environment.

4. Research on writing and reading working together is in its infancy. Further research is needed to explicate the constellations of functions, reasoning operations, learning outcomes, and perspectives that writing and reading working together support. At the same time, research is needed to clarify the saliency of the various dimensions of classroom life and other factors that surround writing and reading experiences.

Chapter Notes

1. Huey, E. (1908). *The psychology and pedagogy of teaching reading.* Boston: MIT Press.

2. Allen, R.V. (1976). *Language experiences in communication.* Boston: Houghton Mifflin.
   Ashton-Warner, S. (1963). *Teacher.* New York: Simon & Schuster.
   Clay, M. (1976). Early childhood and cultural diversity in New Zealand. *The Reading Teacher, 29,* 333–342.
   Montessori, M. (1964). *The Montessori method.* New York: Schocken Books.
   Stauffer, R.G. (1970). *The language-experience approach to the teaching of reading.* New York: Harper & Row.
   Faeder, D., and Shaevitz, M. (1966). *Hooked on books.* New York: Bantam.

3. Bond, G.L., and Dykstra, R. (1967). The cooperative research programs in first grade reading instruction [Special issue]. *Reading Research Quart-*

erly, 2.

Stauffer, R.G., and Hammond, D. (1967). The effectiveness of language arts and basic reader approaches to first grade reading instruction—extended into second grade. *Reading Teacher, 20,* 740–746.

Stauffer, R.G., and Hammond, D. (1969). The effectiveness of language arts and basic reader approaches—extended into third grade. *Reading Research Quarterly, 4,* 468–499.

4. Bissex, G.L. (1980). *GNYS AT WRK: A child learns to read and write.* Cambridge, MA: Harvard University Press.

Chomsky, C. (1979). Approaching reading through invented spelling. In L. Resnick and P. Weaver (Eds.), *Theory and practice of early reading: Vol. 2* (pp. 43–66). Hillsdale, NJ: Erlbaum.

Dyson, A. Haas. (1984). Reading, writing, and language: Young children solving the written language puzzle. In J.M. Jensen (Ed.), *Composing and comprehending.* Urbana, IL: National Council of Teachers of English.

Ferreiro, E., and Teberosky, A. (1982). *Literacy before schooling* (K. Goodman Castro, Trans.). Exeter, NH: Heinemann.

Harste, J.C., Woodward, V.A., and Burke, C.L. (1984). *Language stories and literary lessons.* Exeter, NH: Heinemann.

Read, C. (1971). Preschool children's knowledge of English phonology. *Harvard Educational Review, 41,* 1–34.

5. Harste, Woodward, and Burke (1984); see note 4, p. 218.

6. Chomsky (1979); see note 4.

Read (1971); see note 4.

7. Chomsky (1979); see note 4, pp. 51–52.

8. Atwell, N. (1987). *In the middle.* Upper Montclair, NJ: Boynton/Cook.

Calkins, L.M. (1983). *Lessons from a child.* Exeter, NH: Heinemann.

Giacobbe, M.E. (1982). A writer reads, a reader writes. In T. Newkirk and N. Atwell (Eds.), *Understanding writing: Ways of observing, learning, and teaching* (pp. 114–125). Chelmsford, MA: Northeast Regional Exchange.

Graves, D.H., and Hansen, J. (1983). The author's chair. *Language Arts, 60,* 176–182.

Hansen, J. (1987). *When writers read.* Portsmouth, NH: Heinemann.

9. Calkins (1983); see note 8.

10. Figures 1 and 2 courtesy of Jerome C. Harste.

11. Zolotow, C. (1968). *My friend John.* New York: Harper & Row. 12. Sendak, M. (1967). *Higglety pigglety pop!* New York: Harper & Row.

13. Lobel, A.C. (1976). *Frog and Toad.* New York: Harper & Row.

Yolen, J. (1982). *Commander Toad and the Planet of the Grapes.* New York: Coward, McCann & Geoghegan.

White, E.B. (1970). *The trumpet of the swan.* New York: Harper & Row.

Brown, M.T. (1981). *Arthur's eyes.* New York: Avon Books.

Kellogg, S. (1982). *Pinkerton, behave!* New York: Dial Books.

14. Peck, R. (1974). *Soup.* Westminister, MD: Knopf.

15. Eckhoff, B. (1983). How reading affects children's writing. *Language Arts, 60,* 607–616.

16. National Assessment of Educational Progress (1981). *The reading report card: Trends across the decade.* Princeton, NJ: Educational Testing Service.
National Assessment of Educational Progress (1986). *Writing: Trends across the decade.* Princeton, NJ: Educational Testing Service.

17. Applebee, A.N. (1981). *Writing in the secondary school* (Research Monograph No. 21). Urbana, IL: National Council of Teachers of English.
Applebee, A.N. (1984b). *Context for learning to write: Studies of secondary school instruction.* Norwood, NJ: Ablex.

18. Anderson, R.C., Hiebert, E.H., Scott, J., and Wilkinson, I.A.G. (1984). *Becoming a nation of readers.* (p. 79). Washington, DC: National Institute of Education, National Academy of Education, Commission on Reading.

19. College Entrance Examination Board Commission on Educational Reform (1985). Excellence in our schools: Making it happen. *Proceedings of a national forum on educational reform.* Princeton, NJ: College Entrance Examination Board.

20. Fitzgerald, F.S. (1969). *The great Gatsby.* (p. 8). New York: Scribner's.

21. Poe, E.A. (1984). *The tell-tale heart.* Philadelphia: Franklin Library.

22. Salvatori, M. (1985). The dialogical nature of reading and writing. In D. Bartholomae and A. Petrosky (Eds.), *Facts, artifacts, and counterfacts* (pp. 137–166). Upper Montclair, NJ: Boynton/Cook.

23. Colvin-Murphy, C. (1986). *Enhancing critical comprehension of literary texts through writing.* Paper presented at the National Reading Conference, Austin, TX.

24. McGinley, W. (1987). *The effects of composing as a previewing activity on seventh grade students' understanding of short stories.* Unpublished manuscript.
Denner, P.R., and McGinley, W.J. (1986, March). *The effects of story-impressions as a prereading writing-activity on immediate and delayed story-recall of average and superior readers.* Paper presented at the spring conference of the Idaho Council of the International Reading Association, Burley, ID. (ERIC Document Reproduction Service No. ED 269 743)

25. Marshall, J.D. (1978). The effects of writing on students' understanding of literary text. *Research in the Teaching of English, 21,* 30–63.

26. Bereiter, C., and Scardamalia, M. (1984). Learning about writing from reading. *Written Communication, 1,* 163–188.

27. Wittington, E. (1975). *The foxfire books* (Vols. 1–3). New York: Doubleday.

28. Guthrie, J. (1985). Curriculum reform and strategies related to reading, writing and content areas. In College Entrance Examination Board Commission on Educational Reform; see note 19.

29. Wolfe, T. (1980). *The right stuff.* New York: Bantam Books.

30. Healy, M.K. (1984). *Writing in a science class: A case study of the connections between writing and learning.* Unpublished doctoral dissertation, New York University, New York.

31. Tierney, R.J. (1981). Using expressive writing to teach biology. In A.M. Worting and R.J. Tierney (Eds.), *Two studies of writing in high school science* (pp. 47–68). Berkeley, CA: Bay Area Writing Project.

32. Gould, S.M., Haas, L.W., and Marino, J.L. (1982). *Writing as schema-building: The effects of writing as a pre-reading activity on a delayed recall of narrative text.* Unpublished manuscript.

33. Newell, G.E. (1984). Learning from writing in two content areas: A case study/protocol analysis. *Research in the Teaching of English, 18,* 265–287.

34. Tierney, R.J., Soter, A., O'Flahavan, J., and McGinley, W. (1986, April). *The effects of reading and writing upon thinking critically.* Paper presented at the annual meeting of the American Educational Research Association, San Francisco.

35. Tierney, R.J., and McGinley, W. (1987). *Exploring reading and writing as ways of knowing.* Paper presented at the thirteenth annual conference of the Australian Reading Association.

Appendix:
Learning to Spell/Learning the Written Language System

In writing words, spellers are thought to use two knowledge sources: (1) information about specific words stored in memory and (2) knowledge about how the general spelling system works. Spellers acquire information about specific words from their reading as well as from their spelling experiences. They remember letters as symbols for sounds in the word and also visual properties of the word. Spellers learn how spellings in general are structured from the instruction they receive and also from their experiences reading and spelling specific words. They learn which letters typically symbolize which sounds, how to divide pronunciations into sound units, typical positions of letters in words, how long words tend to be, and so forth. When they spell a word, spellers first look in memory for specific information about the word. If it is not there or only partly there, then they use their general knowledge to invent a spelling or to supplement the recalled spelling.

Researchers have examined the kinds of spellings that young children invent and have proposed several stages to describe the development of their general spelling knowledge.[1] Each stage denotes a period of development. However, its boundaries can be seen to overlap with the next stage. Some of these stages are nicely illustrated in Mary Hurdlow's data shown in Table 1 (see page 180). The earliest stage involves the production of scribbles, strings of randomly selected letters, or numbers to represent words and sentences. At this stage, only a few letters may be known, and they may not be differentiated from numbers. When spellers select letters for words, it is not because they correspond to sounds. For example, some of the spellings in test 1 (*P* for *tack, KO* for *muffin*) bear no relationship to the sounds represented by the letters. This stage may begin very early, when preschoolers begin noticing what written language looks like and where to find it.[2]

The next stage occurs when children learn the names or sounds of letters and use this knowledge to select letters for their spellings. At the onset of this semiphonetic stage, only one or two of the letters may correspond to sounds in the word. This stage is illustrated by *C* (kiss), *BP* (buzz) and *PO* (pickle) from test 1 in Table 1. As children gain more experience with print, they can detect more sounds and represent them with letters; for example, *BZ* (buzz), *PL* (pickle), *KWK* (quick) from test 2 in Table 1. Letter names may be the basis for selecting letters. For example, *Y* was used to spell "wife" as *YUF*; *H*, whose name includes the sound /ch/, might be used to spell "chicken" as *HKN*.[3] Although children's choices may violate spelling conventions, they are nevertheless logical and indicate that learners are attempting to use what they know about letters to figure out how the spelling system works. Adopting this goal is considered to be an extremely important step in learning to spell, as well as in learning to read.

At this stage, children symbolize only some of the sounds with letters, those that are salient and those that they can find in letter names: consonants more often than vowels, long rather than short vowels, single consonants rather than consonant blends, first and final more often than medial sounds. Sometimes extra nonphonetic letters are added at the end because a word does not look long enough. Sometimes boundaries between words are omitted because children lack awareness that the words are separate units; they detect no breaks in their speech (for example, "Gimmeapiceacandy").[4] Sometimes children do not analyze speech the way adults do. They may hear the sound /ch/ at the beginning of "truck" and spell it with *H*, or /j/ at the beginning of "dress" and spell it with *J*, or /sg/ at the beginning of "skate" and spell it with *SG*.[5] These choices are all sensible linguistically. (Say the words and see if you can detect these sounds.) These characteristics typically appear in spelling inventions along the course of development, but subsequently disappear as learners discover that the conventional spelling system works another way.

The next stage occurs when children become able to produce more complete phonetic spellings that contain letters for most of the sounds in words. Vowels as well as consonants and consonant blends are represented; for example, *SIKS* (six), *KWIC* (quick), *WIF* (wife) from test 3 in Table 1. Some kinds of sounds may be delayed in their appearance in spellings during this stage. Nasal consonant blends such as the *M* in "camp" and the *N* in "bend" are typically omitted because the nasal is actually part of the vowel sound and not separately articulated. Note in Table 1 that "camp" was spelled *CAP* or *KAP* before the *M* was finally included in test 5. Vowels in unstressed syllables are also overlooked; for example, "pickle" was spelled *PIKL* in test 4 but *PIKEL* in test 5, "muffin" was *MUFN* in test 3 but *MUFIN* in test 4.

During this stage children become wedded to the belief that every sound they detect in a pronunciation requires a letter or digraph in the spelling. In stretching out pronunciations to spell words, children may even find extra sounds not symbolized in conventional spellings; for example, *DOKTDR* (doctor) in Table 1, *BALAOSIS* (blouses).[6] Acquiring the idea that words consist of a sequence of sound segments or phonemes is considered to be a very important insight for the development of reading as well as spelling skill.[7] In fact, phonemic awareness is one of the best predictors of how well children learn to read.[8] If they have this idea, then reader-spellers are in a good position to make sense of conventional spellings of words, many of which are not completely phonetic. They can recognize which letters correspond to sounds and which do not. This knowledge is thought to be necessary for storing the spellings of specific words in memory so that the words can be spelled and also read accurately.[9]

The final stage might be termed a *morphemic* stage because spellers begin recognizing and using word-based spelling patterns[10] when these are seen as more appropriate than phonetic spellings; for example, spelling past tense verbs consistently with *-ed* rather than according to their sounds as in *WOCHED* rather than *WOCHT* (watched), spelling long vowels with two vowel letters or a final *-e* rather than with one vowel as in *RISE* rather than *RIS* (rice), *SEAD* rather than *CED* (seed).[11] This stage is thought to emerge once children have learned the conventional spellings of several specific words and begin recognizing spelling patterns that recur across words.

The child whose spellings are reported in Table 1 wrote several words correctly with the final *-e* in test 5, indicating that he may have been on the verge of the morphemic stage. However, because the spellings are correct, it is unclear whether they were invented or recalled from memory. The child added the final *-E* incorrectly to a short-vowel word in test 5, "quick" spelled *QUICE*. This may be a case of overgeneralizing a pattern that is newly learned before its correct application is fully understood.[12] Overgeneralization errors are commonplace during the course of both written and oral language development.[13] Such errors are actually to be welcomed as a sign that students are making progress in learning the system.

From this description of the stages of spelling development, it is apparent that children may need to learn how the spelling system works phonetically before they become very skilled at remembering the complete spellings of specific words. This may take some time and practice to accomplish. Also it is apparent that children's spelling errors often reflect the state of their developing knowledge of the system and that various types of errors will inevitably appear and disappear as their knowledge grows and approximates the conventional system. This suggests that teachers should tolerate spelling errors while students are developing competence with the system.

The development of reading skill is related to the development of spelling skill. Several studies have found high positive correlations between reading and spelling, among first graders, $r = .86$,[14] among second graders, $r = .66$, and among fifth graders, $r = .60$.[15] This indicates that better readers tend to be better spellers. Also, training studies have shown that teaching beginners to decode print improves their spelling ability, and teaching beginners to spell improves their reading skill.[16] If one examines the course of development in reading, one can see how spelling and reading contribute to each other's development. There are several processes that can be used to read words. If the words are read in context, contextual cues lead readers to expect certain words or word classes. If readers know how the spelling system works, they can decode words by translating letters into sounds to form recognizable spoken words. If readers have read those specific words before and remember them, then they can find the words in memory to read them. Spelling, then, contributes to readers' knowledge of— and thus their ability to take advantage of—the spelling system to decode words.

Appendix Notes

1. Beers, J.W., and Henderson, E.H. (1977). A study of developing orthographic concepts among first grade children. *Research in the Teaching of English, 11,* 133–148.

   Ehri, L.C. (1986). Sources of difficulty in learning to spell and read. In M.L. Wolraich and D. Routh (Eds.), *Advances in developmental and behavioral pediatrics.* Greenwich, CT: Jai Press.

   Gentry, J. (1982). An analysis of developmental spelling in GYNS AT WRK. *The Reading Teacher, 36,* 192–200.

   Henderson, E.H. (1981). *Learning to read and spell.* DeKalb, IL: Northern Illinois University Press.

   Morris, D., and Perney, J. (1984). Developmental spelling as a predictor of first-grade reading achievement. *The Elementary School Journal, 84,* 441–457.

2. Goodman, Y.M., and Altwerger, B. (1981). *Print awareness in preschool children: A working paper. A study of the development of literacy in preschool children.* Occasional Papers No. 4, Program in Language and Literacy, University of Arizona.

   Harste, J.C., Burke, C.L., and Woodward, V.A. (1982). Children's language and world: Initial encounters with print. In J. Langer and M. Smith-Burke (Eds.), *Bridging the gap: Reader meets author* (pp. 105–131). Newark, DE: International Reading Association.

3. Read, C. (1971). Preschool children's knowledge of English phonology. *Harvard Educational Review, 41,* 1–34.

4. Ehri, L.C. (1979). Linguistic insight: Threshold of reading acquisition. In T.G. Waller and G.E. MacKinnon (Eds.), *Reading research: Advances in theory and practice: Vol. 1* (pp. 63–114). New York: Academic Press.

   Francis, H. (1973). Children's experience of reading and notions of units in language. *British Journal of Educational Psychology, 43,* 17–23.

   Holden, M.H., and MacGinitie, W.H. (1972). Children's conceptions of word boundaries in speech and print. *Journal of Educational Psychology, 63,* 551–557.

5. Read (1971); see note 3.

   Treiman, R. (1985a). Spelling of stop consonants after /s/ by children and adults. *Applied Psycholinguistics, 6,* 261–282.

   Treiman, R. (1985b). Phonemic awareness and spelling: Children's judgments do not always agree with adults'. *Journal of Experimental Child Psychology, 39,* 182–201.

6. Ehri (1986); see note 1.

7. Bradley, L., and Bryant, P.E. (1983). Categorizing sounds and learning to read: A causal connection. *Nature, 301,* 419–421.

   Bryant, P.E., and Bradley, L. (1985). *Children's reading problems.* Oxford: Basil Blackwell.

   Calfee, R.C., Lindamood, P., and Lindamood, C. (1973). Acoustic-phonetic skills and reading: Kindergarten through twelfth grade. *Journal of Educational Psychology, 64,* 293–298.

   Lewkowicz, N.K. (1980). Phonemic awareness training: What to teach and how to teach it. *Journal of Educational Psychology, 72,* 686–700.

   Liberman, I.Y., and Shankwieler, D. (1979). Speech, the alphabet, and teaching to read. In L.B. Resnick and P.A. Weaver (Eds.), *Theory and practice of early reading* (pp. 105–129). Hillsdale, NJ: Erlbaum.

   Lundberg, I., Olofsson, A., and Wall, S. (1980). Reading and spelling skills in the first years predicted from phonemic awareness skills in kindergarten. *Scandinavian Journal of Psychology, 21,* 159–173.

   Torneus, M. (1984). Phonological awareness and reading: A chicken and egg problem. *Journal of Educational Psychology, 76,* 1346–1358.

   Williams, J.P. (1984). Phonemic analysis and how it relates to reading. *Journal of Learning Disabilities, 17,* 240–245.

8. Juel, C., Griffith, P.L., and Gough, P.B. (1986). The acquisition of literacy: A longitudinal study of children in first and second grade. *Journal of Educational Psychology, 78,* 243–255.

Share, D.L., Jorm, A.F., Maclean, R., and Matthews, R. (1984). Sources of individual differences in reading acquisition. *Journal of Educational Psychology, 76,* 1309–1324.

9. Ehri, L.C. (1984). How orthography alters spoken language competencies in children learning to read and spell. In J. Downing and R. Valtin (Eds.), *Language awareness and learning to read.* New York: Springer-Verlag.

10. Becker, W.C., Dixon, R., and Anderson-Inman, L. (1980). *Morphographic and root word analysis of 26,000 high frequency words.* Eugene: University of Oregon Follow Through Project, College of Education.

    Marsh, G., Friedman, M., Welch, V., and Desberg, P. (1980). The development of strategies in spelling. In U. Frith (Ed.), *Cognitive processes in spelling* (pp. 339–354). London: Academic Press.

11. Morris and Perney (1984); see note 1.

12. Mason, J. (1980). Overgeneralization in learning to read. *Journal of Reading Behavior, 8,* 173–182.

13. Berko, J. (1958). The child's learning of English morphology. *Word, 14,* 150–177.

14. Morris and Perney (1984); see note 1.

15. Shanahan, T. (1984). Nature of the reading-writing relation: An exploratory multivariate analysis. *Journal of Educational Psychology, 76,* 466–477.

16. Bradley and Bryant (1983); see note 7.

6 Writing-and-Reading in the Classroom

Planning Group Members

James Britton, Chair
Robert Calfee
Laury Fischer
Lily Wong Filmore
James Gray
Norton Grubb
Don McQuade
James Moffett
Jean Osborn
Art Peterson

Introduction

Mary K. Healy

I would like to center this commentary around two stories that will illustrate what, for me, are the central issues developed in Professor Britton's chapter. The first is the story of a lost tooth, as told in a note written by my niece Elizabeth just after completing her first grade year (see Figure 1 on next page).

No one told her to write to the tooth fairy; my sister was surprised and delighted when Elizabeth placed her note on the dining room table as she was preparing for bed. I was delighted too when I saw it, and in thinking afterwards about the situation in which it was written, I see Elizabeth's act as an exemplar of the sum and total of her experiences with literacy up to that time. She had been read to a great deal in her preschool years and thought of books as sources of pleasure and information. She had been encouraged to draw and to write whatever she wanted, sharing what she did with her family. She had seen some of this work exhibited on several relatives' refrigerator doors. She had received many postcards and notes from those relatives and had learned to work out the approximate meanings. She had seen those same relatives writing and reading, using language in many different functional ways. By age six, Elizabeth had learned that you read for many purposes and you write to communicate and to get things done. Thus her tooth fairy writing shows that she had learned quite well Vygotsky's dictum that "reading and writing are necessary for something."

This quality of necessity is found in many of the writing-reading examples in the chapter that follows. Dialogue journals between pupils and teachers encourage the human relationships that in turn allow thinking to develop. Learning logs kept by students as they explore new subject areas permit the type of "reflective writing" that pushes pupils to reformulate new information in their own words, making individual connections between what they are learning and their own lives. The immediacy of letter writing, with its promise of unpredictable

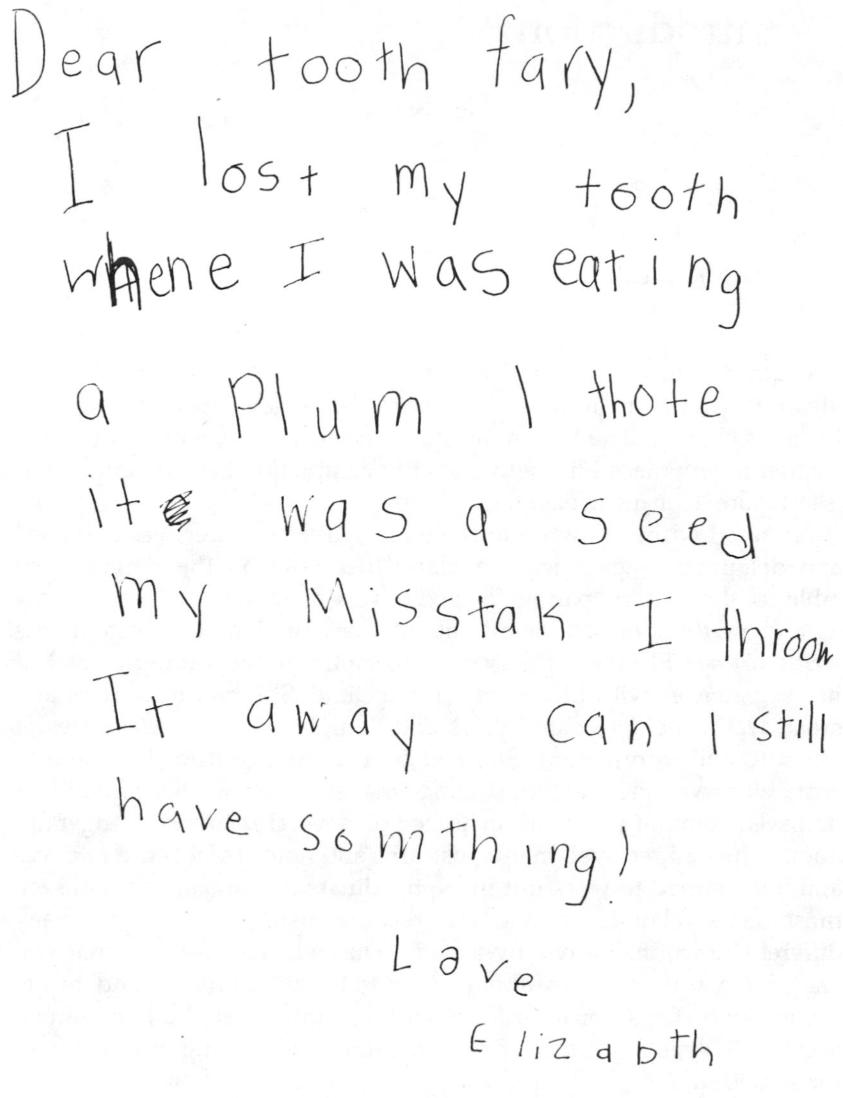

Dear tooth fary,
I lost my tooth
whene I was eating
a Plum I thote
it was a seed
my Misstak I throom
It away Can I still
have somthing)
            Lave
                E lizabth

Figure 1. Elizabeth's note to the tooth fairy.

genuine response, spurs pupils both to write and to anticipate the
pleasure of reading. Students working on writing projects such as
books or reports realize that working together collaboratively will
enable them to achieve their purposes. Throughout the chapter we
find classroom examples of pupils using their developing literacy to
get things done. Clearly, their thoughtful teachers know that, just as

we learn to speak to fulfill our intentions, that same intentionality of purpose fuels the development of writing-reading abilities.

I promised two stories. The second one took place in the late 1960s, a year or two after the Anglo-American Conference on the Teaching of English at Dartmouth. James Britton, then a relatively unknown figure in American educational circles but a key figure at the Dartmouth Conference, came to a northern California school district to give a workshop on teaching literature. I was a part of that group of English teachers and was as astounded as the rest when the central activity of Professor Britton's workshop turned out to be listening to tapes of London secondary school pupils discussing a common literature text in small groups. Although our astonishment seems ludicrous now, after the past twenty years of case-study descriptive research, then it was genuine. We simply had never thought of taping our students and paying close attention to what they were saying to each other. In fact, most of us relied on whole class discussion of readings; we felt we had to direct and channel our students' comprehension and interpretation of texts.

Once the astonishment passed and we concentrated on what we were hearing, we learned much from those British pupils: that they were absorbed in the discussion, listening intently and building on each other's points; that they moved freely from the text to relevant incidents in their own lives and back to the text again; that they could sustain a thoughtful discussion about their reading and work out together a tentative interpretation. In the end, what was perhaps most striking to many of us about the tapes was the absence of the questioning and directing teacher's voice. This was no "class discussion"—that ritual of literature study—but a small group of kids talking seriously about their reading.

For many of us in the room, that workshop was a turning point in our teaching. Subsequently, we attempted many changes in our classrooms: more opportunities for students to discuss in small groups, more emphasis on the students' own responses to texts, and more choices of texts available. In fact, over the years following that experience, I discovered that the more I listened to my students as they wrote and discussed their writing in small groups and as they reported on their reading, the more I understood about what I *could* teach them and about what they *would be ready* to learn.

Teaching writing and reading became for me an exploration rather than a performance. Continuing conversations with students took the place of lectures. I spent far more time gathering and preparing materials and organizing activities than making up tests and marking papers. And because of my new orientation to language learning, I spent more time talking with parents and administrators about what I was doing, showing them the development visible over time in students' writing folders, playing them tapes of students discussing their work.

As a new explorer, I became interested in others' explorations. I began to read research reports and theoretical articles. I began to imagine research I would like to do and to discuss this with others. In sum, once I began to pay close attention to the students in front of me as they struggled with their writing and reading and began to ask questions about what was going on, there was no turning back. And there was no turning back for the teachers Professor Britton describes in this chapter. As one of them, Carol Avery, succinctly puts it, "No schooling prepared me for the powerful unfolding that is taking place around me." This chapter celebrates that unfolding and details the rigorous work necessary in the school community to allow it to happen for all children.

Writing-and-Reading in the Classroom

James Britton

The teaching should be organized in such a way that
reading and writing are necessary for something.
—L.S. Vygotsky, *Mind in Society*

It is in the course of conversational exchanges that young children
learn, little by little, both to listen to and interpret what people say to
them and, at the same time, to put into words their own messages. It
would be a perverse regime that attempted to prevail on them to
separate those two achievements—focusing on listening in one context
and on speaking in another. Yet precisely that dissociation marks the
prevailing methods by which schoolchildren today are taught to write
and read.

This chapter will be concerned with the classroom as an environment
for literacy and literacy learning. In it we shall explore ways in which
teachers have improved upon the prevailing methods and developed
strategies for encouraging children to learn to write-and-read; and we
shall cite research findings that support these efforts and that may
suggest further experimental classroom procedures. We look first at
selected examples of work in the classroom.

Writing-and-Reading—Some Examples

Conversations on Paper

When teaching and learning are seen as genuinely interactive behaviors,
we discover that we cannot effectively teach *children we don't know*.
Getting to know the children in a new group, say at the beginning of
a year, is therefore a first priority. Of course, teachers and children get
to know each other primarily in face-to-face situations and the talk
these promote or permit. But days are short and classes may be large—
and there is no doubt that a written exchange conducted in the right

217

way can greatly assist us in getting to know the children we teach. Moreover—something we cannot underestimate—writing to this end is, for both child and teacher, writing-and-reading to some purpose.

The journal as "written conversation" between child and teacher was something I first appreciated in 1978 in Dundas School, Toronto. Dundas School is in an ethnic area of the city, part Chinese, part Greek. Underachievement in these inner-city schools is a problem that the City of Toronto School Board has taken very seriously—and one to which they have applied positive, optimistic, and enlightened remedies, not the least of which is an agreed-by-consensus school policy for language and learning.

A grade three–grade four class at Dundas in 1978 was taught by Mrs. Irwin, and one of the things the children did for her was to keep a journal, which she would read and write in as she moved around in the classroom. It was clear that journal entries were made only when you had something you wanted to say to Mrs. Irwin—and that made them interesting to read (both for her and for me as a visitor). I quote one or two of the entries made by Linda, a Chinese nine-year-old (the teacher's comments are italicized):

> Friday January 20th, 1978. After my rough copy of my project I am going to rerange my project around. I am going to put growing up first page. What monkeys do to eat in second page. Why do monkeys make faces page three.
> *Sounds interesting!*

> Wednesday Jan 25. It was interesting. Did you think it was very interesting or interesting or just a little interesting? Mrs. I., I'm sorry your husband wouldn't let you have another dog but anyways someone already took the dog. How's Malcolm? I hope he isn't sick or anything.
> *Malcolm is fine thank you—he cries when I leave in the morning and gets very excited when I come home!. . . . .*

> Tuesday Feb 14th. The last time I wrote I told you that I was school sick and you asked me why. Well now I will tell you why, because I like to learn, I also like you, I like to do work and when I was away I miss the class. Today I am glad to be here because I wouldn't like to miss the Valentine party. Mrs. I. can you give me a few suggests for the party. What I mean is to give me a few suggests what to bring for the party.
> *(1) a sharp knife to cut apples (2) serviettes (3) little bags to take goodies home in.*

> Monday Feb 20th. Mrs. I., thank you very much for the suggests for the Valentine party. I'm sorry you were away. What did you come up with?
> *I was very sick!*

When you were away the class had other teachers. The first teacher's name was Mrs. G and the second teacher's name was Mr. M. They were both nice teachers. You know sometimes I wish you were my mother.
Lots of the time I wish I had a little girl like you!

Tues. Feb 21st. It's too bad I'm Chinese because if I was English you could adopt me.

As pedagogues, we too easily lose sight of the realistic judgment that writing that does what we meant it to do must be good writing! Linda, like others in her class, enjoyed writing her journal because it made her feel good about the way "Mrs. I." felt about her. I talked to Linda about her journal and she said, "Yes, we kinda *communicate!*"

I think at this early stage in a writer-reader's progress the journal serves the straightforward purpose of establishing and maintaining relations between pupil and teacher. At later stages we shall demand a double purpose for the journal (as I have done in my courses for adults) and use it both to further interpersonal relationships and to encourage relaxed exploration of the material of the course in the context of the writer's own experience. For either purpose, the teacher's response—even where it may be brief—is responsible for maintaining the tone, and thereby the purpose, of the exchange.

A movement to promote such uses of the journal has come in recent years from the Center for Applied Linguistics in Washington. The journal, in essentially the terms in which I have described it above, has been christened the "Dialogue Journal." Stress has rightly been put on the importance of teacher and pupil *thinking together* in the written exchanges of the journal. Jana Staton describes the exchange in these terms:

> Dialogue journals are private, written conversations between students and the teacher on a daily, semiweekly, or sometimes weekly basis. . . . [S]tudents are free to write about whatever concerns or topics *they* feel are most important. The writing is *functional*; that is, students and teachers write directly to each other, using language to get things done in an active way. Students ask questions, complain about lessons, describe what happened on the playground or at home, reflect on why things happen, express personal feelings, and even argue with the teacher about the fairness of assignments—in other words they think in written language.
>
> The teacher writes a direct, personal response to the *content* of the student's writing, rather than commenting on its form or style, and also brings up new topics of interest. . . . The teacher's responses are natural elaborations and extensions of the students' thinking about issues and experiences.[1]

Staton goes on to quote a student who explains why she prefers the dialogue journal to worksheets: "The worksheets make you answer questions, but the dialogue journal makes *me* ask the questions, and then the teacher helps me think about possible answers."

Dialogue, a newsletter published by the Center for Applied Linguistics, reports a wide variety of situations to which dialogue journals have been applied—both for first language and second language learners, for "regular" and "basic" and "special" English or language arts classes. In a recent issue, Roger Shuy reported on the value of dialogue journals in the early stages of learning to read:

> Dialogue writing is speech-like in nature. (It captures the natural phrasing children already use in understanding what others say.) It is closer by far to the actual talk of both participants than any of their writing in school contexts could be.

On such grounds Shuy finds dialogue journal reading "more functional, more user-responsive, more developmentally adapted for comprehension than basal readers."[2]

The classroom reports that follow will include some variations of the use of journals (for example, "learning logs"): what seems to us essential is that the journal, in any form, should be regarded as an exchange between student and teacher (and available, when appropriate, for sharing with other students), but *not* as an unread student "confessional" or any kind of expendable prewriting activity.

Free-write: Free-read

Since the topic of this chapter is one shared, within the limits of the elementary school, with a collection that owes allegiance to the University of New Hampshire (and to Donald Murray and Donald Graves in particular), it is not surprising that we share also much common concern and that many examples of good practice, particularly at the kindergarten and grade one levels, could have served our purposes here. *Breaking Ground: Teachers Relate Reading and Writing in the Elementary School* was edited by Jane Hansen, Thomas Newkirk, and Donald Graves and was published in 1985.[3] What is particularly noteworthy about the work is that various contributors share a belief that teaching approaches based on the successful experiences of children learning to write are able to create a classroom climate more favorable to learning to read. Indeed, such approaches create climates more favorable to learning in the curriculum as a whole than does the classroom climate currently typical in American schools. And it is two examples of these teaching approaches that we have chosen to present in this chapter. The editors, in their preface, are explicit on this point:

> The philosophy behind writing process instruction is incompatible with the philosophy behind reading worksheets, tests, basals, and the fear that any deviation will endanger students' ability to learn to read. Too many students read fifty worksheets for every book they pick up. Their teachers teach what's next in the teachers' guide instead of what the students need next. Too many classrooms revolve around the teacher.
>
> But in writing classrooms, children say, "I wrote it. I do the work." Writing teachers give students choices and listen when the children talk about what they learn. They affirm what the students know and then learn from them. Writing led many of the teachers in this book to reexamine what they did when they taught reading.[4]

Carol Avery, a grade one teacher in a Pennsylvania school, says of her six-and-a-half-year-old pupil, Lori:

> The first-grade experience for Lori and her classmates would not be a traditional one. The writing process approach has been used in the school district for two years. My experience with it had prompted me, with administrative encouragement, to abandon the commercial reading program used throughout the district and to develop a learning process classroom in which the children's writing would be the beginning impetus and primary instrument for their instruction in learning to read. Reading and writing would be allowed to flow and develop in an interactive process, each supporting and enhancing the other. I had watched the strong effect of writing process on children's reading in previous years and marveled. The two processes seemed to go together naturally.[5]

Avery's account stresses the importance of allowing time, particularly in the early stages, and of creating a cooperative regime:

> We took our time—Lori, the class and I—to get to know and delight in each other. We built an accepting atmosphere. I modeled responses; the children reflected genuine, encouraging comments toward one another and one another's writing. Slowly, carefully, we put together the nuts and bolts of our classroom procedures.[6]

Midterm, the teacher recorded in her journal some sense of a changing role for herself:

> I feel a tension and a tremendous energy in these children working so hard at their reading. There is such an outpouring of effort and strength! At the same time I feel a vulnerability; this is really high-risk activity. I think I function best when I help maintain the atmosphere, remind them of all the strategies they could use and then step back. As I move among them, answering their questions and responding to their successes, I sometimes feel I'm

an intruder. There's a danger that I might throw them off by asking them to deal with *my* priorities and I know that would be a mistake at this point. No schooling prepared me for the powerful unfolding that is taking place around me.[7]

And towards the end of the year she wrote:

> These kids are deeply involved with reading and writing. . . . They've formed a supportive, caring community! It's an environment that encourages risk, and risk-taking seems to be the key for them. To maximize their learning in this environment, I think it's important for me to keep my focus on the kids and to listen—really listen—to them. Then they can show where they are and what they need and I can respond in ways to continually nudge and stimulate their growth.[8]

In a later essay in this same collection, Nancie Atwell, a grade eight teacher, explains in detail how she worked with a group of colleagues to plan a writing course modeled on their own experience as writers and how, subsequently, she radically changed her strategies in teaching reading to bring them into line:

> In the end, the writing program we'd sought to develop was much bigger than a program. It's become a way of life. Writing workshop is perpetual—day in, year out—like breathing, but sometimes much, much harder. We're constantly gathering ideas for writing, planning, writing, conferring, and seeing our writing get things done for us in our real worlds. . . .
>
> A little over two years ago, I began to be aware of the contradictions between my beliefs about writing and my instruction in reading. . . . As a reader I usually decide what I'll read. But I get help—recommendations—from my husband and friends, with whom I talk a lot about books, and from reviews. I also draw on my prior experiences as a reader. I like John Updike's novels; chances are, I'm going to like *The Witches of Eastwick*. And I go back to books I've read, reentering and reconsidering the writing.
>
> Sometimes I engage in activities that involve reading and I can't decide what I'll read. For example, the text is required for the course; the application has to be correctly filled out; I want to serve an interesting, edible dinner. But nobody had better do anything so outright silly as to give me a vocabulary quiz, a comprehension test, or a chance to respond that's limited to the kinds of questions found in teachers' guides or high school essay tests.
>
> I read a lot, at least a couple of books a week. . . . Some of my reading happens away from books. I think about characters, plot twists, and turns of phrase. I playback lines of poetry. I suddenly see, in something that happens in my real world, what an author was getting at.[9]

And so, for Atwell, the reading program in her classroom became much more than a program, more a way of life—or rather part of the way of life already established through writing. Drawing inspiration from the dialogue journals described by Jana Staton, Atwell initiated a letter exchange with the students about their reading. Gradually over time, she began to harvest comments on the reading that clearly reflected the students' experiences *as writers*. And at the same time stories, fictional and autobiographical, began to find a place in what the students wrote. Atwell documents the progress of two students throughout grade eight: they offer us convincing evidence of the way they learned to *write-and-read* and the important role that literature played in that process.

It has been claimed[10]—rightly, we believe—that the experience of reading a work of fiction will tend to have the effect on a reader of making real life more "observable." The "pattern-forming" activity involved in responding to a work of fiction is sustained, perhaps, as a reader returns to contemplating his or her own situation. Similarly, a child who has been moved by a poem may well have taken up a kind of stance from which to write his or her own poem. This is very different, I think, from direct imitation or "modeling"; it is probably a transaction at a deeper level—the *effect of an effect*—one particular way in which writing and reading may be interrelated in the classroom.

Collaborative Learning

When talking, reading, and writing are orchestrated in the classroom in such a way that each can make its unique contribution to a single end, we have surely harnessed language to learning as powerfully as possible. Talk is then, as it were, the catalyst which ensures not only that the impact of reading upon writing shall be felt to the full, but also that writing should have a feedback effect upon reading. (One of the interesting suggestions experts have made in recent years is to the effect that, just as listening to speech must rely upon the ability to produce speech, so the reading process "must somehow borrow the machinery of production.")[11]

While the length and complexity of classroom projects integrating language uses in this way will vary considerably, it is probably true that the long-term undertakings reap the maximum benefit. Lynda Chittenden, a Bay Area Writing Project teacher who had a class of nine- and ten-year-olds in Old Mill School, Mill Valley, California,[12] spent many months producing a book on marine mammals—"a book for kids by kids." It illustrates many kinds of strength: in the first place, the uses of language are firmly grounded in a context of firsthand experience—the school is near enough to coasts from which migrating whales can be watched and is in reach of a marine aquarium, an elephant-seal rookery, and other appropriate sites for field trips. Then it was the teacher's policy to surround the undertaking with reading matter of many kinds—scientific, popular, fictional—and to encourage a variety of kinds of writing both as part of the final product and outside it. She writes that

> the learning process is enhanced when kids are surrounded by the language of the unit they're studying: they need to be read good works of fiction and non-fiction that deal with the content; they need to be involved in animated discussions in which they ponder and exclaim over the wonder of the content.
>
> Puzzling, questioning, imagining, dreaming, pondering: these are all accepted mental activities of learning. They are, however, an even more profound part of learning when kids regularly write in learning logs and reflect on the questions, confusions and fantasies that are included in active, involved learning.[13]

Chittenden saw two purposes for the learning logs: primarily to encourage wide-ranging contemplation and speculation, and secondly to provide an opportunity to marshal a newly acquired learning. She says,

> Listing and ordering new information is necessary at many stages of learning. But I believe that real learning, the kind that changes our lives, comes more as a result of reflection and increased awareness. To me [this] kind of reflective writing . . . demonstrates an awareness and learning far beyond a mere acquisition of factual information.[14]

The students were organized into "chapter groups," cooperative groups in which each student took on a specific assignment, and the group continued to monitor suggestions and discuss first drafts. Where individual "ownership" of a unique contribution combines with a sense of cooperative achievement, the incentive to become involved is likely to be a powerful one.

The final stage in drafting came when individual writers took their sections to the teacher and with her worked out and recorded the definitive version. The published book, *Our Friends in the Waters*,[15] contains two kinds of writing. The running text is the factual account of the topic, presented in such a way as to interest young readers, successfully avoiding the mode that Chittenden, in her postscript, calls "report"—"the traditional form for informational writing by kids, written in a dry, encyclopedia-copied language." Here for example are the closing paragraphs of the account, written by eleven-year-old Steig:

Only five species of great whales are fully protected: Blue, Humpback, Gray, Bowhead and Right Whales. However, even Bowheads are allowed to be killed by native Eskimo whalers. Just recently their allowed quota for Bowheads was raised. Some scientists feel that even though they are protected, there aren't enough Blue Whales left to recover and find each other in the sea and reproduce. The world should stop all hunting of marine mammals or certain species will be totally exterminated.

If the killing is stopped, the possibilities would be fantastic! We could learn so much about them: We could feed a Sperm Whale a fish with a homing device inside that could help us find out how deep this deepest diving whale can really go. We could find out how they are able to stay under water so long. We could even find out *what* they do all that time they're under water!

But the greatest thing that could happen would be for us to be able to totally communicate with our brothers and sisters in the sea! Because Cetaceans have intelligence that has been compared to ours, they'd probably be the most interesting to talk to. A Blue Whale could tell us what it is like to be the biggest creature that ever lived! An Orca could tell us what it's like to be the top predator of the sea and not afraid of anything! A Gray Whale could tell us what they think of us sitting in little boats always watching them! A dolphin could teach us how to play their games!

We could talk to them. We could tell them our dreams about them and ask them, "Do you ever dream about us?" "Do you ever wonder what we're like?"

But, all this will never be possible if all the whales are gone before we become friends.

As for the second kind of writing, Chittenden explains that it was her original intention to include in the book only the factual writing, but that she was so struck with the value of the learning logs and the kinds of writing they introduced that she used short extracts from them along with line drawings to embellish the margins of the text. Here, to conclude, are two such entries, the first by Jill, the second by Laura:

I wish I was rich so I could go out on a boat and go right by one and touch it. Then get some scuba gear and swim with one. That's what I would like to do. I wish that I could go and hear them talk. I want to learn what they are saying. I want to know what they think. I want to be a whale. I want to swim like one and wave my flukes like one and to spout like one. Whales are beautiful.

This weekend I've been wondering. You see we study whales and sometimes when we find something out, we're just so overwhelmed. So what I was wondering, if whales study us? Like if you're standing watching whales and a whale comes up to your boat. You usually think that the whale is there just for you to

look at. But did you ever think that it was there to look at
you? . . . When I was little I used to think that a whale was a
whale and they were big and that's it.

Letters and Learning

A letter exchange between two people, sustained over a period of time
in the absence of face-to-face contact, will clearly tend to bring the
process of writing and the process of reading into a complex reciprocal
relationship, a relationship that affects the writing behaviors and the
reading behaviors of both participants.

How this may be applied to create a learning situation is dramatically
illustrated in an account of Amanda Branscombe's ninth grade classroom.[16] The school she taught in was a high school in the Deep South
of the United States. The school ran two tracks, one "general" for the
average and above average students, the other "basic" for the special
education students and low scorers. Branscombe's class was a basic
class of eighteen students, fourteen black and four white.

She aimed to turn her class into a learning community where
students of diverse interests and abilities could find scope for their
activities and where they were encouraged to see themselves as writers
and readers, able to use those powers both in school and in the
community. She stressed writing and reading as complementary processes. She did not "teach" grammar or spelling, and she did not
"red-pencil" their writings.

The course lasted a school year of nine months. In the first semester,
students were asked to write a letter introducing themselves—describing who they were and what they were interested in—and on this
basis they were paired with a grade eleven-twelve senior in a regular
English class in the same school. The school was large, so there was
little likelihood of the ninth graders ever meeting their opposite
numbers. No attempt was made to bring them together, since the idea
was that they should have to rely on a written exchange to develop,
over a period of time, satisfactory communication based on mutual
understandings. There were no prescriptions as to topic, manner, or
mode of approach. Each week a fifty-minute class session was allowed
for the reading and discussing of letters received and the writing of
replies.

One member of the class introduced herself as follows:

> My name is Cassandra. There's not much too say, except that I
> have a lot of ups and down's. I love to play sports, especially
> volley ball. I hope whoever reads this letter finds the personal
> Cassandra. We'll are your going to the game Friday. Well as for

me, I'm not sure. My boyfriend wants me to go with him, but with things like they are now, I'm not sure what my next move is. . . . I would appreciate if you wouldn't inform me about this letter. But it's o.k. because most of this stuff is just in the head. Well so-long kid. And have a nice day. P.S.—Hope that you don't mind me saying kid.[17]

Several letters later her correspondent complained:

Hello. I just discovered you haven't written me a letter this week. I guess I'll have to struggle through this without your letter of response. . . . Although your letters never were much to begin with. I'm probably better off talking to myself because your always so *damn* confusing. May-be if you re-read or proof read your letters you might catch some of the strange things you've been saying.

To this Cassandra replied:

But you and I are to different person's you know. And I've tried to explain myself as much as I could, but somewho you just don't get the message. What do you mean about my letters being confusing. I explain the things I write about the best I know how. Maybe they are confusing to you but I understand what I write. I don't think that it's confusing to you. I think that you just felt like getting me told a little. . . . We're still friends in my book, and if it's something you want to know I'll try and make myself clear. I hope that this is not so *damn confusing*. And if it is the Hell with the stuff.[18]

In fact, through these exchanges, which lasted one semester, ninth graders who had no previous opportunity in class to attempt continuous, interpersonal, written communication quite rapidly developed the ability to initiate topics and to respond to those raised in the letters they received. The students also grew in their ability to anticipate their readers' responses and their difficulties in responding and to employ the conventional formats both of address (salutation and signing off) and of recapitulatory signals that bring coherence to written exposition.

In the article written jointly by Heath and Branscombe, this part of the course is commented on as follows:

The increase in voluntary extended prose length, use of format features, idea initiations, types of conjunctions, and metalinguistic comments came not through teacher-directed revisions of the same pieces, but through "natural" needs that evolved as the ninth graders developed more topics on which they wanted to share information with the upperclassmen and as they became more inquisitive about how the upperclassmen felt about social issues and ideas. . . . Thus their development as writers came about for one of the primary reasons writing in the real world occurs:

> when direct face-to-face interaction or oral verbal communication
> by telephone is not possible.

The authors observe how this mode of learning parallels the procedures by which an infant acquires mastery of the spoken language: "The students' maturity as writers developed in accord with situations similar to those of young children who want something, are misunderstood, and must use oral language to have their needs met."[19]

All this proved to be excellent preparation for the next phase of the course. The regular English eleventh-twelfth grade course came to an end and with it the paired letter exchanges. What took their place, surprisingly enough, was a corporate undertaking in liaison with a stranger the students had never met. Shirley Brice Heath, anthropologist of Stanford University, wrote letters to the class as a whole, enlisting their help in making and forwarding field notes that would contribute to an ethnographic study of their communities. Interpersonal communication was to some extent maintained in the letters students wrote to Heath, but the emphasis shifted in the direction of impersonal expository discourse:

> Branscombe saw the autobiographies, paragraphs, and letters to Heath as occasions to force the students to communicate to distant unknowing audiences the following types of information: 1) detailed explanations and assessments of past events, 2) descriptions of current scenes, actions and people, and 3) arguments defending their course of action, point of view, or interpretation.

That transition was not always easy. Although Heath's letters were photocopied so that each member of the class received one, some students were unhappy at the lack of personal, direct response to the questions they raise:

> Yet by the end of the term, they had learned to negotiate through oral discussion the meaning of the depersonalized and decontextualized passages of Heath's letters. Perhaps most important, they retained their questioning habits from their correspondence with the upperclassmen, continually asking Heath to explain herself, to clarify points, to add more information, and to relate points she made in her letters to points of information she or they had included in earlier letters.[20]

Branscombe organized class work that provided anthropological background, and she played a key role in the discussions aimed at interpreting Heath's letters and in the fine-honing of the drafts of field notes submitted to her. Heath's visit to the class, late in the year, provided one kind of culmination to the course, but threads of follow-up activity arising from the cooperation are still in existence.

Heath and Branscombe are of the firm opinion that this piece of teaching and learning is in sharp contrast to much that is traditional practice in American schools:

> We argue that previous schooling had in essence denied writing as a form of communication to these students; in many ways, this extended denial of a channel of communication by an institution is analogous to the severe and extremely rare cases of parents who shut their children off from verbal and social interaction at birth and prevent them from learning to talk. However, the school's shutting off of written communication for students designated as not "intelligent" enough to write extended prose is an accepted event which occurs frequently.[21]

And they conclude their account by claiming that "the intelligence of a nation" depends upon communicator-audience relations, and that the one-time "special education" students in this ninth grade class were helped "to become 'intelligent' writers within such an audience community."[22]

"Real-World" Writing-Reading

Art Peterson, a participant in the Reading-Writing Planning Conference group that planned this chapter, teaches an advanced composition class, composed primarily of Asian students, at Lowell High School in San Francisco. Most of the students taking that class are studious and hard working. In Peterson's opinion they tended to spend far too much time studying, so that when they expressed an interest in sharing information on "how to enjoy yourself in San Francisco," he encouraged them to produce a magazine under the title *The Best of Teenage San Francisco*.[23]

It is in any case his policy to stock his classroom with "real-world models of strong writing" covering a wide range of types and purposes—baseball almanacs, *Harpers*, examples of advertising, letters to the editor of the newspaper, stories, literature. They serve both as sources of inspiration and models for the students' own writing. It is part of his deliberate policy that students read aloud what they write and listen to fellow students doing the same.

In the present instance he was also particularly concerned to correct what seemed to him to be a tendency on the students' part to express and maintain unsupported judgments. (Clearly, to describe one's prime sources of enjoyment in realistic terms constitutes a fair test.)

The Best of Teenage San Francisco provides for a wide range of interests, including:

The Best Sushi Bar: A few years ago, teenagers were not particularly fond of raw fish. But, now all that has changed, and the search is on for the best sushi bar in San Francisco.

The Best Place to Get a New Look: Glemby does not just style hair. They also do manicures and makeovers. Glass counters are stacked with lipsticks of more than thirty shades, blushers, . . . lipglosses, and an assortment of eyeshadows.

The Best Playground: The Children's Playground, San Francisco's best playground, located near the edge of Golden Gate Park, attracts people of all ages. On any clear as a bell Sunday, chubby-faced pre-schoolers create their "mud-sculptures" while their grandparents lounge at the benches and reminisce about the last time the weather was "this good."

Best Library: San Francisco State Library . . . is an ideal place to study and research; quiet, open until late hours, and full of six stories of wall to wall books. . . . Just as any library, State has some librarians who are glad to help and some who make you feel like a dunce when you ask them to help. Use the library often enough and you'll be able to time your visits to coincide with the tyrant's day off.

Understanding What It Is Writers Do

Writing workshops are a familiar enough phenomenon as freshman composition courses in American colleges and universities. They are in essence courses where student writing is drafted, read, discussed, and, where indicated, revised. The writing, reading, and discussion are typically the work of small groups of students, which may sometimes include the teacher. The teacher's primary responsibility lies in devising assignments that set the writing in motion and in monitoring the final evaluation of student performance.

Carl Klaus of the University of Iowa introduces a series of workshop courses (devised by members of the National Endowment for the Humanities/Iowa Writing Institute in 1979 and 1980) in the following terms:

> The workshop . . . is flexibly designed to allow for a variety of arrangements, so that student writing is sometimes examined by "the class as a whole, sometimes in small groups, sometimes in pairs." . . . The teacher sometimes guides class discussion, sometimes rotates among the small groups and pairs, at other times works one-on-one with individual students as they request. Responses to writing are sometimes conveyed entirely through

discussion, sometimes entirely in writing, sometimes in a combi-
nation of forms. The process of responding is sometimes conducted
according to highly structured guidelines, sometimes in a relatively
open-ended way. . . . And the material under discussion sometimes
consists of notes and rough outlines, sometimes early drafts,
sometimes finished pieces. As these variable arrangements suggest,
the workshop is typically adapted to suit a variety of instructive
purposes—all of which can be seen as contributing to the goal of
writing and learning through experience.

By virtue of repeatedly bringing students together to consider
each other's writing, the workshop is intended to develop within
the group a community of writers and learners.[24]

The twenty courses outlined in the book vary greatly in the degree
in which they involve the reading of texts *not* written by students and
in the nature of such texts. For our purposes here of illustrating good
practice that relates writing to reading, I shall describe two courses
that are differentiated in the kind of discourse they invite students to
read and, hence, the kinds of writing they set out to promote.

The first is a course entitled "Literature and Exploratory Writing,"
devised by Karen Pelz for freshman composition classes at Dartmouth
College. She explains that her intention was to "tap the faculty's
interest and enthusiasm for literature, and at the same time create a
course which would be a genuine freshman composition course, not
just a course in which students wrote themes about literature." Her
object was to give students experience in expressive discourse with
opportunities for extension into various kinds of writing that grow out
of it. The focus of the course is certainly an "exploratory discourse":

Rather than seeking to explain, analyze, or persuade, its main aim
is to allow writers to probe their own experience, to reflect upon
it, and to experiment, with the intention of discovering and
developing their own attitudes, beliefs, feelings, and ideas about
the experience, whether that experience be something they have
done or witnessed in their own lives, a concept or an idea they
have encountered, or a literary text they have read.[25]

Early assignments invite students to write about some "natural"
area of the campus, as experienced at different times and under
different circumstances: then to imagine that scene, before ever the
college existed, as a wilderness in which they are to spend a summer.
This imaginative projection is an approach to the first literary text
presented, Thoreau's *Walden*. Thus

through language, through internal dialogue, through writing,
students begin to explore the world of ideas, and the written
expression of those ideas, by starting with what they know best—

the world which they have experienced and can continue to experience directly—and moving into the world of indirect experience through literature.[26]

The outline goes on to introduce a second literary text, Conrad's *Heart of Darkness*, which students explore by keeping "a reading journal, a collection of writing-in-progress." Finally, with the help of the journal, students write on a topic raised by the novel in any way they like ("analytic, personal response, interpretive") and conclude the course by attempting a final assessment of what has been discovered, what it all means to them.

A brief account of the second course will illustrate the broad range of purposes and contexts covered in the Iowa Writing Institute collection. The texts that Frank Hubbard asks students to read in his course are drawn from a variety of well-known sources, for example the Pledge of Allegiance, the National Anthem, the Lord's Prayer.[27] They represent a focus on language itself: at one level a study of "automatic language"—ritual and formulaic discourse, cliches, set-pieces known by heart—but at a deeper level a concern for the principles and practice of *design in language*.

Hubbard's method is to invite students to encounter a stretch of discourse, to "re-experience it in writing" (for example, by commenting, interpreting, paraphrasing), and finally to analyze the experience. By such metalinguistic activity he hopes to reintroduce meaning in taken-for-granted utterances and thereby to promote the study of the *ways in which discourse conveys meaning*. He believes a course of this nature will equip students to tackle—on their own, by deliberate design— the production of unfamiliar and original forms of discourse.

His closing comment represents the course as a community undertaking and spells out what he hopes it will achieve:

> We tell each other not to accept any advice about writing that isn't rooted in positive response from an audience and developed out of activities each of us designs to suit himself or herself. So, the course at last depends on what the students bring and contribute. The content of the course becomes what we tell ourselves and one another as people and as writers. . . . I want students to formulate for themselves, in terms of experiences they have just had, what the course means, so that they can have similar experiences in the future and formulate again for themselves what the experiences signify; this procedure insures, I hope, that they will understand, rather than memorize before they are able to understand, what it is writers do.[28]

Hallmarks of Good Practice

It seems reasonable at this stage to ask what common features characterize classroom practices we have judged to be *good*. Our answer, however, has to be guarded: in the first place, good practice must be responsive to a great range of variations in the nature of classroom communities and in their organizational contexts. It follows that what is good practice in one situation will not of necessity be good practice in another. Organizational contexts, moreover, will offer a range of constraints, some highly concrete and visible, others abstract, ambiguous perhaps, and difficult to identify. Practices that succumb in some degree to such pressures may nevertheless powerfully reflect good judgment in the features they salvage.

Our focuses will be upon teacher behavior—upon actions and decisions over which the teacher has control. There may be aspects of good practice for which the responsibility lies elsewhere, and we shall have to make this clear in our commentary.

First, as for the Teacher...

Priority must go to a proper conception of the teaching-learning relationship and its implications for the power structure of the classroom. It is our belief that a good teacher does not dominate the class, but seeks to create an active, cooperative community capable of taking initiatives, able to draw upon individual strengths, and contributing to the elimination of individual weaknesses. Rather than relying on the teacher as the go-between in all learning, group members expect to learn with each other and from each other. It is an important corollary here to recognize that the teacher is, first and foremost, a member of the group and is willing to that end to forgo privileges that would promote him or her out of that status.

Such a regime recognizes the principle that experience is a prime source of learning, but adds the notion that shared experience should enrich or extend the learning. (Attitudes, interests, intentions—the motive forces that get enterprises going—tend to be contagious.)

Notice that it is the teacher's initiative that establishes and sustains such a regime. This is achieved partly by reason of what the teacher *says* but becomes effective primarily by his or her example. Thus the teacher is likely to try to cut down on teacher talk and make *listening* a major target. By the same token, however successful teachers may be in encouraging students to write for real purposes to real audiences, they are likely themselves to remain privileged first readers of what the students write.

Other behaviors teachers will forgo include *because I say so* justifications and the habit of asking questions to which they know the answers, and probably the habit of whipping up a little spurious enthusiasm by imposing a competitive framework upon learning activities.

We must stress that none of this should be taken as denying the fact that teachers have ultimately the responsibility of "managing" the class, that is to say, of ensuring conditions in which learning can take place. This responsibility and the authority required to back it constitute, in the regime as we have described it, an invisible pedagogy: the management role is something that underlies but is distinct from the teaching role: in good practice the teaching role takes over and the management role remains latent—a backup potential.

This general view of the teaching-learning relationship has many specific applications to the handling of writing and reading in class. Because an individual's language so intimately reflects his or her identity, it is important that the classroom community should openly acknowledge ethnic, class, and cultural differences, encouraging an appreciation of language variety, a sense of the richness of the corporate group. Many of the examples we have quoted refer to the need to establish an "accepting" environment, one in which students feel secure enough to take risks.

This respect for cultural and other differences will involve the questioning of many traditional assumptions: our views of language norms, of accepted modes of perceiving the world, of behavior rituals and routines need to be tentative, open to complication and subdivision in the light of our experience of individuals and their communities.

If writing and reading are to be mastered by using them to achieve the users' own purposes, provision must be made for choice in what is written and what is read. Balancing the resulting diversity with the desirability of corporate undertakings becomes an important logistic, and curriculum decisions become a matter for negotiation.

The classroom needs to be rich in verbal stimuli—books (fiction and nonfiction, mainstream and ethnic), spare magazines, newspapers, printed ephemera, writings by students and teachers (in many languages, where this is appropriate), records, audio and video tapes, and so forth. And the classroom must be rich, too, in opportunities to use language in a variety of modes and functions—reflecting the developmental importance of expressive talk and writing.

Taking up a point that Carl Klaus has made,[29] we would claim that both writing and reading are (1) profoundly personal and (2) profoundly social activities. Such activities will best be served by a flexible organization that provides ample opportunities for individuals to work on their own or in pairs or in small groups but intersperses such sequences with whole group sessions, for example a coming together to watch a student presentation or hear a reading.

In this connection, we believe there is a special value—particularly but not exclusively at the earlier levels of schooling—in having the teacher read aloud to the class. The written language has its own rhythms and cadences, and having an inner sense of these becomes an essential resource to a writer.

We would put great stress on setting up a situation in which it is not only the students who write but also the teacher. Teaching and learning are not truly interactive if the teacher plays only from the touchline.

Classroom regimes that place great stress on grades or frequent testing have the effect of undermining the learning value of the class undertakings; they discourage the risk-taking necessary to discovery. Summative evaluation may well be part of a teacher's responsibility, but it is better carried out as an operation distinct from teaching; this can be done by periodic assessment of accumulated performances. (It is only too easy for the classroom to degenerate into the only place in the world where *everything we do, we do in order to have someone else tell us how well we've done it!*) As a general principle, it seems to us desirable that we should keep our teaching role clear of our evaluating role—preferably by having students collect a portfolio of work over a period and, at the close of the period, make their own selection (under guidance) of work on which to be assessed.

Writing and reading can be intimately interrelated only by floating both on a sea of talk; but to achieve this requires time and patience on the teacher's part, since traditionally we have shown that we do not value student talk.

Next, for Administrators and Others...

To itemize now the kinds of constraint that may affect what can be done in classrooms is, in one sense, to move from the *pros* to the *cons* of good practice. In doing so we shall be indicating some limitations upon what a teacher can achieve and pointing to action required of other agencies.

Timetabling can make or mar a classroom program. While in general there is greater freedom of action for a class that has longer rather than shorter time allocations, and while it might be argued that English and language arts teaching relies particularly heavily on the personality of the teacher, hence continuity of class with teacher is desirable (for example, an elementary classroom teacher covering two or more grades within one group), the only really satisfactory solution lies in internal discussion and negotiation before timetable decisions are made.

If, as we have suggested, talk is the catalyst that relates reading to writing and both to firsthand and secondary experience, allowance must be made for active, animated, extended discussion. Where architectural inadequacies or authoritarian attitudes place too great a value on a quiet classroom, what a class can achieve may be severely restricted. We would point out, in this context, that we believe many teachers took their first steps towards an interactive view of teaching and learning not via a writing workshop approach as did the teachers referred to above in the New Hampshire publication, but by testing out and discovering the learning potential of student talk. Easy access to tape recorders made it possible for groups of teachers to *listen* to student talk when no teacher was present, and many of us were amazed at what the talk could sometimes achieve.[30]

Administrators need to recognize that, while objective and criterion-referenced tests can give us information about individual and group progress, the information they yield is partial only. Test results need to be supplemented by the holistic, experience-based judgments of teachers who have worked with the students. Where reliability is valued at the expense of validity, testing procedures deteriorate to the point where whatever can be reliably measured is worth measuring— a procedure that has been likened to pulling up a plant at frequent intervals to see how the root is developing. An authoritative report to the National Institute of Education in 1974 from leading psychologists and linguists stated their view this way:

> If we could somehow convey the notion that diagnosis and teaching are inseparable, we might reduce the need for large-scale efforts in instrument development and rely more on the intuition and sensitivity of experienced teachers to evaluate the preparation, competence, and needs of their students.[31]

That diagnosis and teaching are inseparable is something we accept without affecting our recommendation above that teaching and summative evaluation should be kept separate. Diagnosis is teachers' way of monitoring their own performance, deriving information for their own use. Summative evaluation is a response to the justified external demand for a progress report: it is information for the student, parents, other teachers and—on occasions—prospective employers or college admission agents.

Good practice has benefited a great deal in the past fifty years or so by what we have learned from observing and studying "natural learning processes." As a result, many of the features of good practice show marked differences from the practices of a generation or more ago—the period during which the parents of children now in our schools were educated. It seems to us to be an important part of a teacher's responsibility to keep the parents informed of new procedures and their rationale. At the same time, we must stress here the responsibility of administrators to assist in this process and the responsibility of parents to listen and be open to new potentials. In the final analysis, we recognize that some needed changes in classrooms can be achieved only when the community recognizes and supports them.

There have been repeated references above, by teachers citing examples of good practice, to the need for an accepting environment, one that makes possible the risk-taking that is involved in genuine, exploratory learning. But teaching is also a high-risk undertaking and teachers themselves need to operate in an accepting environment. A system that initiates a regime of surveillance rather than a regime of trust may succeed in weeding out individual weak spots, but will undermine by loss of morale the general level of teacher performance. Similarly, a school that as an institution operates a regime of surveillance will militate against the effectiveness of good practice in its classrooms.

If "instruction" is to remain a customary word to label the teacher's role in American education, its connotations will have to be considerably widened. We venture to quote here a claim made in the British Government Report on Reading and the Uses of Language in School (the "Bullock Report") since it bears particularly on the teaching-learning of English and language arts:

1. all genuine learning involves discovery, and it is as ridiculous to suppose that teaching begins and ends with "instruction" as it is to suppose that "learning by discovery" means leaving children to their own resources;
2. language has a heuristic function; that is to say a child can learn by talking and writing as certainly as he can by listening and reading;
3. to exploit the process of discovery through language in all its uses is the surest means of enabling a child to master his mother tongue.[32]

Research and the Classroom

A fuller account of relevant research having been given in earlier chapters, it is our concern here to refer briefly to studies that throw— or seem to throw—direct light on classroom procedures in the teaching of writing and reading. By way of introduction, we must report that there was disagreement within the planning group as to the value of research studies to classroom practitioners. Certainly, teachers are not in any position to wait upon research findings: as problems arise, they must act from intuition and experience to effect as good a solution as they can. In general, from intuition, experience, and the slow fruits of reflection, teachers know, better than they are able to perform; that is to say, more often than not, it is not lack of knowledge but lack of opportunity to put that knowledge into practice that rules out or restricts good practice. On the other hand, it can hardly be denied that educational practice has, over the years, benefited widely from the thinking that has contributed to and resulted from research.

To set the scene for the studies we shall describe, we could do no better than refer to an analysis based on observations and carried out by Russian psychologist L.S. Vygotsky more than fifty years ago. It is described in the last chapter of a posthumous publication, prepared by four American editors, entitled *Mind in Society*.[33] The chapter itself is called "The Prehistory of Written Language." Vygotsky introduces it by claiming that teachers have made the mistake of focusing upon, on the one hand, the motor skills needed to learn to read and, on the other, the motor skills needed to learn to write. Psychologists, moreover, have followed suit, so that both theorists and practitioners have "paid remarkably little attention to the question of written language as such, that is, a particular system of symbols and signs whose mastery heralds a critical turning-point in the entire cultural development of the child."[34] Vygotsky traces contributory developments towards mastery of written language in children's use of gesture, drawing, make-believe play (and the role that speech plays in these activities). He concludes that, rather than receiving reading and writing "at the hands of the teacher," children should master the written language through and by means of their own activities, primarily their play. Hence the statement with which we opened this chapter: "The teaching should be organized in such a way that reading and writing are necessary for something."

I think we may learn from Vygotsky that the development of *writing-cum-reading* will be a complex, many-faceted, often discontinuous progress, rooted in early drawing and play activity, and that in the process of discovering that they "can draw not only objects but also speech," children are likely to move through a topographical stage (where the position of marks on a page carries meaning) to a pictographic stage (where, for example, an 0-shape may represent an egg) and thence to the stage of conventional signs.[35] It is worth noting that in a number of schools, with such conclusions from Vygotsky in mind, kindergarten teachers have provided, along with every sheet of drawing paper, smaller and perhaps colored sheets for writing on. By establishing this procedure, the teachers are able to study the initial stages that children move through as they accompany their drawings with a parallel activity they conceive of as "writing."

In a masterly review of research on written composition Scardamalia and Bereiter[36] turn aside briefly to suggest that Vygotsky's notion of "internalization" could profitably be investigated in the context of the forms of "facilitation" by which teachers attempt to influence the composing behaviors of students, including conferencing:

> On first thought, conferencing would seem to be well designed for internalization: the thinking, carried out jointly at first, comes in time to be carried out in the mind of the student. But the form of the conference is dialogue, and there is no indication from research to suggest that the mature composing process has the form of an internal dialogue. . . . Serious research is needed to determine what students internalize from what teachers have helped or induced them to do.[37]

We might point out here that, though evidence does not suggest that adults operate an internalized dialogue, there is certainly evidence that young children talk to themselves, and sometimes to other people, in the course of composing.

In this context Scardamalia and Bereiter take up the question of the value of expressive writing:

> Although data collected with a view to external validity are close to nonexistent, there seems little reason to doubt the abundance of case material indicating that, given a reasonably supportive context, most children will take readily to opportunities for expressive writing. . . . There thus seems to be substantial merit in the current enthusiasm for expressive activity approaches to writing, especially as regards developing written language fluency and a sense of the personal satisfactions that can come from writing.[38]

They go on, however, to point out certain limitations: for example, because of the limited nature of the demands made on a writer in producing expressive writing, it may prove to be a means of fostering only relatively simple kinds of levels of composing. This would indicate that it should be regarded as a bridge, a transitional stage towards more developed forms of discourse (a recommendation that is certainly in line with examples of good practice we have quoted earlier). Further, since in current active approaches to writing the teacher is regarded as collaborator rather than as expert instructor, the degree to which a learner profits eventually from this collaboration must depend to some extent upon his or her success in internalizing the teacher's contribution.

Clearly, a fuller understanding of internalization would also throw light on the relationship of writing to reading, perhaps in a variety of ways. Scardamalia and Bereiter report two kinds of cognitive study along these lines: research into the effects of various literary devices on readers, and research on the effects of literary models upon students' writing.[39] The problem of providing operational definitions of literary devices (as distinct from existing literary-critical characterizations) has tended to hold up progress in the former type of study, and systematic enquiries of the second type are at an early stage and seem so far to have yielded little that was not already obvious. The classroom will certainly be the appropriate setting for further researches of both kinds.

There is one problem on which I have long thought grassroots evidence from the classroom was urgently needed: that is, the question as to how far implicit rule systems supplement and how far they may substitute for explicit knowledge of rules. Theorists, it seems, offer conflicting and confusing views on this point.

In comparing inexperienced with expert writers, Scardamalia and Paris suggest that, whereas all writers use implicit knowledge of text features, adults use also explicit knowledge of such features (for example, "argument," "introduction," "example") in the course of composing.[40] Their experiments showed that grade four and grade six schoolchildren *could be taught* to use such explicit knowledge, *but its use made their writing less and not more coherent.*

The means by which learners acquire knowledge of genre is a key issue in this connection. In a carefully controlled observation of the reading and writing performances of children in grades three, six, and nine, Langer found that, while stories and reports are firmly differentiated by the third grade, knowledge and control of story form is well in advance of that of report form: report writing undergoes dramatic change between grades six and nine.[41] Langer suggests that the source of children's knowledge of genre as it is revealed both in their reading and their writing lies in the *"functional forms they hear and use in their daily lives"*—knowledge which we must therefore presume is likely to be predominately implicit rather than explicit.

Such a conclusion is borne out by Freedman, Carey, and Miller's study of six students who, although not regular law students, were taking a law course at Carleton University and thus acquiring a genre of academic discourse new to them.[42] This, the researchers found, is how they did it:

1. The learners approach the task with a "dimly felt sense" of the new genre they are attempting.
2. They begin composing by focusing on the specific content to be embodied in this genre.
3. In the course of the composing, the "dimly felt sense" of the genre is both formulated and modified as (a) this "sense," (b) the composing processes, and (c) the unfolding text interrelate and modify each other.
4. On the basis of the external feedback (the grade assigned), the learners either confirm or modify their map of the genre.[43]

The authors stress that it is the purposeful addressing of the question set by the assignment that plays a vital part in the interaction by which the genre is constructed: compare Langer's reference above to rhetorical forms as *functional*.

Perhaps this is a process John Dewey can help us to understand: in *Democracy and Education* he wrote:

> For the person approaching a subject, the simple thing is his purpose—the use he desires to make of material, tool or technical process, no matter how complicated the process of execution may be. The unity of the purpose, with the concentration upon details which it entails, confers simplicity upon the elements which have to be reckoned with in the course of the action. It furnishes each with a single meaning according to its service in carrying on the whole enterprise.[44]

A growing knowledge and understanding of how writing relates to reading and how both are founded upon development of spoken language has been the outcome of psychological, sociological, and linguistic studies over recent years. Yet, more recently, we have been sharply reminded that such studies are based principally upon observations of mainstream, middle-class families and that the picture needs to be considerably complicated if it is to do justice to the situation within our multicultural schools and societies. A major contribution in this field—and one that is gaining increasing recognition—is the work of Shirley Brice Heath, notably her book *Ways with Words*.[45] Her ethnographic study of three communities located in neighboring areas of Carolina raises the problem of the gap between the linguistic expectations, demands, and assumptions of the average elementary school, and the language habits and attitudes of many of the children who go there: a gap, moreover, that, under present educational circumstances, will widen with the years.

We cannot leave the subject of research without remarking that if the current concern with the role of teacher-researcher makes the kind of headway it promises in the United States, there can hardly be a more suitable field for such classroom inquiries than the topic of this present chapter.

Teachers and Change

There are educational practitioners and theorists who have operated long enough in the recognition that teaching and learning are interactive behaviors to have become aware that any agency outside the classroom can influence learning outcomes only as its demands are mediated by and represented in the teacher's behavior. Such a realization is derived from an increasing sensitivity to the nature of individual learning patterns, the role of intentionality in learning, and the importance of the classroom community as a source of knowledge and understanding. These are insights not yet widely accepted, and there are researchers who still speak of "teacher-proof kits" and administrators who still look for outcomes predictable in terms of measured behaviors. (In contrast, the best teachers, we believe, secure rich outcomes by the initial and progressive planning of *input*, in the light of their knowledge of the subject, their experience of the world, and their familiarity with the needs and interests of the particular students they teach. This is planning, moreover, that allows for choice and negotiation on the part of those students.)

Our concern here is to claim that our target audience for the kind of thing we have been saying about good practice, about integration in the teaching of writing and reading, will be primarily the classroom teacher. Schools and educational systems tend to be slow to change, but when they do initiate deliberate change, it is usually by a kind of movement that spreads from teacher to teacher.

We shall be addressing teachers of all subjects, not only English and language arts teachers. A movement that began in England with a group of London teachers in the late sixties has become worldwide, still under the title they gave it, Language across the Curriculum. The lively presence of that movement on the American continent provides us with an audience already sympathetic to the kinds of insights that lie behind the good practice we have described. For teachers of the elementary grades, the Language across the Curriculum campaign indicates little more than the need to coordinate teaching and learning strategies concerning language throughout a school staff, since the classroom teacher is already responsible for whatever is achieved by writing and reading in all subject areas. At the secondary school level, however, the campaign must try to recruit the concern of teachers of varied interests, many of whom are inclined to feel that language is the concern of the English department and nobody else. Our approach must indicate that what is at issue is the quality of learning achieved by students in the subject they teach, and it must suggest that what is needed is an agreed policy for language in the school: a document prepared by staff in consultation that shall be at one and the same time the agenda for further periodic staff discussion and an instrument of agreed policy for action.

This is a procedure that cannot be rushed: English and language arts teachers are likely to be called on to initiate action, but will need to do so with tact and caution. Experience suggests that the best plan is to begin in a small way, working with a few allies and attempting to extend the circle gradually.

We see our appeal to classroom teachers as part of a process of *professionalization*, a move towards equipping teachers to manage more completely their educational function in society, and in doing so to earn the confidence of the community they serve and the professional status that goes with that responsibility. As such, we look to the National Writing Project as a model of the appropriate disseminating procedures—procedures that draw fully upon the resources participants bring with them and at the same time provide a genuine learning experience in the context of a supportive group.

Laury Fischer, another member of the Reading-Writing Planning Conference group that planned this chapter and a teacher in Washington High School, Fremont, California, stressed these issues in his comments to the group. He pointed out the importance of consultation among teachers—opportunities to observe each other in action and to discuss the whys and wherefores of particular practices. Grants may be used to provide time in the school day for such procedures. Without opportunities of this kind, teachers new to the task are above all likely to model their teaching on the practices of traditional, established, senior colleagues. Change in such a context comes hard: new insights and understandings have to fight for acceptance into practice. Fischer thus sees teacher education, properly handled, as a major opportunity to break through this resistance.

Looking at the present state of affairs from the point of view of strategies for change, we feel that what is above all lacking is administrative support for the innovations that classroom teachers are ready to attempt. For this reason we would put a high priority on the need to provide professional development opportunities for principals and other administrators. It is no denial of anything we have said about the primary role of classroom teachers to add now that many initiatives are likely to come to nothing for lack of encouragement and support at the right moment from administrators. We believe this lack is as likely to be due to failure to understand what is at issue as it is to result from a lack of concern. After all, teachers are in the classrooms, where first order problems arise and must be dealt with, and this is a learning experience denied to administrators.

There is, we believe, a complementary need for support in a variety of ways from universities. Degree structures are not always adaptable to the kinds of professional development of teachers most in demand; and where suitable courses are provided, the staff concerned may receive scant recognition, either professional or financial. Again, university teaching styles deemed appropriate for a typical student population will often reflect an undervaluing of the experiences the schoolteachers themselves can contribute to the course. (As we have suggested, it is in their classrooms that the problems arise and are dealt with: where the practitioner's wisdom and experience can interact with the specialist's expertise, learning and teaching may genuinely become a two-way affair.)

But finally, when in England the Bullock Report was published, with its firm recommendations for change, a teacher wrote to the *Daily Telegraph* to say that "failure to implement the Bullock Report was built into the timetable." That was in 1975, and the years since then have proven her right. The professionalization of the teacher, which prospered in our countries during the period of post-world-war expansion and right through the sixties, has suffered a sharp decline since that time. If last words carry solemn and portentous messages, our last words shall be a plea for the provision of more time for staff consultation within the school day. We believe that only in this way can the potential for change that we have been concerned with be brought to fruition.

Notes

1. Staton, J. (1984). Thinking together: The role of language interaction in children's reasoning. In C. Thaiss and C. Suhor (Eds.), *Speaking and writing, K-12* (pp. 178–179). Urbana, IL: National Council of Teachers of English.
2. Shuy, R.W. (1985). Dialogue journals and reading comprehension. *Dialogue, 3*, 2–3, p. 2.

3. Hansen, J., Newkirk, T., and Graves, D. (Eds.) (1985). *Breaking ground: Teachers relate reading and writing in the elementary school.* Portsmouth, NH: Heinemann.

4. Hansen et al. (Eds.) (1985), p. ix.

5. Hansen et al. (Eds.) (1985), p. 16.

6. Hansen et al. (Eds.) (1985), p. 17.

7. Hansen et al. (Eds.) (1985), p. 20.

8. Hansen et al. (Eds.) (1985), p. 26.

9. Hansen et al. (Eds.) (1985), pp. 150–151.

10. Iser, W. (1978). *The art of reading* (p. 140). London: Routledge & Kegan Paul.

11. Cooper, F.S. (1972). How is language conveyed by speech? In J.F. Kavanagh and I.G. Mattingly (Eds.), *Language by ear and by eye* (p. 36). Cambridge, MA: MIT Press.

12. Chittenden, L. (1982). What if all the whales were gone before we become friends? In M. Barr, P. D'Arcy, and M.K. Healy (Eds.), *What's going on?* (pp. 36–51). Upper Montclair, NJ: Boynton/Cook.

13. Chittenden (1982), p. 37.

14. Chittenden (1982), p. 43.

15. *Our friends in the waters* (1979). Mill Valley, CA: Old Mill School.

16. A full account of this experimental teaching is given in Heath, S.B., and Branscombe, A. (1985). "Intelligent writing" in an audience community: Teacher, students, and researcher. In S.W. Freedman (Ed.), *The acquisition of written language: Response and revision* (pp.3–32). Norwood, NJ: Ablex.

17. Heath and Branscombe (1985), p. 10.

18. Heath and Branscombe (1985), p. 11.

19. Heath and Branscombe (1985), p. 29.

20. Heath and Branscombe (1985), p. 23.

21. Heath and Branscombe (1985), p. 23.

22. Heath and Branscombe (1985), p. 31.

23. *Best of teenage San Francisco* (1985). San Francisco: Lowell High School.

24. Klaus, C.H., and Jones, N. (Eds.) (1984). *Courses for change in writing: A selection from the N.E.H./Iowa Institute* (p. xx). Upper Montclair, NJ: Boynton/Cook and University of Iowa.

25. Klaus and Jones (Eds.) (1984), p. 59.

26. Klaus and Jones (Eds.) (1984), p. 61.

27. Klaus and Jones (Eds.) (1984), p. 4.

28. Klaus and Jones (Eds.) (1984), p. 8.

29. Klaus and Jones (Eds.) (1984), p. xvii.

30. To document this aspect of professional development as it took place among London teachers, see:

     Rosen, C., and Rosen, H. (1973). *The language of primary school children.* Harmondsworth, England: Penguin Books.

     Britton, J. (1970). *Language and learning.* Harmondsworth, England: Penguin Press.

31. Miller, G.A. (Ed.) (1974). *Linguistic communication: Perspectives for research: Report of the Study Group on Linguistic Communication to the National Institute of Education* (p. 27). Newark, DE: International Reading Association.

32. Great Britain Department of Education and Science (1975). *A language for life: Report of the committee of inquiry appointed by the Secretary of State for Education and Science under the chairmanship of Sir A. Bullock.* London: H.M.S.O.

33. Vygotsky, L.S. (1978). *Mind in society* (M. Cole, V. John-Steiner, S. Scribner, and E. Souberman, Eds.). Cambridge, MA: Harvard University Press.

34. Vygotsky (1978), p. 106.

35. Donaldson, M. (1984). Speech and writing and modes of learning. In H. Goelman, A.A. Oberg, and F. Smith (Eds.), *Awakening to literacy* (pp. 174–184). Exeter, NH: Heinemann.

    Dyson, A. Haas. (1984a). Emerging alphabetic literacy in school contexts: Towards defining the gap between school curriculum and child mind. *Written Communication, 1,* 5–55.

    Ferreiro, E., and Teberosky, A. (1982). *Literacy before schooling.* Exeter, NH: Heinemann.

    Luria, A.R. (1983). The development of writing in the child. In M. Martlew (Ed.), *The psychology of written language* (pp. 237–277). London: Wiley.

36. Scardamalia, M., and Bereiter, C. (1986). Research on written composition. In M.C. Wittrock (Ed.), *The handbook of research on teaching* (pp. 778–803). New York: Macmillan.

37. Scardamalia and Bereiter (1986), pp. 797–798.

38. Scardamalia and Bereiter (1986), p. 793.

39. Scardamalia and Bereiter (1986), p. 798.

40. Scardamalia, M., and Paris, P. (1985). The function of explicit discourse knowledge in the development of text representations and composing strategies. *Cognition and Instruction, 2,* 1–39.

41. Langer, J.A. (1985). Children's sense of genre: A study of performance on parallel reading and writing tasks. *Written Communication, 2,* 157–187, p.185.

42. Freedman, A., Carey, J., and Miller, T. (1986). *Learning to write again: Six students acquiring a new genre of academic discourse.* Ottawa: Carleton University Department of Linguistics.

43. Freedman et al. (1986), p. 35.

44. Dewey, J. (1916). *Democracy and education.* (p. 234). New York: Macmillan.

45. Heath, S.B. (1983). *Ways with words: Language, life, and work in communities and classrooms.* Cambridge: Cambridge University Press.

7 Commentary

The Writing-Reading Connection: Taking Off the Handcuffs

Art Peterson

I wish I could remember that French phrase for the retort that comes to mind the moment one leaves a party. I could use it now. Of course, the conference on writing-reading relationships had not been a party, and the ideas I was mulling over would hardly pass for a Gallic witticism, but as I emerged from the Berkeley Faculty Club into a February drizzle, I did keep reformulating a thought I wished I had had the nerve to express: Most of the classrooms I know about would be healthier learning environments if writing and reading were less connected. Driving home, I waited for my imaginary audience to stop the hisses, boos, and cries of "throw the bum out." Then I explained.

From what I have seen, the writing-reading connection too often becomes a restrictive yolk rather than a liberating merger. In many high school English classrooms the writing-reading connection comes down to a single exercise: A literary work is to be deciphered. The teacher guides the class through the text as decoded by one or another critical essay in *Twentieth Century Views*. The students, amazed that the teacher "sees all this stuff," are not about to argue with Norman O. Brown as filtered through Ms. Gundersen. In the obligatory writing that follows the completion of each work, students are asked either to regurgitate what they have been told or to become nervous players in the teacher's "What Is This Symbol I Am Holding Behind My Back" game. When the relationship between writing and reading comes to mirror the graduate school model, the link between the two becomes more an exercise in cryptology than an opportunity for self-discovery.

I may be overstating the case. While many teachers send their students fishing for the flute motif in "Death of a Salesman," others ask their students to use the play as a way of examining their own lives, relating the play to their experience and to the fathers, sons, salesmen, and others they have known. Further, it need hardly be added that the search for a flute motif—or an analysis of this kind— provides an exercise in careful reading, ordering of ideas, and understanding of a writer's technique and purpose. What I object to are four years of writing and reading dedicated entirely to the equivalent of flute motif searches.

Teachers of college freshmen seem almost terminally depressed reading the voiceless, prefabricated prose submitted, sometimes even proudly, by their students. "Did these people read or write *anything* in high school?" these teachers ask. The answer is: Yes, many of these students have been exposed to the standard repertoire of high school classics, and they have written about these works. The catch is, they have brought to this writing the degree of passion and originality normally reserved for a note thanking a distant aunt for a totally inappropriate birthday gift.

As the possessor of these jaded views, I was a bit nervous about participating in a conference that seemed to have as its goal the reinforcement of a link that has too often atrophied into a marriage turned sour. At the conference I was assigned to the "classroom" group, along with some of the most prominent people associated with English language arts instruction: James Britton, James Moffett, James Gray. I was feeling a little bit like a first-year rabbinical student who had wandered into a reunion of Old Testament prophets. But as the meeting proceeded, I relaxed a bit. As it turned out, the discussion was, as they say at the State Department, "wide ranging." Particularly in the general sessions, we often talked past each other. We all seemed to have our own shtick. I was curious as to how James Britton, charged with writing the chapter for the "classroom" group, would bring all this together. I certainly did not envy his task.

But when Britton sent along the draft of his chapter, I was genuinely delighted. The thread of meaning he had pulled from our discussion was compatible with all the things I wish I had said. Britton was defining the writing-reading connection in the broadest possible terms. The connection could be made through dialogue journals, in which two people communicate through writing and reading; it could be made by middle school students who read everything they can find about whales and supplement this reading with personal experience, so that the student writers become expert enough to bring a personal voice to their subject; it could be encouraged by asking college students, before they read *Walden*, to write their imaginings of their campus as wilderness. Other groups at the conference were also cataloguing techniques for linking literature and writing that would prod creative expression and personal voice. (See, for instance, Rebekah Caplan's suggestions in this volume for teaching style.) The message that emerges is that written analysis of literature is only one of the writing-reading connections.

Finally now, I would like to make my own contribution. In what ways have I encouraged the writing-reading connection? Here are thirty-two ways I was able to recall in the ten minutes I allotted myself. They are meant to supplement, not replace, the reading and analysis of literature.

Reading	*Writing*
Advertising placards on public transportation	Analysis of these ads in the context of primary human concerns: work, food, sex, health, and so forth
The travel section of the newspaper	Parody: your neighborhood as a tourist attraction
An antismoking pamphlet	Script and shot sequence for TV spot propagandizing one of the points made in the pamphlet
The section of the Declaration of Independence that lists grievances against the king	Model: teens list grievances against adults and vice versa
A book of dream interpretation	Analysis of your dreams applying the book's principles
The Nieman Marcus Christmas catalogue	An essay on American excess
Principal's directives	Revision for clarity and style
The Driver's License Handbook	Rewrite of ordinances as poetry
A thirty-year-old copy of *Life* magazine	An analysis of the times
Teen or *Tiger Beat* magazine	Essay questioning or defending the values of today's youth
Dog-training manual	Contrast with the experiences trying to train a real dog
Entry in the *Dictionary of American Biography*	Personal ad for the biographee
Report in *Omni* or *Discovery* about a future development	Dialogue between two future people confronting this innovation
A story written by a classmate	An interview with the classmate about her story

Reading	Writing
A story intended for primary grade readers	Adaptation to make appealing to teenagers
Any news story in today's paper	Imaginary follow-up news story reporting what happens tomorrow
Any list of rules	A film-shot sequence illustrating one of these rules
An encyclopedia article about a president	Partial adaptation to serve as a moral tale for young children
Who's Who in America	An entry for someone you know
The Ten Commandments	An explanation in terms of modern experience
Some pages of a Stephen King novel	Adaptation to a screenplay
Police reports	Analysis of types of crime in the community
Newspaper weather reports	Script for an entertaining TV weather person
Old joke books	Analysis of social change
Magazine reporting an election campaign three years ago	Analysis of charges and promises made at that time
Book of grand opera plot summaries	Revision to suit modern setting and circumstances
A favorable and a negative review of the same movie or concert	Contrast of diction and choice of detail in the two reviews
A letter to the editor	An argument in opposition
Two city telephone books, ten years apart	Analysis of social and economic change
Album liner notes	Sorting out of fact and opinion
Prepared food ingredient labels	Analysis and contrast
Machiavelli's *The Prince*	Evaluation of modern leaders, using Machiavelli's criteria

I could keep going. Anyone could, including a young and enthusiastic beginning teacher who asked me at a recent workshop, "What can students write about if they don't write about literature?" For her, a copy of this essay is in the mail.

Comprehensive References

Adams, M.J., and Bruce, B. (1982). Background knowledge and reading comprehension. In J.A. Langer and T. Smith-Burke (Eds.), *Reader meets author/bridging the gap: A psycholinguistic and sociolinguistic perspective* (pp. 2–25). Newark, DE: International Reading Association.

Allen, R.V. (1976). *Language experiences in communication.* Boston: Houghton Mifflin.

Amastae, J., and Elias-Olivares, L. (Eds.) (1982). *Spanish in the United States: Sociolinguistic aspects.* Cambridge: Cambridge University Press.

Anderson, A., and Stokes, S. (1984). Social and institutional influences on the development and practice of literacy. In H. Goelman, A. Oberg, and F. Smith (Eds.), *Awakening to literacy* (pp. 24–37). Exeter, NH: Heinemann.

Anderson, P. (1985). What survey research tells us about writing at work. In L. Odell and D. Goswami (Eds.), *Writing in non-academic settings.* New York and London: Guilford Press.

Anderson, R.C., Hiebert, E.H., Scott, J., and Wilkinson, I.A.G. (1984). *Becoming a nation of readers.* Washington, DC: National Institute of Education, National Academy of Education, Commission on Reading.

Anderson, R.C., Pichert, J.W., Goetz, E.T., Schallert, D.L., Stevens, K.V., and Trollip, S.R. (1976). Instantiation of general terms. *Journal of Verbal Learning and Verbal Behavior, 15,* 667–679.

Applebee, A.N. (1974). *Tradition and reform in the teaching of English: A history.* Urbana, IL: National Council of Teachers of English.

Applebee, A.N. (1981). *Writing in the secondary school* (Research Monograph No. 21). Urbana, IL: National Council of Teachers of English.

Applebee, A.N. (1982). Literature. In H.E. Mitzel (Ed.), *Encyclopedia of educational research* (5th ed.) (pp. 1105–1118). New York: Free Press.

Applebee, A.N. (1984a). Writing and reasoning. *Review of Educational Research, 54,* 577–596.

Applebee, A.N. (1984b). *Contexts for learning to write: Studies of secondary school instruction.* Norwood, NJ: Ablex.

Applebee, A.N. (1986). Problems in process approaches: Toward a reconceptualization of process instruction. In A.R. Petrosky and D. Bartholomae (Eds.), *The teaching of writing. 85th Yearbook of the National Society for the Study of Education* (pp. 95–113). Chicago: University of Chicago Press.

Artley, A.S. (1950). Research concerning interrelationships among the language arts. *Elementary English, 27,* 527–537.

Ash, S., and Myhill, J. (1983). *Linguistic correlates of interethnic contact.* Philadelphia: University of Pennsylvania, Linguistics Laboratory.

255

Ashton-Warner, S. (1963). *Teacher.* New York: Simon & Schuster.

Atlas, M. (1979, April). *Expert-novice differences in the writing process.* Paper presented at the annual meeting of the American Educational Research Association, San Francisco. (ERIC Document Reproduction Service No. ED 170 769)

Atwell, N. (1987). *In the middle.* Upper Montclair, NJ: Boynton/Cook.

Baker, F.T. (1913). Composition. In P. Monroe (Ed.), *A cyclopedia of education: Vol. 2* (pp. 165–168). New York: Macmillan.

Baker, L., and Brown, A. (1984). Metacognitive skills and reading. In D. Pearson, M.L. Kamil, R. Barr, and P. Mosenthal (Eds.), *Handbook of reading research* (pp. 353–394). New York: Longman.

Bataille, R. (1982). Writing in the world of work: What undergraduates report. *College Composition and Communication, 33,* 226–283.

Baugh, J. (1981). Design and implementation of writing instruction for speakers of non-standard English: Perspectives for a national neighborhood literacy program. In B. Cronnell (Ed.), *The writing needs of linguistically different students* (pp. 17–44). Los Alamitos, CA: Southwest Research Laboratory Education Research and Development.

Bauman, R., and Sherzer, J. (Eds.) (1974). *Explorations in the ethnography of speaking.* Cambridge: Cambridge University Press.

Becker, W.C., Dixon, R., and Anderson-Inman, L. (1980). *Morphographic and root word analysis of 26,000 high frequency words.* Eugene: University of Oregon Follow Through Project, College of Education.

Beers, J.W., and Henderson, E.H. (1977). A study of developing orthographic concepts among first grade children. *Research in the Teaching of English, 11,* 133–148.

Bereiter, C., and Scardamalia, M. (1984). Learning about writing from reading. *Written Communication, 1,* 163–188.

Bereiter, C., and Scardamalia, M. (1985). Cognitive coping strategies and the problem of "inert knowledge." In S. Chipman, J. Segal, and R. Glaser (Eds.), *Thinking and learning skills: Vol. 2* (pp. 65–80). Hillsdale, NJ: Erlbaum.

Berg, I. (1972). *Education and jobs: The great training robbery.* New York: Praeger.

Berko, J. (1958). The child's learning of English morphology. *Word, 14,* 150–177.

Berlin, J.A. (1984). *Writing instruction in nineteenth century American colleges.* Carbondale, IL: Southern Illinois University Press.

Best of teenage San Francisco (1985). San Francisco: Lowell High School class magazine.

Birnbaum, J.C. (1982). The reading and composing behavior of selected fourth- and seventh-grade students. *Research in the Teaching of English, 16,* 241–261.

Bissex, G.L. (1980). *GNYS AT WRK: A child learns to write and read.* Cambridge, MA: Harvard University Press.

Bledstein, B. (1976). *The culture of professionalism: The middle class and the development of higher education in America.* New York: Norton.

Blount, N.S. (1973). Research on teaching literature, language, and composition. In R.M.W. Travers (Ed.), *Second handbook of research on teaching* (pp. 1072–1097). Chicago: Rand McNally.

Bond, G.L., and Dykstra, R. (1967). The cooperative research programs in first grade reading instruction [Special issue]. *Reading Research Quarterly*, 2.

Bowen, J.D. (1970). The structure of language. In A. Marckwardt (Ed.), *Linguistics in school programs. 69th Yearbook of the National Society for the Study of Education, Part I* (pp. 36–63). Chicago: University of Chicago Press.

Braddock, R. (1969). English composition. In R.E. Ebel (Ed.), *Encyclopedia of educational research: Vol. 4* (4th ed.) (pp. 443–461). New York: Macmillan.

Bradley, L., and Bryant, P.E. (1983). Categorizing sounds and learning to read: A causal connection. *Nature, 301,* 419–421.

Bransford, J.D., and Johnson, M.K. (1972). Contextual prerequisites for understanding. Some investigations of comprehension and recall. *Journal of Verbal Learning and Verbal Behavior, 11,* 717–726.

Brewer, W.F., and Hay, A. (1981, April). *Children's understanding of the author's point of view in stories.* Paper presented at the meeting of the Society for Research in Child Development, Boston.

Bridwell, L. (1980). Revising strategies in twelfth grade students' transactional writing. *Research in the Teaching of English, 14,* 197–222.

Britton, J. (1970). *Language and learning.* Harmondsworth, England: Penguin Press.

Britton, J. (1977). Language and the nature of learning: An individual perspective. In J.R. Squire (Ed.), *The teaching of English. 76th Yearbook of the National Society for the Study of Education* (pp. 1–38). Chicago: University of Chicago Press.

Brown, A. (1980). Metacognitive development and reading. In R.J. Spiro, B.C. Bruce, and W.F. Brewer (Eds.), *Theoretical issues in reading comprehension* (pp. 453–482). Hillsdale, NJ: Erlbaum.

Brown, A., Armbruster, B., and Baker, L. (1986). The role of metacognition in reading and studying. In J. Orasanu (Ed.), *Reading comprehension: From research to practice* (pp. 49–76). Hillsdale, NJ: Erlbaum.

Brown, A., and Day, J. (1983). Macrorules for summarizing texts: The development of expertise. *Journal of Verbal Learning and Verbal Behavior, 22,* 1–14.

Brown, A., and Palinscar, A.S. (1985). *Reciprocal teaching of comprehension strategies: A natural history of one program for enhancing learning* (Tech. Rep. No. 334). Urbana–Champaign, IL: University of Illinois, Center for the Study of Reading.

Brown, A., and Smiley, S. (1977). Rating the importance of structural units of prose passages: A problem of metacognitive development. *Child Development, 48,* 1–8.

Brown, E. Eagle. Unpublished papers, Newberry Library, Chicago.

Brown, M.T. (1981). *Arthur's eyes.* New York: Avon Books.

Brown, M.W., and Charlip, R. (1958). *The dead bird.* New York: Harper and Row.

Brown, R. (1974). Development of the first language in the human species. In E. Haugen and M. Bloomfield (Eds.), *Language as a human problem* (pp. 121–136). New York: W.W. Norton.

Bruce, B. (1981). A social interaction model of reading. *Discourse Process, 4,* 273–311.

Bruffee, K. (1984). Collaborative learning and the "conversation of mankind." *College English, 46,* 635–652.

Bryant, P.E., and Bradley, L. (1985). *Children's reading problems.* Oxford: Basil Blackwell.

Burrows, A.T. (1977). Composition: Prospect and retrospect. In H.A. Robinson (Ed.), *Reading and writing instruction in the United States: Historical trends* (pp. 17–43). Newark, DE: International Reading Association.

Burtis, P.J., Bereiter, C., Scardamalia, M., and Tetroe, J. (1983). The development of planning in writing. In C.J. Wells and B.M. Kroll (Eds.), *Explorations in the development of writing: Theory, research, and practice* (pp. 153–174). Chicester, England: Wiley.

Calfee, R., and Drum, P. (1986). Research on teaching reading. In M.C. Wittrock (Ed.), *Handbook of research on teaching* (3rd ed.) (pp. 804–849). New York: Macmillan.

Calfee, R.C., Lindamood, P., and Lindamood, C. (1973). Acoustic-phonetic skills and reading: Kindergarten through twelfth grade. *Journal of Educational Psychology, 64,* 293–298.

Calhoun, D. (1973). *The intelligence of a people.* Princeton, NJ: Princeton University Press.

Calkins, L.M. (1980). Children's rewriting strategies. *Research in the Teaching of English, 14,* 331–341.

Calkins, L.M. (1983). *Lessons from a child.* Exeter, NH: Heinemann.

Carroll, J.B., and Chall, J.S. (Eds.) (1975). *Toward a literate society* (Report of the Committee on Reading of the National Academy of Education). New York: McGraw-Hill.

Cazden, C., John, V., and Hymes, D. (1972). *Functions of language in the classroom.* New York: Teachers College Press.

Cazden, C., Michaels, S., and Tabors, P. (1985). Spontaneous repairs in sharing time narratives: The intersection of metalinguistic awareness, speech event, and narrative style. In S.W. Freedman (Ed.), *The acquisition of written language: Response and revision* (pp. 51–64). Norwood, NJ: Ablex.

Chall, J.S., and Conard, S.S. (1984). Resources and their use for reading instruction. In A.C. Purves and O.S. Niles (Eds.), *Becoming readers in a complex society. 83rd Yearbook of the National Society for the Study of Education* (pp. 209–232). Chicago: University of Chicago Press.

Chall, J.S., and Stahl, S.A. (1982). Reading. In H.E. Mitzel (Ed.), *Encyclopedia of educational research* (5th ed.) (pp. 1535–1559). New York: Free Press.

Charrow, V.R. (1981). The written English of deaf adolescents. In M.F. Whiteman (Ed.), *Writing: The nature, development and teaching of written communication: Vol. 1. Variation in writing: Functional and linguistic-cultural differences* (pp. 179–196). Hillsdale, NJ: Erlbaum.

Cherry Wilkinson, L. (Ed.) (1982). *Communicating in the classroom.* New York: Academic Press.

Chittenden, L. (1982). What if all the whales were gone before we become friends? In M. Barr, P. D'Arcy, and M.K. Healy (Eds.), *What's going on?* (pp. 36–51). Upper Montclair, NJ: Boynton/Cook.

Chomsky, C. (1979). Approaching reading through invented spelling. In L. Resnick and P. Weaver (Eds.), *Theory and practice of early reading: Vol. 2* (pp. 43–66). Hillsdale, NJ: Erlbaum.

Church, R.L. (1976). *Education in the United States: An interpretive history.* New York: Free Press.

Clark, M. (1976). *Young fluent readers: What they can teach us.* London: Heinemann.

Clay, M. (1976). Early childhood and cultural diversity in New Zealand. *The Reading Teacher, 29,* 333–342.

Clifford, G.J. (1978). Words for schools: The applications in education of the vocabulary researches of Edward L. Thorndike. In P. Suppes (Ed.), *Impact of research on education: Some case studies* (pp. 107–198). Washington, DC: National Academy of Education.

Clifford, G.J. (1981). The past is prologue. In K. Cirincioni-Coles (Ed.), *The future of education: Policy issues and challenges* (pp. 25–34). Beverly Hills, CA: Sage.

Clifford, G.J. (1984). Buch und lesen: Historical perspectives on literacy and schooling. *Review of Educational Research, 54,* 472–500.

Clifford, G.J. (1987). The impact of technology in American education. In S. Bruchey and J. Cotton (Eds.), *Technology, the economy and society: The American experience* (pp. 251–277). New York: Columbia University Press.

Cohen, S. (Ed.) (1974). *Education in the United States: A documentary history: Vol. 1.* New York: Random House.

Coleman, J.S. (1972). The children have outgrown the schools. *Psychology Today, 5,* 72–76.

College Entrance Examination Board Commission on Educational Reform (1985). Excellence in our schools: Making it happen. *Proceedings of a national forum on educational reform.* Princeton, NJ: College Entrance Examination Board.

College Entrance Examination Board Commission on English (1965). *Freedom and discipline in English.* Princeton, NJ: College Entrance Examination Board.

Collins, A., Brown, J.S., and Larkin, K.M. (1980). Inference in text understanding. In R.J. Spiro, B.C. Bruce, and W.F. Brewer (Eds.), *Theoretical issues in reading comprehension* (pp. 385–410). Hillsdale, NJ: Erlbaum.

Colvin-Murphy, C. (1986). *Enhancing critical comprehension of literary texts through writing.* Paper presented at the National Reading Conference, Austin, TX.

Commager, H.S. (1962). Introduction. In H.S. Commager (Ed.), *Noah Webster's American spelling book.* New York: Teachers College Press.

Conant, J.B. (1959). *The American high school today.* New York: McGraw-Hill.

Connors, R.J. (1986). The rhetoric of mechanical correctness. In T. Newkirk (Ed.), *Only connect: Uniting reading and writing* (pp. 27–58). Upper Montclair, NJ: Boynton/Cook.

Cook-Gumperz, J. (1986). Literacy and schooling: An unchanging equation? In J. Cook-Gumperz (Ed.), *The social construction of literacy* (pp. 16–44). New York: Cambridge University Press.

Cooper, F.S. (1972). How is language conveyed by speech? In J.F. Kavanagh and I.G. Mattingly (Eds.), *Language by ear and by eye*. Cambridge, MA: MIT Press.

Copeland, K.A. (1984). *The effect of writing upon good and poor writers' learning from prose*. Unpublished doctoral dissertation, University of Texas, Austin.

Corbett, E.P.J. (1981). The status of writing in our society. In M.F. Whiteman (Ed.), *Writing: The nature, development, and teaching of written communication: Vol. 1. Variation in writing: Functional and linguistic-cultural differences* (pp. 47–52). Hillsdale, NJ: Erlbaum.

Counts, G.S. (1952). *Education and American civilization*. New York: Teachers College Press.

Crandall, J. (1981). *A sociolinguistic investigation of the literacy demands of clerical workers*. Unpublished doctoral dissertation, Georgetown University, Washington, DC.

Crane, R. (1984). *The quality of American high school graduates: What personnel officers say and do about it* (Final Report to the National Institute of Education). Washington, DC: Office of Educational Research and Improvement, U.S. Office of Education.

Cremin, L.A. (1970). *American education: The colonial experience, 1607–1783*. New York: Harper & Row.

Cremin, L.A. (1980). *American education: The national experience, 1783–1876*. New York: Harper & Row.

Cronnell, B. (Ed.) (1981). *The writing needs of linguistically different students*. Los Alamitos, CA: Southwest Regional Laboratory Education Research and Development.

Cuban, L. (1984). *How teachers taught: Constancy and change in American classrooms, 1890–1980*. New York: Longman.

Denner, P.R., and McGinley, W.J. (1986, March). *The effects of story-impressions as a prereading writing-activity on immediate and delayed story-recall of average and superior readers*. Paper presented at the spring conference of the Idaho Council of the International Reading Association, Burley, ID. (ERIC Document Reproduction Service No. ED 269 743)

Devine, T.G. (1971). Reading in high schools. In L.C. Deighton (Ed.), *Encyclopedia of education: Vol. 7* (pp. 402–406). New York: Macmillan.

Dewey, J. (1916). *Democracy and education*. New York: Macmillan.

Diederich, P.B. (1966). The use of external tests in public schools in the United States. In J.R. Squire (Ed.), *A common purpose: The teaching of English in Great Britain, Canada, and the United States* (pp. 146–152). Urbana, IL: National Council of Teachers of English.

Dixon, J. (1967). *Growth through English*. Reading, England: National Association for the Teaching of English.

Dixon, J. (1975). *Growth through English, set in the perspective of the seventies*. Huddersfield, England: National Association for the Teaching of English.

Donaldson, M. (1978). *Children's minds*. New York: Norton.

Donaldson, M. (1984). Speech and writing and modes of learning. In H. Goelman, A.A. Oberg, and F. Smith (Eds.), *Awakening to literacy* (pp. 174–184). Exeter, NH: Heinemann.

Douglas, W.W. (1970). The history of language instruction in the schools. In H.G. Richey (Ed.), *Linguistics in school programs. 69th Yearbook of the National Society for the Study of Education, Part II* (pp. 155–166). Chicago: University of Chicago Press.

Durkin, D. (1966). *Children who read early.* New York: Teachers College Press.

Durst, R.K. (1986). The cognitive and linguistic dimensions of analytic writing. *Dissertation Abstracts International, 46,* 12A. (University Microfilms No. DA8602471)

Dyson, A. Haas (1984a). Emerging alphabetic literacy in school contexts: Towards defining the gap between school curriculum and child mind. *Written Communication, 1,* 5–55.

Dyson, A. Haas (1984b). Reading, writing, and language: Young children solving the written language puzzle. In J.M. Jensen (Ed.), *Composing and comprehending* (pp. 165–176). Urbana, IL: ERIC Clearinghouse on Reading and Communication Skills and National Conference on Reading in English.

Dyson, A. Haas (in press). *The multiple worlds of child writers: A study of friends learning to write.* New York: Teachers College Press.

Eckhoff, B. (1983). How reading affects children's writing. *Language Arts, 60,* 607–616.

Edelsky, C. (1986). *Writing in a bilingual program: Habia una vez.* Norwood, NJ: Ablex.

Edelsky, C., and Smith, K. (1984). Is that writing—or are those marks just a figment of your curriculum? *Language Arts, 61,* 24–32.

Ehri, L.C. (1979). Linguistic insight: Threshold of reading acquisition. In T.G. Waller and G.E. MacKinnon (Eds.), *Reading research: Advances in theory and practice: Vol. 1* (pp. 63–114). New York: Academic Press.

Ehri, L.C. (1984). How orthography alters spoken language competencies in children learning to read and spell. In J. Downing and R. Valtin (Eds.), *Language awareness and learning to read.* New York: Springer-Verlag.

Ehri, L.C. (1986). Sources of difficulty in learning to spell and read. In M.L. Wolraich and D. Routh (Eds.), *Advances in developmental and behavioral pediatrics.* Greenwich, CT: Jai Press.

Elson, R.M. (1964). *Guardians of tradition: American schoolbooks in the nineteenth century.* Lincoln, NE: University of Nebraska Press.

Emig, J. (1982). Writing, composition, and rhetoric. In H.E. Mitzel (Ed.), *Encyclopedia of education research* (5th ed.) (pp. 2021–2036). New York: Free Press.

Erickson, F. (1984). Rhetoric, anecdote, and rhapsody: Coherence strategies in a conversation among black American adolescents. In D. Tannen (Ed.), *Coherence in spoken and written discourse* (pp. 81–154). Norwood, NJ: Ablex.

Evans, B., and Lynch, J.J. (1960). *Dialogues on the teaching of literature.* New York: Bookman.

Faeder, D., and Shaevitz, M. (1966). *Hooked on books.* New York: Bantam.

Faigley, L., Miller, T.P., Meyer, P.R., and Witte, S.P. (1981). *Writing after college: A stratified survey of the writing of college-trained people.* Austin: University of Texas.

Farning, M., Boyce, E., and Mahnke, R. (1975). *Developing a list of competencies for the communication skills area of vocational-technical post-secondary education.* Madison: Wisconsin State Board of Vocational, Technical, and Adult Education. (ERIC Document Reproduction Service No. ED 112 194)

Farr, M. (1982, March). *Learning to write English: One dialogue journal writer's growth in writing.* Paper presented at the annual meeting of the American Educational Research Association, New York.

Farr, M. (1984). Writing growth in young children: What we are learning from research. In C. Thaiss and C. Suhor (Eds.), *Speaking and writing, K–12* (pp. 126–143). Urbana, IL: National Council of Teachers of English.

Farr, M. (1986). Language, culture, and writing: Sociolinguistic foundations of research on writing. In E. Rothkopf (Ed.), *Review of research in education: Vol. 13.* Washington, DC: American Educational Research Association.

Farr, M., and Daniels, H. (1986). *Language diversity and writing instruction.* Urbana, IL: National Council of Teachers of English.

Fasold, R. (1972). *Tense marking in Black English.* Washington, DC: Center for Applied Linguistics.

Ferguson, C. (1977). Linguistic theory. In *Bilingual education: Current perspectives* (pp. 43–52). Washington, DC: Center for Applied Linguistics.

Ferreiro, E. (1983). The development of literacy: A complex psychological problem. In F. Coulmas and K. Ehlich (Eds.), *Focus on writing* (pp. 270–299). Berlin: Mouton.

Ferreiro, E. (1986). The interplay between information and assimilation in beginning literacy. In W. Teale and E. Sulzby (Eds.), *Emergent literacy: Writing and reading* (pp. 15–49). Norwood, NJ: Ablex.

Ferreiro, E., and Teberosky, A. (1982). *Literacy before schooling* (K. Goodman Castro, Trans.). Exeter, NH: Heinemann.

Fitzgerald, F.S. (1969). *The great Gatsby.* New York: Scribner's.

Flateley, M.E. (1982). A comparative analysis of the written communication of managers of various organizational levels in the private business sector. *Journal of Business Communication, 19,* 35–49.

Flower, L. (1979). Writer-based prose: A cognitive basis for problems in writing. *College English, 41,* 19–37.

Flower, L. (1980). Planning to be creative. *Composition and Teaching, 2,* 61–67.

Flower, L. (1985). *Problem-solving strategies in writing.* San Diego, CA: Harcourt Brace Jovanovich.

Flower, L., and Hayes, J.R. (1980). The cognition of discovery: Defining a rhetorical problem. *College Composition and Communication, 33,* 21–32.

Flower, L., and Hayes, J.R. (1981a). Plans that guide the composing process. In C.H. Frederiksen and J.F. Dominic (Eds.), *Writing: The nature, development, and teaching of written communication: Vol. 2. Process, development, and communication* (pp. 39–58). Hillsdale, NJ: Erlbaum.

Flower, L., and Hayes, J.R. (1981b). The pregnant pause: An inquiry into the nature of planning. *Research in the Teaching of English, 15,* 229–243.

Flower, L., and Hayes, J.R. (1984). Images, plans, and prose: The representation of meaning in writing. *Written Communication, 1,* 120–160.

Flower, L., Hayes, J.R., Carey, L., Schiver, K., and Stratman, J. (1986). Detection, diagnosis, and the strategies of revision. *College Composition and Communication, 37,* 16–56.

Francis, H. (1973). Children's experience of reading and notions of units in language. *British Journal of Educational Psychology, 43,* 17–23.

Franks, J., Vye, N., Auble, P., Mezynski, K., Perfetti, C.A., Bransford, J., and Littlefield, J. (1982). Learning from explicit vs. implicit text. *Journal of Experimental Psychology: General, 111,* 414–422.

Frazier, A. (Ed.), and NCTE Commission on the English Curriculum (1966). *Ends and issues: 1965–66.* Urbana, IL: National Council of Teachers of English.

Freedman, A., Carey, J., and Miller, T. (1986). *Learning to write again: Six students acquiring a new genre of academic discourse.* Ottawa: Carleton University Department of Linguistics.

Freedman, S., Dyson, A. Haas, Flower, L., and Chafe, W. (1985). Mission statement. In *A proposal to establish a Center for the Study of Writing.* Submitted by the University of California–Berkeley and Carnegie-Mellon University to the National Institute of Education, Washington, DC.

Freeman, F.N. (1913). Writing: Historic evolution. In P. Monroe (Ed.), *A cyclopedia of education: Vol. 5* (pp. 819–827). New York: Macmillan.

Fulwiller, T., and Young, A. (Eds.) (1982). *Language connections: Writing and reading across the curriculum.* Urbana, IL: National Council of Teachers of English.

Gantry, L. (Ed.) (1982). *Research and instruction in practical writing.* Los Alamitos, CA: Southwest Regional Laboratory Education Research and Development.

Gardner, J. (1968). *No easy victories.* New York: Harper & Row.

Geertz, C. (1983). *Local knowledge.* New York: Basic Books.

Gentes, H. (1986, June 18). The importance of dairy farming. *Home News,* p. 7.

Gentry, J. (1982). An analysis of developmental spelling in GYNS AT WRK. *The Reading Teacher, 36,* 192–200.

Giacobbe, M.E. (1982). A writer reads, a reader writes. In T. Newkirk and N. Atwell (Eds.), *Understanding writing: Ways of observing, learning, and teaching* (pp. 114–125). Chelmsford, MA: Northeast Regional Exchange.

Gilmore, P., and Glatthorn, A. (Eds.) (1982). *Children in and out of school: Ethnography and education.* Washington, DC: Center for Applied Linguistics.

Gilmore, W.J. (1982). *Elementary literacy on the eve of the industrial revolution: Trends in rural New England, 1760–1830.* Worcester, MA: American Antiquarian Society.

Goelman, H., Oberg, A., and Smith, F. (Eds.) (1984). *Awakening to literacy.* Exeter, NH: Heinemann.

Goodman, K.S. (1984). Unity in reading. In A.C. Purves and O.S. Niles (Eds.), *Becoming readers in a complex society. 83rd Yearbook of the National Society for the Study of Education* (pp. 79–114). Chicago: University of Chicago Press.

Goodman, K.S. (1986). *What's whole in whole language?* Exeter, NH: Heinemann.

Goodman, Y.M., and Altwerger, B. (1981). *Print awareness in preschool children: A working paper. A study of the development of literacy in preschool children.* Occasional Papers No. 4, Program in Language and Literacy, University of Arizona.

Gould, S.M., Haas, L.W., and Marino, J.L. (1982). *Writing as schema-building: The effects of writing as a pre-reading activity on a delayed recall of narrative text.* Unpublished manuscript.

Grant family papers (1841). Unpublished papers, Sophia Smith Collection, Smith College, Northampton, MA.

Graves, D.H. (1980). A new look at writing research. *Language Arts, 57,* 913–918.

Graves, D.H. (1982). *A case study observing the development of primary children's composing, spelling and motor behavior during the writing process* (Final Report to the National Institute of Education, NIE-G-78-0174). Durham, NH: University of New Hampshire.

Graves, D.H. (1983). *Writing: Teachers and children at work.* Exeter, NH: Heinemann.

Graves, D.H., and Hansen, J. (1983). The author's chair. *Language Arts, 60,* 176–182.

Gray, W.S., and Larrick, N. (Eds.) (1956). Better readers for our times. *International Reading Association Conference Proceedings: Vol. 1.* New York: Scholastic Magazine.

Great Britain Department of Education and Science (1975). *A language for life: Report of the committee of inquiry appointed by the Secretary of State for Education and Science under the chairmanship of Sir A. Bullock.* London: H.M.S.O.

Green, G.M., and Laff, M.O. (1981). *Five-year-olds' recognition of authorship by literary style* (Tech. Rep. No. 181). Champaign, IL: University of Illinois, Center for the Study of Reading.

Green, J. (1983). Research on teaching as a linguistic process: A state of the art. In E.W. Gordon (Ed.), *Review of research in education: Vol. 10* (pp. 151–252). Washington, DC: American Educational Research Association.

Green, J., and Wallat, C. (Eds.) (1981). *Ethnography and language in educational settings.* Norwood, NJ: Ablex.

Griscom, J. (1859). *Memoir of John Griscom, LL.D.* New York: Robert Carter & Brothers.

Grubb, N. (1984). The bandwagon once more: Vocational preparation for high tech occupations. *Harvard Educational Review, 54,* 429–451.

Gumperz, J.J. (1982a). *Discourse strategies.* Cambridge: Cambridge University Press.

Gumperz, J.J. (Ed.) (1982b). *Language and social identity.* Cambridge: Cambridge University Press.

Gundlach, R.A. (1982). Children as writers: The beginnings of learning to write. In M. Nystrand (Ed.), *What writers know: The language, process, and structure of written discourse* (pp. 129–147). New York: Academic Press.

Gundlach, R.A., McLane, J.B., Stott, F.M., and McNamee, G.D. (1985). The social foundations of children's early writing development. In M. Farr (Ed.),

Advances in writing research: Vol. 1. Children's early writing development (pp. 1–58). Norwood, NJ: Ablex.

Guthrie, J. (1985). Curriculum reform and instructional strategies related to reading, writing, and content areas. In *Excellence in our schools: Making it happen. Proceedings of a national forum on educational reform.* Princeton, NJ: College Entrance Examination Board.

Haas, C., and Flower, L. (1988). Rhetorical reading and the construction of meaning. *College Composition and Communication, 39,* 167–183.

Hall, O., and Carlton, R. (1977). *Basic skills at home and work.* Toronto: Ontario Economic Council.

Hall, W., and Guthrie, L. (1980). On the question of dialect and reading. In R.J. Spiro, B.C. Bruce, and W.F. Brewer (Eds.), *Theoretical issues in reading comprehension* (pp. 439–452). Hillsdale, NJ: Erlbaum.

Hansen, J. (1981). The effects of inference training and practice on young children's reading comprehension. *Reading Research Quarterly, 16,* 391–417.

Hansen, J. (1987). *When writers read.* Portsmouth, NH: Heinemann.

Hansen, J., Newkirk, T., and Graves, D. (Eds.) (1985). *Breaking ground: Teachers relate reading and writing in the elementary school.* Portsmouth, NH: Heinemann.

Hansen, J., and Pearson, P.D. (1983). An instructional study: Improving the inferential comprehension of 4th grade and poor readers. *Journal of Educational Psychology, 79,* 821–829.

Harris, T.L. (1969). Reading. In R.L. Ebel (Ed.), *Encyclopedia of educational research* (4th ed.) (pp. 1069–1104). New York: Macmillan.

Harste, J.C., Burke, C.L., and Woodward, V.A. (1982). Children's language and world: Initial encounters with print. In J. Langer and M. Smith-Burke (Eds.), *Bridging the gap: Reader meets author* (pp. 105–131). Newark, DE: International Reading Association.

Harste, J.C., Woodward, V.A., and Burke, C.L. (1984). *Language stories and literary lessons.* Exeter, NH: Heinemann.

Hartwell, P. (1980). Dialect interference in writing: A critical view. *Research in the Teaching of English, 14,* 101–118.

Hartwell, P. (1985). Grammar, grammars, and the teaching of grammar. *College English, 47,* 105–127.

Hatlin, B. (1986). Old wine and new bottles: A dialectical encounter between the old rhetoric and the new. In T. Newkirk (Ed.), *Only connect: Uniting reading and writing* (pp. 59–86). Upper Montclair, NJ: Boynton/Cook.

Healy, M.K. (1984). *Writing in a science class: A case study of the connections between writing and learning.* Unpublished doctoral dissertation, New York University, New York.

Heath, S.B. (1981). Toward an ethnohistory of writing in American education. In M.F. Whiteman (Ed.), *Writing: The nature, development and teaching of written communication: Vol. 1. Variation in writing: Functional and linguistic-cultural differences* (pp. 25–46). Hillsdale, NJ: Erlbaum.

Heath, S.B. (1982a). What no bedtime story means. *Language in Society, 11,* 49–76.

Heath, S.B. (1982b). Protean shapes in literacy events: Ever-shifting oral and literate traditions. In D. Tannen (Ed.), *Spoken and written language: Exploring orality and literacy* (pp. 91–118). Norwood, NJ: Ablex.

Heath, S.B. (1983). *Ways with words: Language, life, and work in communities and classrooms.* Cambridge: Cambridge University Press.

Heath, S.B. (1986). Critical factors in literacy development. In S. deCastell, A. Luke, and K. Egan (Eds.), *Literacy, society, and schooling: A reader* (pp. 209–229). Cambridge: Cambridge University Press.

Heath, S.B., and Branscombe, A. (1985). "Intelligent writing" in an audience community: Teacher, students, and researcher. In S.W. Freedman (Ed.), *The acquisition of written language: Response and revision* (pp. 3–32). Norwood, NJ: Ablex.

Henderson, E.H. (1981). *Learning to read and spell.* DeKalb, IL: Northern Illinois University Press.

Hendrix, R. (1981). The status and politics of writing instruction. In M.F. Whiteman (Ed.), *Writing: The nature, development and teaching of written communication: Vol. 1. Variation in writing: Functional and linguistic-cultural differences* (pp. 53–70). Hillsdale, NJ: Erlbaum.

Henry, G.H. (1986). What is the nature of English education? *English Education, 18,* 4–41.

Herber, H.C., and Nelson-Herber, J. (1984). Planning the reading program. In A.C. Purves and O.S. Niles (Eds.), *Becoming readers in a complex society. 83rd Yearbook of the National Society for the Study of Education* (pp. 174–208). Chicago: University of Chicago Press.

Higgins, L. (1986). *Inference and argument: An exploratory study.* Unpublished manuscript, Carnegie-Mellon University, Pittsburgh, PA.

Hillocks, G. (1984). What works in teaching composition: A meta-analysis of experimental treatment studies. *American Journal of Education, 93,* 133–170.

Hillocks, G. (1986). *Research on written communication: New directions for teaching.* Urbana, IL: National Council of Teachers of English.

Hoagland, N. (1982). A report on the occupational writing of developmental English students. In D. Gallehr, R. Gilstrap, A. Legge, M. Mohr, and M. Wilson-Nelson (Eds.), *The writing process of college students.* Fairfax, VA: George Mason University.

Holden, M.H., and MacGinitie, W.H. (1972). Children's conceptions of word boundaries in speech and print. *Journal of Educational Psychology, 63,* 551–557.

Holt, S.L., and Vacca, J.L. (1984). Reading with a sense of writer: Writing with a sense of reader. In J.M. Jensen (Ed.), *Composing and comprehending* (pp. 177–184). Urbana, IL: ERIC Clearinghouse on Reading and Communication Skills and National Conference on Reading in English.

Hosic, J.F. (Compiler) (1917). *Reorganization of English in secondary schools* (Bulletin 1917, No. 2). Washington, DC: United States Bureau of Education.

Huey, E. (1908). *The psychology and pedagogy of teaching reading.* Boston: MIT Press.

Hyde, W.D. (1894). Educational values as assessed by the Committee of Ten. *School of Review, 2,* 628–645.

Hymes, D. (1971). Competence and performance in linguistic theory. In R. Huxley and E. Ingram (Eds.), *Language in acquisition: Models and methods* (pp. 3–28). London: Academic Press.

Hymes, D. (1974). *Foundations of sociolinguistics: An ethnographic approach.* Philadelphia: University of Pennsylvania Press.

Hymes, D. (1980). *Language in education: Ethnolinguistic essays.* Washington, DC: Center for Applied Linguistics.

Hymes, D. (1984). [Review of J.J. Gumperz, *Discourse strategies*]. *American Journal of Sociology, 90,* 469–471.

Iser, W. (1978). *The art of reading.* London: Routledge & Kegan Paul.

Jacobs, E. (1982). Research on practical writing in business and industry. In L. Gantry (Ed.), *Research and instruction in practical writing* (pp. 37–50). Los Alamitos, CA: Southwest Regional Laboratory Education Research and Development.

Jeffrey, C. (1981). Teachers' and students' perceptions of the writing process. *Research in the Teaching of English, 15,* 215–228.

Jenkins, W.A. (1977). Changing patterns in teacher education. In J.R. Squire (Ed.), *The teaching of English. 76th Yearbook of the National Society for the Study of Education* (pp. 260–281). Chicago: University of Chicago Press.

Jensen, J.M. (Ed.) (1983). Language arts at sixty: A retrospective [Special issue]. *Language Arts, 60.*

Jerrolds, B.W. (1978). *Reading reflections: The history of the International Reading Association.* Newark, DE: International Reading Association.

Jewett, A. (1959). *English language arts in American high schools* (Bulletin 1958, No. 13). Washington, DC: United States Department of Health, Education, and Welfare.

Juel, C., Griffith, P.L., and Gough, P.B. (1986). The acquisition of literacy: A longitudinal study of children in first and second grade. *Journal of Educational Psychology, 78,* 243–255.

Kaufer, D., Geisler, C., and Neuwirth, C. (in press). *The architecture of argument: A cross-disciplinary rhetoric.* San Diego, CA: Harcourt Brace Jovanovich.

Kavanagh, J.F., and Mattingly, I.G. (Eds.) (1972). *Language by ear and by eye.* Cambridge, MA: MIT Press.

Kellogg, S. (1982). *Pinkerton behave.* New York: Dial Books.

Kennedy, M.L. (1985). The composing processes of college students writing from sources. *Written Communication, 2,* 434–456.

King, M.L., and Rentel, V.M. (1981). *How children learn to write: A longitudinal study* (Final Report to the National Institute of Education, NIE-G-79-0137 and NIE-G-79-0039). Columbus: Ohio State University.

King, M.L., and Rentel, V.M. (1982). *Transition to writing* (Final Report to the National Institute of Education, NIE-G-0137 and NIE-G-79-0031). Columbus: Ohio State University.

King, M.L., and Rentel, V.M. (1983). *A longitudinal study of coherence in children's written narratives* (Final Report to the National Institute of Education, NIE-G-81-0063). Columbus: Ohio State University.

Kintsch, W., and van Dijk, T.A. (1978). Toward a model of text comprehension and production. *Psychological Review, 85,* 363–394.

Klaus, C.H., and Jones, N. (Eds.) (1984). *Courses for change in writing: A selection from the N.E.H./Iowa Institute.* Upper Montclair, NJ: Boynton/ Cook and University of Iowa.

Knott, T.A. (1940). Observations on vocabulary problems. *Elementary English Review, 17,* 63–67.

Kochman, T. (Ed.) (1972). *Rappin' and stylin' out: Communication in urban black America.* Urbana, IL: University of Illinois Press.

Kochman, T. (1981). *Black and white styles in conflict.* Chicago: University of Chicago Press.

Kreeft, J.P., Shuy, R.W., Staton, J., Reed, L., and Morroy, R. (1984). *Dialogue writing: Analysis of student-teacher interactive writing in the learning of English as a second language* (Final Report to the National Institute of Education, NIE-G-83-0030). Washington, DC: Center for Applied Linguistics. (ERIC Document Reproduction Service No. ED 252 097)

Kroll, B.M. (1984). Audience adaptation in children's persuasive letters. *Written Communication, 1,* 407–428.

Krug, E. (1964). *The shaping of the American high school.* Madison: University of Wisconsin Press.

Labov, W. (1969). On the logic of non-standard English. *Georgetown Monographs on Language and Linguistics, 22.* Washington, DC: Georgetown University Press.

Labov, W. (1970). The logic of non-standard English. In F. Williams (Ed.), *Language and poverty* (pp. 153–189). Chicago: Markham.

Labov, W. (1972a). *Language in the inner city: Studies in the Black English Vernacular.* Philadelphia: University of Pennsylvania Press.

Labov, W. (1972b). *Sociolinguistic patterns.* Philadelphia: University of Pennsylvania Press.

Labov, W. (Ed.) (1980). *Locating language in time and space.* New York: Academic Press.

Labov, W. (1983). Recognizing Black English in the classroom. In J. Chambers, Jr. (Ed.), *Black English: Educational equity and the law* (pp. 29–55). Ann Arbor, MI: Karoma.

Labov, W., and Harris, W. (1983, April). *De facto segregation of black and white vernaculars.* Paper presented at the annual conference on New Ways of Analyzing Variation in English, Montreal, Canada.

LaConte, R.T., and Barber, B.S. (1986). English in the eighties: A midpoint international perspective. *English Journal, 75,* 27–31.

Langer, J.A. (1984). The effects of available information on responses to school writing tasks. *Research in the Teaching of English, 18,* 27–44.

Langer, J.A. (1985). Children's sense of genre: A study of performance on parallel reading and writing tasks. *Written Communication, 2,* 157–187.

Langer, J.A. (1986a). Learning through writing: Study skills in the content areas. *Journal of Reading, 29,* 400–406.

Langer, J.A. (1986b). *Children reading and writing: Structures and strategies.* Norwood, NJ: Ablex.

Langer, J.A., and Applebee, A. (1987). *How writing shapes thinking: A study of teaching and learning.* (Res. Rep. No. 22). Urbana, IL: National Council of Teachers of English.

Levine, K. (1982). Functional literacy: Fond illusions and false economies. *Harvard Educatonal Review, 52,* 249–266.

Lewkowicz, N.K. (1980). Phonemic awareness training: What to teach and how to teach it. *Journal of Educational Psychology, 72,* 686–700.

Liberman, I.Y., and Shankwieler, D. (1979). Speech, the alphabet, and teaching to read. In L.B. Resnick and P.A. Weaver (Eds.), *Theory and practice of early reading* (pp. 105–129). Hillsdale, NJ: Erlbaum.

Liebling, C. (1989). *Children's comprehension of inside view and character plans in fiction: A pilot investigation* (Tech. Rep. No. 459). Urbana–Champaign, IL: University of Illinois, Center for the Study of Reading.

Litowitz, B. (1985). The speaking subject in adolescence: Response to Theodore Shapiro's essay. *Adolescent Psychiatry, 12,* 312–326.

Litowitz, B., and Gundlach, R.A. (1987). When adolescents write: Semiotic and social dimensions of adolescents' personal writing. *Adolescent Psychiatry, 14,* pp. 82–111.

Lloyd, S.M. (1979). *A singular school: Abbot Academy, 1828–1973.* Hanover, NH: Phillips Academy, Andover.

Lobel, A.C. (1976). *Frog and toad.* New York: Harper & Row.

Lundberg, I., Olofsson, A., and Wall, S. (1980). Reading and spelling skills in the first years predicted from phonemic awareness skills in kindergarten. *Scandinavian Journal of Psychology, 21,* 159–173.

Luria, A.R. (1983). The development of writing in the child. In M. Martlew (Ed.), *The psychology of written language* (pp. 237–277). London: Wiley.

Mandler, J.M., and DeForest, M. (1979). Is there more than one way to recall a story? *Child Development, 50,* 886–889.

Mandler, J.M., Scribner, S., Cole, M., and DeForest, M. (1980). Cross-cultural invariance in story recall. *Child Development, 51,* 19–26.

Markman, E. (1981). Comprehension monitoring. In W.P. Dickinson (Ed.), *Children's oral communication skills* (pp. 61–84). New York: Academic Press.

Markman, E. (1985). Comprehension monitoring: Developmental and educational issues. In S.F. Chipman, J.W. Segal, and R. Glaser (Eds.), *Thinking and learning skills: Vol. 2* (pp. 275–292). Hillsdale, NJ: Erlbaum.

Marsh, G., Friedman, M., Welch, V., and Desberg, P. (1980). The development of strategies in spelling. In U. Frith (Ed.), *Cognitive processes in spelling* (pp. 339–354). London: Academic Press.

Marshall, J.D. (1978). The effects of writing on students' understanding of literary text. *Research in the Teaching of English, 21,* 30–63.

Marshall, J.D. (1984). *The effects of writing on students' understanding of literary texts.* Paper presented at the annual meeting of the National Council of Teachers of English, Detroit. (ERIC Document Reproduction Service No. ED 252 842)

Mason, J. (1980). Overgeneralization in learning to read. *Journal of Reading Behavior, 8,* 173–182.

Mathews, M.M. (1966). *Teaching to read, historically considered.* Chicago: University of Chicago Press.

McGinley, W. (1987). *The effects of composing as a previewing activity on seventh grade students' understanding of short stories.* Unpublished manuscript.

Meckel, H.C. (1963). Research on teaching composition and literature. In N.L. Gage (Ed.), *Handbook of research on teaching* (pp. 966–1000). Chicago: Rand McNally.

Meyer, B.J.F., Brandt, D.M., and Bluth, G.J. (1980). Use of top-level structure in text: Key for reading comprehension of ninth-grade students. *Reading Research Quarterly, 16,* 72–103.

Michaels, S. (1981). Sharing time: Children's narrative style and differential access to literacy. *Language in Society, 10,* 423–442.

Michaels, S., and Collins, J. (1984). Oral discourse styles: Classroom interaction and the acquisition of literacy. In D. Tannen (Ed.), *Coherence in spoken and written discourse* (pp. 219–244). Norwood, NJ: Ablex.

Mikulecky, L. (1982a). Functional writing in the workplace. In L. Gantry (Ed.), *Research and instruction in practical writing* (pp. 51–72). Los Alamitos, CA: Southwest Regional Laboratory Education Research and Development.

Mikulecky, L. (1982b). Job literacy: The relationship between school preparation and workplace actuality. *Reading Research Quarterly, 17,* 400–419.

Miller, G.A. (Ed.) (1974). *Linguistic communication: Perspectives for research: Report of the Study Group on Linguistic Communication to the National Institute of Education.* Newark, DE: International Reading Association.

Mitchell, R. (1982). Negative entropy at work: A theory of practical writing. In L. Gantry (Ed.), *Research and instruction in practical writing* (pp. 9–36). Los Alamitos, CA: Southwest Regional Laboratory Education Research and Development.

Moffett, J. (1985). Hidden impediments to improving English teaching. *Phi Delta Kappan, 67,* 50–56.

Moll, L., and Diaz, R. (1986). Teaching writing as communication: The use of ethnographic findings in classroom practice. In D. Bloome (Ed.), *Literacy, language and schooling.* Norwood, NJ: Ablex.

Montessori, M. (1964). *The Montessori method.* New York: Schocken Books.

Moore, A.E., Betzner, J., and Lewis, M. (1927–1928). *The classroom teacher.* Chicago: The Classroom Teacher.

Morris, D., and Perney, J. (1984). Developmental spelling as a predictor of first-grade reading achievement. *The Elementary School Journal, 84,* 441–457.

Muller, H.J. (1967). *The uses of English.* New York: Holt, Rinehart, & Winston.

Murray, D. (1982). Teaching the other self: The writer's first reader. *College Composition and Communication, 33,* 140–147.

Myers, G. (1986). Reality, consensus, and reform in the rhetoric of composition teaching. *College English, 48,* 154–174.

National Assessment of Educational Progress (1981). *The reading report card: Trends across the decade.* Princeton, NJ: Educational Testing Service.

National Assessment of Educational Progress (1986). *Writing: Trends across the decade.* Princeton, NJ: Educational Testing Service.

NCTE (1939). *Conducting experiences in English.* New York: Appleton-Century.

NCTE Commission on the English Curriculum (1952). *The English language arts.* New York: Appleton-Century-Crofts.

NCTE Commission on the English Curriculum (1954). *Language arts for today's children.* Urbana, IL: National Council of Teachers of English.

NCTE Commission on the English Curriculum (1956). *The English language arts in the secondary school.* New York: Appleton-Century-Crofts.

NCTE Commission on the English Curriculum (1968). *English curriculum development projects.* Urbana, IL: National Council of Teachers of English.

NCTE Committee on Correlation (1936). *A correlated curriculum.* New York: Appleton-Century.

NCTE Committee on National Interest (1961). *The national interest and the teaching of English.* Urbana, IL: National Council of Teachers of English.

NCTE Curriculum Commission (1935). *An experience curriculum in English.* New York: Appleton-Century.

NCTE Steering Committee on Social and Political Concerns (1976). What are the basics of English? *Slate Newsletter, 1,* 1–4.

NCTE Task Force on Class Size and Workload in the Secondary School, W.L. Smith (Chair) (1986). *Class size and English in the secondary school.* Urbana, IL: National Council of Teachers of English.

Nelson, K. (1985). *Making sense: The acquisition of shared meaning.* Orlando, FL: Academic Press.

Newell, G.E. (1984). Learning from writing in two content areas: A case study/protocol analysis. *Research in the Teaching of English, 18,* 265–287.

Newkirk, T. (1982). Young writers as critical readers. In T. Newkirk and N. Atwell (Eds.), *Understanding writing: Ways of observing, learning, and teaching* (pp. 106–113). Chelmsford, MA: Northeast Regional Exchange.

Newkirk, T. (1986). Background and introduction. In T. Newkirk (Ed.), *Only connect: Uniting reading and writing* (pp. 1–10). Upper Montclair, NJ: Boynton/Cook.

Newman, D. (1981). *Children's understanding of strategic interaction.* Unpublished doctoral dissertation, City University of New York.

Newman, D. (in press). The role of mutual belief in the development of perspective-taking. *Developmental Review.*

Newman, D., and Bruce, B. (1986). Interpretation and manipulation in human plans. *Discourse Process, 9,* 167–195.

Ninio, A., and Bruner, J. (1978). The achievement and antecedents of labelling. *Journal of Child Language, 5,* 1–5.

Nystrand, M. (1987). *The structure of written communication.* Orlando, FL: Academic Press.

Odell, L. (1981). Business writing: Observation and implications for teaching composition. *Theory into Practice, 13,* 225–232.

Odell, L., and Goswami, D. (1982). Writing in a non-academic setting. *Research in the Teaching of English, 16,* 201–223.

Odell, L., and Goswami, D. (1985). Introduction. In L. Odell and D. Goswami (Eds.), *Writing in non-academic settings.* New York and London: Guilford Press.

Odell, L., Goswami, D., and Herrington, A. (1983). The discourse-based interview: A procedure for exploring the tacit knowledge of writers in non-academic settings. In P. Mosenthal, L. Tamar, and S. Walmsley (Eds.), *Research on writing: Principles and methods* (pp. 220–235). London and New York: Longman.

Ohmann, R. (1986). Reading and writing: Work and leisure. In T. Newkirk (Ed.), *Only connect: Uniting reading and writing* (pp. 11–26). Upper Montclair, NJ: Boynton/Cook.

O'Neil, W. (1970). Properly literate. *Harvard Educational Review, 40,* 260–263.

Our friends in the waters (1979). Mill Valley, CA: Old Mill School.

Palinscar, A.S., and Brown, A. (1984). Reciprocal teaching of comprehension-fostering and monitoring activities. *Cognition and Instruction, 1,* 117–175.

Paradis, J., et al. (1985). Writing at Exxon I.T.D.: Notes on the writing environment of an R & D organization. In L. Odell and D. Goswami (Eds.), *Writing in non-academic settings.* New York and London: Guilford Press.

Pearson, P.D., and Tierney, R.J. (1984). On becoming a thoughtful reader: Learning to read like a writer. In A.C. Purves and O.S. Niles (Eds.), *Becoming readers in a complex society. 83rd Yearbook of the National Society for the Study of Education* (pp. 144–173). Chicago: University of Chicago Press.

Peck, R. (1974). *Soup.* Westminster, MD: Knopf.

Penrose, A. (1986). What do we know about writing as a way to learn? *English Record, 37,* 10–13.

Perfetti, C.A., Bransford, J.D., and Franks, J.J. (1983). Constraints on access in a problem-solving context. *Memory and Cognition, 11,* 24–31.

Philips, S.U. (1972). Participant structures and communicative competence: Warm Springs children in community and classroom. In C. Cazden, V. John, and D. Hymes (Eds.), *Functions of language in the classroom* (pp. 370–394). New York: Teachers College Press.

Philips, S.U. (1983). *The invisible culture: Communication in classroom and community on the Warm Springs Indian Reservation.* New York: Longman.

Poe, E.A. (1984). *The tell-tale heart.* Philadelphia: Franklin Library.

Project English (1964). Project English curriculum studies: A progress report. In *Iowa English Yearbook: Vol. 9.* Iowa City, IA: Iowa Council of Teachers of English.

Purves, A.C. (1977). Evaluating growth in English. In J.R. Squire (Ed.), *The teaching of English. 76th Yearbook of the National Society for the Study of Education* (pp. 231–259). Chicago: University of Chicago Press.

Purves, A.C. (1984). The challenge of education to produce literate students. In A.C. Purves and O.S. Niles (Eds.), *Becoming readers in a complex society. 83rd Yearbook of the National Society for the Study of Education* (pp. 1–15). Chicago: University of Chicago Press.

Radar, M., and Wunsch, A. (1980). A survey of communicative practices of business school graduates by job category and undergraduate major. *Journal of Business Communication, 17,* 33–41.

Read, C. (1971). Preschool children's knowledge of English phonology. *Harvard Educational Review, 41,* 1–34.

Read, C. (1981). Writing is not the inverse of reading for young children. In C.H. Fredericksen and J.F. Dominic (Eds.), *Writing: The nature, development and teaching of written communication: Vol. 2. Process, development and communication* (pp. 105–118). Hillsdale, NJ: Erlbaum.

Redish, J. (1985). *Adult writers: Using and learning job-related skills.* Unpublished manuscript.

Reed, C. (1981). Teaching teachers about teaching writing to students from varied linguistic social and cultural groups. In M.F. Whiteman (Ed.), *Writing: The nature, development and teaching of written communication: Vol. 1. Variation in writing: Functional and linguistic-cultural differences* (pp. 139–152). Hillsdale, NJ: Erlbaum.

Resnick, D.P., and Resnick, L. (1977). The nature of literacy: An historical explanation. *Harvard Educational Review, 47,* 370–385.

Robinson, H.A. (Ed.) (1977). *Reading and writing instruction in the United States: Historical trends.* Newark, DE: International Reading Association.

Robinson, H.A., and Schatzberg, K. (1984). The development of effective teaching. In A.C. Purves and O.S. Niles (Eds.), *Becoming readers in a complex society. 83rd Yearbook of the National Society for the Study of Education* (pp. 233–270). Chicago: University of Chicago Press.

Robinson, H.M. (1971). Reading instruction: Research. In L.C. Deighton (Ed.), *Encyclopedia of education: Vol. 7* (pp. 406–412). New York: Macmillan.

Rodriguez, R. (1982). *Hunger of memory: The education of Richard Rodriguez.* New York: Bantam Books.

Rose, M. (1980). Rigid rules, inflexible plans, and the stifling of language: A cognitivist analysis of writer's block. *College Composition and Communication, 31,* 389–401.

Rosen, C., and Rosen, H. (1973). *The language of primary school children.* Harmondsworth, England: Penguin Books.

Rosenblatt, L. (1978). *The reader, the text, the poem.* Carbondale, IL: Southern Illinois University Press.

Roundy, N., and Mair, D. (1982). The composing process of technical writers. *Journal of Advanced Composition, 3,* 89–101.

Rubin, D. (1979). The myth of dialect interference in written composition. *Arizona English Bulletin, Spring.*

Ruddell, R.B., and Speaker, R.B. (1985). The interactive reading process: A model. In H. Singer and R.B. Ruddell (Eds.), *Theoretical models and processes of reading* (3rd ed.) (pp. 571–593). Newark, DE: International Reading Association.

Rumelhart, D. (1975). Notes on a schema for stories. In D. Bobrow and A. Collins (Eds.), *Representation and understanding: Studies in cognitive science* (pp. 211–236). New York: Academic Press.

Rumelhart, D., and Ortony, A. (1977). The representation of knowledge in memory. In R.C. Anderson, R.J. Spiro, and W.E. Montague (Eds.), *Schooling and the acquisition of knowledge* (pp. 99–136). Hillsdale, NJ: Erlbaum.

Russell, D., and Fea, H.R. (1963). Research on teaching reading. In N.L. Gage (Ed.), *Handbook of research on teaching* (pp. 865–928). Chicago: Rand McNally.

Salvatori, M. (1985). The dialogical nature of reading and writing. In D. Bartholomae and A. Petrosky (Eds.), *Facts, artifacts, and counterfacts* (pp. 137–166). Upper Montclair, NJ: Boynton/Cook.

Sarason, S. (1982). *The culture of the school and the problem of change* (2nd ed.). Boston: Allyn & Bacon.

Scardamalia, M., and Bereiter, C. (1982). Assimilative processes in composition planning. *Educational Psychologist, 17,* 165–171.

Scardamalia, M., and Bereiter, C. (1986). Research on written composition. In M.C. Wittrock (Ed.), *Handbook of research on teaching* (3rd ed.) (pp. 778–803). New York: Macmillan.

Scardamalia, M., and Bereiter, C. (1987). Knowledge telling and knowledge transforming in written composition. In S. Rosenberg (Ed.), *Advances in applied psycholinguistics: Vol. 1* (pp. 142–175). Cambridge: Cambridge University Press.

Scardamalia, M., Bereiter, C., and Sternbach, R. (1984). Teachability of reflective processes in written composition. *Cognitive Science, 8,* 173–190.

Scardamalia, M., and Paris, P. (1985). The function of explicit discourse knowledge in the development of text representations and composing strategies. *Cognition and Instruction, 2,* 1–39.

Schein, E.H. (1972). *Professional education: Some new directions.* New York: McGraw-Hill.

Schieffelin, B.B., and Cochran-Smith, M. (1984). Learning to read culturally: Literacy before schooling. In H. Goelman, A. Oberg, and F. Smith (Eds.), *Awakening to literacy* (pp. 3–23). Exeter, NH: Heinemann.

Scollon, R., and Scollon, S. (1981). *Narrative, literacy and face in interethnic communication.* Norwood, NJ: Ablex.

Scribner, S., and Cole, M. (1981). *The psychology of literacy.* Cambridge, MA: Harvard University Press.

Sendak, M. (1967). *Higglety pigglety pop!* New York: Harper & Row.

Shanahan, T. (1984). Nature of the reading-writing relation: An exploratory multivariate analysis. *Journal of Educational Psychology, 76,* 466–477.

Share, D.L., Jorm, A.F., Maclean, R., and Matthews, R. (1984). Sources of individual differences in reading acquisition. *Journal of Educational Psychology, 76,* 1309–1324.

Short, E.J., and Ryan, E.B. (1984). Metacognitive differences between skilled and less skilled readers: Remediating deficits through story grammar and attribution training. *Journal of Educational Psychology, 76,* 225–235.

Shugrue, M.F. (1966). New materials for the teaching of English: The English program of the USOE. *Publications of the Modern Language Association of America, 81,* 1–36.

Shuman, A. (1986). *Storytelling rights: The uses of oral and written texts by urban adolescents.* Cambridge: Cambridge University Press.

Shuy, R.W. (1985). Dialogue journals and reading comprehension. *Dialogue, 3,* 2–3.

Shuy, R.W. (1987). Research currents: Dialogue as the heart of learning. *Language Arts, 64,* 890–897.

Shuy, R.W., and Schnukcal, A. (Eds.) (1980). *Language use and the uses of language*. Washington, DC: Georgetown University Press.

Slobin, D.I. (1979). *Psycholinguistics*. Glenview, IL: Scott, Foresman.

Smith, F. (1977). Making sense of reading—and of reading instruction. *Harvard Educational Review, 47*, 386–395.

Smith, F. (1984). Reading like a writer. In J.M. Jensen (Ed.), *Composing and comprehending* (pp. 47–56). Urbana, IL: ERIC Clearinghouse on Reading and Communication Skills and National Conference on Research in English.

Smith, N.B. (1965). *American reading instruction*. Newark, DE:International Reading Association.

Smith-Burke, T., and Ringler, L. (1986). STAR: Teaching reading and writing. In J. Orasanu (Ed.), *Reading comprehension: From research to practice* (pp. 215–234). Hillsdale, NJ: Erlbaum.

Smitherman, G. (1977). *Talkin' and testifyin': The language of black America*. Boston: Houghton Mifflin.

Snow, C.E. (1983). Literacy and language: Relationships during the preschool years. *Harvard Educational Review, 53*, 165–189.

Snow, C.E., and Ninio, A. (1986). The contracts of literacy: What children learn from learning to read books. In W. Teale and E. Sulzby (Eds.), *Emergent literacy: Writing and reading* (pp. 116–138). Norwood, NJ: Ablex.

Sowers, S. (1982). Reflect, expand, and select: Three responses in the writing conference. In T. Newkirk and N. Atwell (Eds.), *Understanding writing: Ways of observing, learning, and teaching* (pp. 76–90). Chelmsford, MA: Northeast Regional Exchange.

Spillich, G.J., Vesonder, G.T., Chiesi, H.L., and Voss, J.F. (1979). Text processing of domain-related information for individuals with high and low domain knowledge. *Journal of Verbal Learning and Verbal Behavior, 18*, 275–290.

Spivey, N. (1983). *Discourse synthesis: Constructing texts in reading and writing*. Austin: University of Texas Press.

Squire, J.R. (Ed.) (1966). *A common purpose: The teaching of English in Great Britain, Canada, and the United States*. Urbana, IL: National Council of Teachers of English.

Squire, J.R. (1969). English literature. In H.E. Mitzel (Ed.), *Encyclopedia of educational research* (4th ed.) (pp. 461 473). New York: Free Press.

Squire, J.R., and Applebee, R.K. (1968). *High school English instruction today: The national study of high school English programs*. New York: Appleton-Century-Crofts.

Staton, J. (1982). *Analysis of dialogue journal writing as a communicative event* (Final Report to the National Institute of Education, NIE-G-80-0122). Washington, DC: Center for Applied Linguistics.

Staton, J. (1984). Thinking together: The role of language interaction in children's reasoning. In C. Thaiss and C. Suhor (Eds.), *Speaking and writing, K–12* (pp. 144–187). Urbana, IL: National Council of Teachers of English.

Staton, J. (1988). *Dialogue journal writing: Linguistic, cognitive, and social views*. Norwood, NJ: Ablex.

Staton, J., Shuy, R., Kreeft, J., and Reed, L. (1982). *Dialogue journal writing as a communicative event* (Final Report to the National Institute of Education, NIE G-80-0122). Washington, DC: Center for Applied Linguistics.

Staton, J., Shuy, R., Kreeft, J., and Reed, L. (1987). *Dialogue journal writing: Linguistic, cognitive, and social views.* Norwood, NJ: Ablex.

Stauffer, R.G. (1970). *The language-experience approach to the teaching of reading.* New York: Harper & Row.

Stauffer, R.G., and Hammond, D. (1967). The effectiveness of language arts and basic reader approaches to first grade reading instruction—extended into second grade. *Reading Teacher, 20,* 740–746.

Stauffer, R.G., and Hammond, D. (1969). The effectiveness of language arts and basic reader approaches—extended into third grade. *Reading Research Quarterly, 4,* 468–499.

Stein, N., and Glenn, C.G. (1979). An analysis of story comprehension in elementary school children. In R. Freedle (Ed.), *New directions in discourse processing* (pp. 53–120). Norwood, NJ: Ablex.

Stiles, L. (1969). Revolution in instruction. In E.D. Hemsing (Compiler), *A decade of thought on teacher education. The Charles W. Hunt Lectures, 1960–1969* (pp. 29–53). Washington, DC: American Association of Colleges for Teacher Education.

Stitcht, T. (1980). *Literacy and vocational competence.* Columbus, OH: National Center for Research in Vocational Education.

Storms, C.G. (1983). What business school graduates say about the writing they do at work: Implications for the business communication course. *ACBA Bulletin, 46,* 13–18.

Street, B. (1984). *Literacy in theory and practice.* Cambridge: Cambridge University Press.

Strickland, R. (1964). The contributions of structural linguistics to the teaching of reading, writing, and grammar in the elementary school. *Bulletin of the School of Education, Indiana University, 40,* 1–39.

Suchman, L. (1985). *Plans and situated actions: The problem of human-machine communication* (Research document). Palo Alto, CA: Xerox Parc.

Suzzallo, H. (1913). Reading, teaching beginners. In P. Monroe (Ed.), *A cyclopedia of education: Vol. 5* (pp. 118–122). New York: Macmillan.

Swift, J. (1984). A modest proposal. In A. Ross and D. Woolley (Eds.), *Jonathan Swift* (pp. 492–499). Oxford: Oxford University Press. (Original work published 1792)

Szwed, J.F. (1981). The ethnography of literacy. In M.F. Whiteman (Ed.), *Writing: The nature, development, and teaching of written communication: Vol. 1. Variation in writing: Functional and linguistic-cultural differences* (pp. 13–24). Hillsdale, NJ: Erlbaum.

Tannen, D. (1985). Relative focus on involvement in oral and written discourse. In D.R. Olson, N. Torrance, and A. Hildyard (Eds.), *Literacy, language, and learning* (pp. 124–147). New York: Cambridge University Press.

Taylor, D. (1983). *Family literacy.* Exeter, NH: Heinemann.

Teale, W. (1986). Home background and young children's literacy development. In W. Teale and E. Sulzby (Eds.), *Emergent literacy: Writing and reading* (pp. 173–206). Norwood, NJ: Ablex.

Teale, W., and Sulzby, E. (1986). Introduction: Emergent literacy as a perspective for examining how young children become writers and readers. In W. Teale and E. Sulzby (Eds.), *Emergent literacy: Writing and reading*. Norwood, NJ: Ablex.

Tetroe, J. (1981, April). *The effect of planning on children's writing*. Paper presented at the annual meeting of the American Educational Research Association, Los Angeles.

Tierney, R.J. (1981). Using expressive writing to teach biology. In A.M. Worting and R.J. Tierney (Eds.), *Two studies of writing in high school science* (pp. 47–68). Berkeley, CA: Bay Area Writing Project.

Tierney, R.J., and Leys, M. (1986). What is the value of connecting reading and writing? In B. Peterson (Ed.), *Convergences: Essays on reading, writing, and literacy* (pp. 15–29). Urbana, IL: National Council of Teachers of English.

Tierney, R.J., and McGinley, W. (1987). *Exploring reading and writing as ways of knowing*. Paper presented at the thirteenth annual conference of the Australian Reading Association.

Tierney, R.J., Soter, A., O'Flahavan, J., and McGinley, W. (1986, April). *The effects of reading and writing upon thinking critically*. Paper presented at the annual meeting of the American Educational Research Association, San Francisco.

Torneus, M. (1984). Phonological awareness and reading: A chicken and egg problem. *Journal of Educational Psychology, 76,* 1346–1358.

Townsend, L.F. (1986, April). *The gender effect: A comparison of the early curricula of Beloit College and Rockford Female Seminary*. Paper presented at the annual meeting of the American Educational Research Association, San Francisco.

Treiman, R. (1985a). Phonemic awareness and spelling: Children's judgments do not always agree with adults'. *Journal of Experimental Child Psychology, 39,* 182–201.

Treiman, R. (1985b). Spelling of stop consonants after /s/ by children and adults. *Applied Psycholinguistics, 6,* 261–282.

Valdéz, C. (1981). Identity, power and writing skills: The case of the Hispanic bilingual student. In M.F. Whiteman (Ed.), *Writing: The nature, development and teaching of written communication: Vol. 1. Variation in writing: Functional and linguistic-cultural differences* (pp. 167–178). Hillsdale, NJ: Erlbaum.

Vygotsky, L.S. (1962). *Thought and language*. Cambridge, MA: MIT Press. (Original work published 1934)

Vygotsky, L.S. (1978). *Mind in society* (M. Cole, V. John-Steiner, S. Scribner, and E. Souberman, Eds.). Cambridge, MA: Harvard University Press.

Welty, E. (1984). *One writer's beginning*. Cambridge, MA: Harvard University Press.

West, W.W. (1971). Teaching of composition. In L.C. Deighton (Ed.), *Encyclopedia of education: Vol. 2* (pp. 363–370). New York: Macmillan.

White, E.B. (1970). *The trumpet of the swan*. New York: Harper & Row.

Whiteman, M.F. (1981). Dialect influence in writing. In M.F. Whiteman (Ed.), *Writing: The nature, development and teaching of written communication: Vol. 1. Variation in writing: Functional and linguistic-cultural differences* (pp. 153–166). Hillsdale, NJ: Erlbaum.

Whyte, J. (1980). Stories for young children: An evaluation. *International Journal of Early Childhood, 12,* 23–26.

Williams, J.P. (1984). Phonemic analysis and how it relates to reading. *Journal of Learning Disabilities, 17,* 240–245.

Winograd, P.N. (1984). Strategic difficulties in summarizing texts. *Reading Research Quarterly, 19,* 404–425.

Wittington, E. (1975). *The foxfire books* (Vols. 1–3). New York: Doubleday.

Wolfe, T. (1980). *The right stuff.* New York: Bantam Books.

Wolfram, W. (1969). *Sociolinguistic description of Detroit negro speech.* Washington, DC: Center for Applied Linguistics.

Wolfram, W. (1974). *Sociolinguistic aspects of assimilation: Puerto Rican English in New York City.* Washington, DC: Center for Applied Linguistics.

Wolfram, W., and Christian, D. (1976). *Appalachian speech.* Washington, DC: Center for Applied Linguistics.

Wolfram, W., Christian, D., Potter, L., and Leap, W. (1979). *Variability in the English of two Indian communities and its effects on reading and writing* (Final Report to the National Institute of Education, NIE-G-77-0006). Washington, DC: Center for Applied Linguistics.

Wresch, W. (Ed.) (1984). *The computer in composition: A writer's tool.* Urbana, IL: National Council of Teachers of English.

Yolen, J. (1982). *Commander toad and the planet of the grapes.* New York: Coward, McCann & Geoghegan.

Young, R.E., Becker, A.L., and Pike, K.L. (1970). *Rhetoric: Discovery and change.* New York: Harcourt, Brace, & World.

Zeller, R. (1985). *Developing the inferential reasoning abilities of basic writers.* Paper presented at Penn State Conference on Rhetoric and Composition.

Zentella, A.C. (1981). Language variety among Puerto Ricans. In C. Ferguson and S.B. Heath (Eds.), *Language in the U.S.A.* (pp. 218–238). Cambridge: Cambridge University Press.

Zolotow, C. (1968). *My friend John.* New York: Harper & Row.

Editor

Anne Haas Dyson is an associate professor of education in language and literacy at the University of California at Berkeley and a project director for the Center for the Study of Writing. A former preschool and primary grade teacher, Dr. Dyson now researches children's oral and written language use in classroom settings. She has published articles and chapters on her studies of young children's language use and is author of the forthcoming book *The Multiple Worlds of Child Writers: A Study of Friends Learning to Write*. She is also coauthor of *Language Assessment in the Early Years* with Celia Genishi, with whom she coedits the "Research Currents" column in *Language Arts*.

Contributors

Betsy A. Bowen is an assistant professor of English at Fairfield University. She has served as director of computation at the Bread Loaf School of English, Middlebury College, and is an associate of the Center for the Study of Writing at Carnegie-Mellon University. She is currently collaborating with John Elder, Jeffrey Schwartz, and Dixie Goswami on *Learning to Write with a Word Processor*. Her recent research examines the cognitive processes involved in collaborative revision.

James Britton is emeritus professor of education at the University of London, having been for twenty years head of the English department at the London Institute of Education. He taught in state secondary schools for eight years and was educational editor to John Murray, Publisher, for fifteen years. He directed the Schools Council Research Project on the Development of Writing Abilities, 11–18, was a member of the Bullock Committee, was awarded an honorary doctorate at the University of Calgary in 1977 and, in the same year, NCTE's David H. Russell Award for Distinguished Research in the Teaching of English. His publications include *Language and Learning* (author), *The Development of Writing Abilities 11–18* (editor and coauthor), *Prospect and Retrospect* (contributor). *The Word for Teaching Is "Learning,"* edited by Martin Lightfoot and Nancy Martin, was recently published to celebrate his eightieth birthday.

Bertram Bruce is a principal scientist at BBN Laboratories in Cambridge, Massachusetts. He has been active in the development of computer natural language understanding systems. Since 1976 he has been associate director of OERI's Center for the Study of Reading. He is known for his theory of story understanding based on the interacting plans of characters and for his analyses of stories in basal readers and trade books. He has designed educational software—notably QUILL, an integrated computer-based reading and writing program, and ELASTIC, an interactive system for learning statistical reasoning—and studies its use in schools. He is currently researching the development of literacy, especially the ways that assumptions about learning and modes of discourse shape classroom practices. His publications concern the teaching of reading and writing, discourse structures, artificial intelligence, computational models of language use, educational software design, and the consequences of computer use in classrooms.

Rebekah Caplan is codirector of the Bay Area Writing Project at the University of California, Berkeley, and a teacher at Foothill High School in Pleasanton,

California. In addition to conducting the Writing Project's school-year in-service programs and teaching English, she conducts workshops on the teaching of writing for the Bay Area and National Writing Projects. She is the author of *Showing-Writing: A Training Program to Help Students Be Specific*, a classroom research project published by the Bay Area Writing Project, and *Writers in Training*.

Wallace Chafe is a professor of linguistics at the University of California, Santa Barbara. His long-term research interests include the study of discourse and of cognitive factors underlying language production. Some of his project work is reported in *The Pear Stories: Cognitive, Cultural, and Linguistic Aspects of Narrative Production*. In recent years he has focused on the differences between spoken and written languages; his research is sponsored by the Center for the Study of Writing.

Geraldine Jonçich Clifford is a professor of education in the Graduate School of Education, University of California at Berkeley. She also teaches in the social science field major and the Women's Studies Program. She is the author of *The Sane Positivist: A Biography of Edward L. Thorndike, The Shape of American Education, Ed School: A Brief for Professional Education* (with James W. Guthrie), and *Lone Voyagers: Academic Women in American Co-educational Universities, 1880–1937* (forthcoming). Professor Clifford began her career in education as a third grade teacher in 1954. Her scholarly honors include a Guggenheim Fellowship (the first awarded to a woman in the field of education), a Rockefeller Fellowship, and support for her research on nineteenth-century American education from the Spencer Foundation.

Jenny Cook-Gumperz is a research sociologist at the National Center for Research in Vocational Education at the University of California, Berkeley. Her academic and research interests include adult literacy, child language socialization and family dynamics, interactional sociolinguistics, and cross-cultural communication. Her publications include *Socialization and Social Control*, a study of language and socialization practices of mothers and their children in London; *Children's Worlds and Children's Language*, an edited collection with W. Cosaro and Jurgen Streeck; and *Social Construction of Literacy*. She is at present working on another book on literacy in adults and children.

Linnea C. Ehri is a professor of education at the University of California, Davis campus. She has conducted and published numerous studies on the processes that explain how people learn to read and spell. Her more recent papers on beginning-level processes have appeared in the *Reading Research Quarterly*, the *Journal of Educational Psychology*, and the *Journal of Reading Behavior*. She teaches courses on educational psychology, cognitive and language development, and the psychology of reading. She makes presentations regularly at the American Educational Research Association meetings.

Marcia Farr is an associate professor of English at the University of Illinois at Chicago, where she teaches and conducts research on theoretical and pedagogical issues in literacy use and acquisition. She is currently researching oral language use among Mexican Americans in Chicago. She was previously at the National Institute of Education, where she developed a national research program on writing. Dr. Farr has taught at the secondary level and has designed and taught inservice workshops on nonstandard dialects and language arts instruction. She is series editor of *Writing Research: Multidisciplinary Inquiries into the Nature of Writing* and coauthor, with Harvey Daniels, of *Language Diversity and Writing Instruction*.

Linda Flower is a professor of rhetoric at Carnegie-Mellon University and codirector of the Center for the Study of Writing. Author of *Problem-Solving Strategies for Writing*, her research on cognitive processes in writing includes a study of "Detection, Diagnosis and Strategies of Revision," which won the 1988 Braddock award. A recent collaborative project at the center tracks how a group of freshmen integrate the processes of reading and writing as they try to enter the academic discourse of college. This work will appear in the forthcoming *Reading-to-Write: Exploring a Cognitive and Social Process*. As director of the "Making Thinking Visible" project, she also works with the Pittsburgh schools to develop classroom research teams that use collaborative planning to help students reflect on their own thinking process as writers.

Robert Gundlach directs the Writing Program in the College of Arts and Sciences and teaches in the Linguistics Department at Northwestern University.

Mary K. Healy is the research and training coordinator of the Puente Project in the Office of the President of the University of California. She is also the regional director for International Sites of the National Writing Project and coeditor of the NCTE journal *English Education*. Formerly she was the codirector of the Bay Area Writing Project and supervisor of teacher education at the University of California, Berkeley. In addition to writing journal articles and book chapters, she was coeditor of *What's Going On: Language Learning Experiences in British and American Classrooms*.

Mary K. Hurdlow was an elementary teacher in Livermore, California, for thirty years. For eight years she was also an active teacher/consultant for the Bay Area Writing Project. She gave in-service workshops in Germany, Texas, Alaska, Florida, Nevada, and extensively in the San Francisco Bay area. In addition, she taught courses for the University of California Extension Division, Berkeley. Mary passed away in December 1988 after a long illness.

Margaret Kantz has taught writing at the college and university level for more than twenty years. A recent graduate of the Carnegie-Mellon rhetoric program, she taught for a year as a visiting professor at Cleveland State University and now has a joint appointment with the Writing Center and the Department of English at Texas Christian University. She recently published an article in *Poetics* on needed research on reading processes.

James Moffett is an author and consultant in education. He has been on the faculties of Phillips Exeter Academy, the Harvard Graduate School of Education, the University of California at Berkeley, San Diego State University, and the Bread Loaf School of English of Middlebury College. His publications include *Teaching the Universe of Discourse; Student-centered Language Arts and Reading; Coming on Center,* a recently revised edition of collected essays; and *Storm in the Mountains: A Case Study of Censorship, Conflict, and Consciousness.*

Sandra Murphy taught high school English for three years in Pleasant Hill, California. She is now an associate professor in the Department of Secondary/Postsecondary Education at San Francisco State University. She is an associate director of the Bay Area Writing Project and has been a consultant to the Maryland State Department of Education, the Association of American Medical Colleges, and the National Assessment of Educational Progress on the assessment of writing. Coauthor of *Designing Writing Tasks for the Assessment of Writing* and author of articles on both reading and writing, she is now interested in the relationship between assessment and curriculum in the language arts.

Ann M. Penrose is an assistant professor of English at North Carolina State University, where she teaches courses in composition and in writing theory and research. She is an affiliated researcher with the Center for the Study of Writing and the former director of the Research-for-Teaching Seminar Series from the Center at Carnegie-Mellon. Her research and publications explore interactions between writing and reading and the role of individual differences in writing-to-learn.

Art Peterson teaches English at Lowell High School in San Francisco. A fellow of the Bay Area Writing Project, he has developed curriculum materials for writing, literature, and social studies classes, junior high school through college. In addition to text materials, simulation games, and journal articles, he has written two books of humor: *Teachers: A Survival Guide for the Grown Up in the Classroom* and, with his wife Norma, *The Unofficial Mother's Handbook.* While recently on sabbatical leave, he worked on books about critical thinking, prose style, and Shakespeare in the modern classroom.

Ann S. Rosebery is a scientist at BBN Laboratories, Cambridge, Massachusetts, and a senior researcher for the Reading Research and Education Center. Her research interests lie in the areas of language processing and language learning and in the application of basic research and technology to education. Currently she is developing an inquiry-based science curriculum for students of limited-English-proficiency. Dr. Rosebery has taught reading and writing to middle and high school students and courses in the use of microcomputers in the reading-language arts classroom at Harvard University, Graduate School of Education.

Robert J. Tierney is on the faculty at The Ohio State University, where he teaches graduate courses in reading and writing and conducts classroom-based research on the thought processes students engage in during reading and writing. His articles have appeared in journals such as *Reading Research Quarterly, Journal of Reading Behavior, Research in the Teaching of English, The Reading Teacher,* and *Language Arts.* He has been involved in several books as an author or editor, including *Reading Strategies and Practices, Understanding Readers' Understanding,* and *Learning to Read in American Schools.*

Guadalupe Valdés is a professor in the Division of Language and Literacy in the Graduate School of Education at the University of California, Berkeley. A sociolinguist, she specializes in the study of English/Spanish bilingualism. In addition to her work on language choice in bilingual communities, she has authored a number of Spanish-language textbooks. One of these, *Composición: Proceso y Síntesis,* focuses on the development of writing skills in the foreign language learner. She recently completed a project entitled "Identifying Priorities in the Study of the Writing of Hispanic Background Students" for the Center for the Study of Writing. She is a member of CCCC's Committee on Language Policy and of the MLA's Advisory Committee on Foreign Language Programs. She also serves as a member of NCTE's Standing Committee on Research.

Beth Warren is a scientist in the Education Department at BBN Laboratories and a senior researcher with the Reading Research and Education Center. Her research is currently focused on formulating a model of historical understanding, on relationships between science learning and literacy development in limited-English-proficient students, and on developing computer tools to support translation and foreign language learning. She has published several articles on reading and on the use of computers to enhance reading skill.

 Institute for the Advancement of Urban Education
NJDHE 1989-91